101 703 841 4

# ONE WEEK LOAN

D1351318

The Migration and Settlement of Refugees in Britain

# The Migration and Settlement of Refugees in Britain

Alice Bloch

*Goldsmiths College*
*University of London*

First published 2002 by
PALGRAVE MACMILLAN
Houndmills, Basingstoke, Hampshire RG21 6XS and
175 Fifth Avenue, New York, N.Y. 10010
Companies and representatives throughout the world

PALGRAVE MACMILLAN is the global academic imprint of the Palgrave Macmillan division of St. Martin's Press, LLC and of Palgrave Macmillan Ltd. Macmillan® is a registered trademark in the United States, United Kingdom and other countries. Palgrave is a registered trademark in the European Union and other countries.

ISBN 0–333–96923–5

This book is printed on paper suitable for recycling and made from fully managed and sustained forest sources.

A catalogue record for this book is available from the British Library

Library of Congress Cataloging-in-Publication Data

Bloch, Alice, 1964–
   The migration and settlement of refugees in Britain/Alice Bloch
      p. cm.
   Includes bibliographical references and index.
   ISBN 0-333-96923-5
   1. Refugees–Government Policy–Great Britain. 2. Refugees–Government policy–European Union countries. I. Title.

JV7682 .B56 2002
324'.21'0941–dc21
                                                                    2002022076

10   9   8   7   6   5   4   3   2   1
11   10   09   08   07   06   05   04   03   02

Printed and bound in Great Britain by
Anthony Rowe Ltd, Chippenham and Eastbourne

# Contents

# List of Tables

# List of Figures

# Acknowledgements

I would like to thank those who participated in the research and the survey interviewers. Also thanks to Stratford Development Partnership and the European Commission for their financial support for the fieldwork and the Department of Sociology and Anthropology at the University of East London and the London Borough of Newham for their assistance.

I am grateful to family, friends and colleagues, too numerous to mention, who have provided support, help and guidance at different stages of this work. In particular, thanks to Liza Schuster, John Solomos, Les Back, Amal Treacher, Jill Enterkin and Rita Davies.

# 1
# Introduction

Refugee migration has been a constant feature of the twentieth century. Refugee flows have occurred for a number of reasons including international wars, civil wars, the rise in fascism, decolonization, national liberation struggles and the creation of nation states. The twentieth century has also seen the development of international, regional and national responses to refugees.

This book explores the settlement of refugees in Britain through a case study of refugees from Somalia, Sri Lanka and the Democratic Republic of Congo (DRC)[1] living in the London Borough of Newham, a local authority area in east London. The book will show that the social and economic settlement of refugees is affected by the characteristics and experiences that refugees bring with them on arrival to Britain, attitudes and aspirations about the migration, access to economic and social institutions, the presence of community organizations and social networks and structural factors that relate to refugee policies. The diversity of experience among the three communities is also significant and among Somalis, there is a strong gender dimension.

## Theoretical and thematic concerns

Existing literature on refugee migration and settlement raise a number of relevant theoretical issues that are examined in this book. The theoretical paradigms around migration and settlement are explored in

---

1. When the fieldwork was carried out the Democratic Republic of Congo (DRC) was called Zaire. In the presentation of the findings the terms DRC and Congolese will be used.

detail in Chapters 4 and 5 while this section introduces the main issues and their application to this case study.

The research points to a number of key determinants in the settlement of refugees and their ability to gain access to the social and economic institutions in the country of asylum. Of particular significance are language skills, length of residence, gender, childcare responsibilities, employment, education, the presence of an ethnic community, participation in community activities and immigration status.

On arrival in exile refugees bring with them a range of skills, experiences, cultural norms, aspirations and social and kinship networks all of which are thought to affect settlement. The pre-migration characteristics of refugees vary by country of origin and gender. Aspirations for the migration are affected in part by the circumstances of the migration, while social and kinship networks depend upon the migration patterns of different communities. The three case study communities offer a contrast in terms of pre-migration characteristics as well as migration patterns and established networks in Britain.

In terms of pre-migration characteristics, the most significant are the ability to speak the language of the country of asylum, educational qualifications and labour market experience. Certainly for those unable to speak the language of the country of asylum, the acquisition of language skills is crucial and has been identified as the first stage in the settlement process (Robinson, 1986).

Language skills of refugees vary by country of origin and gender. While some Somalis and Sri Lankans learned English in school, due to their countries' former colonial links with Britain, the official language in DRC was French reflecting its colonial past. There were significant gender differences among Somali respondents with women, for the most part, unable to speak English as they had participated little in formal schooling in Somalia. Once in Britain, some Somali women were excluded from language classes for cultural reasons or due to child care responsibilities and this has left many isolated. In contrast, Congolese refugees arrived in Britain with virtually no knowledge of the English language but with high levels of literacy skills in their first language and most were also multilingual. As a result Congolese acquired English language skills more easily than many others.

Not having adequate language skills of the country of asylum leaves refugees unable to obtain employment or negotiate with statutory agencies and members of the wider community. Thus for many refugees from the Somali community and to a lesser extent the Tamil community, lack of English language was the main barrier to settlement. Indeed, according to one Tamil respondent: 'All refugees must undergo a proper English training course so that they can read, write and speak fluently. Hence English language courses must be made compulsory to all refugees.'

Educational and employment backgrounds also affect settlement. Refugees were, for the most part, well educated though there were differences by community and gender. Somali women were least likely to have participated in any formal schooling, as mentioned above, and were more likely to be looking after the home and family prior to their migration. Even where refugees do have qualifications and employment experiences from their country of origin their skills may not be transferable to the British labour market and some may not have the tools to obtain new skills. Even those with relevant professional qualifications and experience from their country of origin are often unable to practice their profession because their qualifications are not recognized in the UK. Transferring qualifications at a level that enables them to practice their chosen profession often requires retraining. As one Tamil respondent observed: 'Most of the Sri Lankans are unable to get into their professions because their degrees and diplomas are not recognized in Britain.'

Participation in education and employment in the country of asylum are also important predictors of settlement. There were differences between the communities in terms of participation. Of the three case study groups, Tamils were the most likely to have participated in education, training and employment in Britain. Men were more likely than women to have studied in Britain and participation in education was also affected by length of residence and feeling settled. The longer refugees had been in the UK, the more likely that they would have participated in education. One striking feature was the high rates for non-completion of courses often due to a lack of ability to concentrate.

The three case study groups also had different migration patterns to Britain that affected the networks that existed and the level of community activity. There was a strong network of community organizations for Tamils and Somalis who have had a lengthy history of migration to Britain while there was comparatively little community formation among the Congolese, due to their more recent arrival.

Of the three case study groups Somali migration to Britain has the longest history. Somalis first arrived in Britain during the second half of the nineteenth century, almost exclusively as seafarers forming transient communities in the dock areas of London's east end as well as Cardiff and smaller port towns like Liverpool. Most were from

Northern Somalia, which at the time was a British Protectorate, and so were entitled to British citizenship.

At the end of the 1950s there were changes in Somali settlement patterns. The economic boom in Britain, coupled with a decline in the merchant navy, led to settlement in industrial towns such as Manchester. At this time Somali men also began to bring their families to the UK (El-Solh, 1991). As a result, there were already established Somali communities in Britain prior to the arrival of refugees. Refugees began arriving in 1981 as a result of armed opposition in northern Somalia against the Siad Barre regime that resulted in increasing numbers of Isaaq clan members (the group most affected by the struggle) fleeing from political persecution. Political refugees were joined in Britain by students and Somali youth from the Gulf states (El-Solh, 1991).

May 1988 saw all out civil war in northern Somalia. The profile of the new arrivals was different from their predecessors and tended to be comprised of victims of the civil war, including single mothers and their children, the elderly, the disabled and single young people. In January 1991 the demise of Siad Barre's regime led to fights among rival clan factions. In the same year the Gulf war resulted in the arrival to Britain of Somalis who had been working in the Gulf states (Griffiths, 1997).

Migration from Sri Lanka to Britain also originated due to the colonial links between the two countries. Sri Lanka was a British colony that gained independence in 1948. Prior to the 1960s much of the migration from Sri Lanka to Britain was among returning colonial migrants. However, from the 1960s onwards there was a large increase in the size of the Sri Lankan born population living in Britain. This was due to high levels of unemployment in Sri Lanka, especially among the highly educated, so many of the early migrants were professionally qualified and most were Sinhalese. Since the mid-1980s however, the main migratory movement from Sri Lanka to Britain comprised Tamil refugees (Siddhisena and White, 1999).

The conflict in Sri Lanka dates back to the 1970s when there was a rise in militant Tamil nationalism after successive Sinhalese governments failed to guarantee the rights of the minority Tamil population. In 1976, for the first time, the Tamil United Liberation Front called for a separate state for Tamils in the northeast of Sri Lanka. Inter-community violence escalated in 1983 and the following years saw the onset of civil war. The result was an increase in the numbers Tamils fleeing Sri Lanka and seeking asylum in the Indian state of Tamil Nadu, home to 55 million

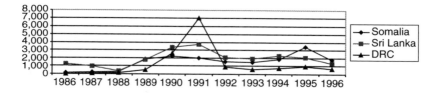

*Figure 1.1* Applications for asylum received from Somali, Sri Lankan and Congolese nationals between 1990 and 1996.

Tamils. In addition, Tamils began to arrive as asylum seekers in Europe and North America (www.unhcr.ch/refworld/country/cdr/cdrlka.htm). The Indian government intervened in 1987 by dispatching a peacekeeping force to the island. However, the subsequent involvement of the peacekeeping force in the conflict and the withdrawal of the Liberation Tigers of Tamil Eelam (LTTE) from a constitutional arrangement, involving a degree of self-government in Tamil majority areas, resulted in the resumption of war. The conflict in Sri Lanka continued in the 1990s (www.refugeecouncil.org.uk).

The pattern of migration of Congolese to the UK is in contrast to that of Somalis and Sri Lankans. There are no colonial ties between the DRC and the UK and so migration began with refugees in the late 1980s rather than earlier cohorts of voluntary migrants, as was the case among Somalis and Sri Lankans. The conflict in DRC (formally Zaire) is relatively recent. Refugees started arriving in the UK from the DRC in 1989 and peaked in 1991(see Figure 1.1). This was in direct response to the political changes – the result of which was a huge increase in human rights abuses (Amnesty International, 1993). Between 1965 and 1990 the only legal political organization in Zaire was the *Mouvement Populaire de la Révolution* (MPR) led by President Mobutu. Opposition demonstrations in the 1980s motivated changes towards a multiparty system. The first major development towards political reform was in 1991 with the establishment of the Sovereign National Conference whose objective was to draft a new constitution. However, from its inception, the Conference was in conflict with President Mobutu (www.unhcr.ch/refworld/country/cdr/cdrsrc.htm). A succession of short-lived governments ensued and after 1992, when Mobutu's power began to be eroded, the stability of the country began to decline. In 1997 Laurent Kabila declared himself President of the DRC following an offensive by the Alliance of Democratic Forces for the Liberation of Congo-Zaire.

One of the significant effects of migration patterns is the extent to which social and community organizations have evolved. There was diversity among the three communities in terms of the extent that organizations had developed, but also in terms of participation and use of networks and community organizations. Tamils had a large network of organizations and of the three case study groups were most involved in community activities. This is explained, in part, by the clustering of residence among Sri Lankans in Britain. Most reside in greater London and within certain localities in London including east London (Siddhisena and White, 1999). Those from the DRC who were involved in community activities were most likely to be involved in political activities. This reflects their reasons for seeking asylum, which were based on political activity. Somalis were the least likely to participate in any community-based activities though they did seek advice and assistance from community-based volunteers. Thus the pattern of use and the role of community varied between the three communities reflecting not only their different migration patterns, but also the circumstances of the migration and cultural differences.

Increasingly structural barriers have emerged in Britain, and in other European countries of asylum, that impede the freedom of forced migrants especially their access to the social and economic institutions in the country of asylum. Those without refugee status – that is asylum seekers, those with Exceptional Leave to Remain and most recently those on temporary protection – lack many basic rights and this in turn affects settlement. Those with refugee status, in this study, were most likely to feel settled in Britain and were most likely to participate socially or economically than others. The significance of differential rights between different categories of forced migrants will be examined throughout the book.

## The categorization of forced migrants

The 1951 Convention relating to the Status of Refugees forms the basis of international refugee law. It contains 46 articles that establish the minimum rights for refugees. Refugees are those who are recognized as such under Article 1 of the Convention. The Convention was drafted by the United Nations and was concerned primarily with refugees in postwar

Europe and, as such, was restricted to refugees from Europe and to those who had emerged as a result of events that occurred before 1 January 1951. Under the 1951 Convention a refugee is any person who:

> owing to a well-founded fear of being persecuted for reasons of race, religion, nationality, membership of a particular social group or political opinion, is outside the country of his [sic] nationality and is unable to or, owing to such a fear, is unwilling to avail himself of the protection of that country; or who, not having a nationality and being outside the country of his former habitual residence as a result of such events, is unable or, owing to such fear, is unwilling to return to it.

The UK has been a signatory to the 1951 Convention since 1954 and is also governed by the 1967 Bellagio Protocol. The Protocol took account of the failure of the Convention on refugees to recognize refugee flows in other continents that remained outside the jurisdiction of the international community (Zolberg *et al.*, 1989). This was because the United Nations High Commissioner for Refugees was Eurocentric reflecting the distribution of international power (Suhrke, 1997). The addition of new members to the United Nations allowed for a widening of the remit of UNHCR and this was reflected in the Bellagio Protocol, signed by nearly 100 countries. The Protocol adopted the Geneva Convention's definition of a refugee but removed the geographical and temporal limitations of the Convention, giving the United Nations High Commissioner for Refugees responsibility for refugees from all over the world as well as for refugees who had been displaced after January 1951.

In 1969, soon after the 1967 Protocol, the Organization of African Unity (OAU) agreed to a Convention Governing the Specific Aspects of Refugee Problems in Africa. The OAU definition included:

> The term 'refugee' shall apply to every person who, owing to external aggression, occupation, foreign domination or events seriously disturbing public order in either part or the whole of his [sic] country of origin or nationality, is compelled to leave his place of habitual residence in order to seek refuge in another place outside his country of origin or nationality (Article 1(2)).

The introduction of the OAU Convention recognized the upheaval and displacement of people in Africa following decolonization and the creation of nation-states (Kushner and Knox, 1999).

The 1951 Convention is still the cornerstone of refugee protection. The Convention guarantees some basic refugee rights, to which signatories must adhere. Under the Convention refugees have the right not to be forcibly removed or refouled (returned) to a country in which the refugee has reason to fear persecution. In addition, refugees have the right to work, the right to education, the right to public relief or assistance, freedom of religion, access to courts, freedom of movement and the right to be issued with identity and travel documents.

Britain, like many other countries, has introduced national legislation that governs entry to the UK as a country of asylum and the rights conferred on those who are not recognized as refugees under the terms of the Geneva Convention. Asylum policy is governed by three pieces of legislation: Asylum and Immigration Appeals Act, 1993; Asylum and Immigration Act, 1996 and the Immigration and Asylum Act, 1999. National legislation has been cumulative in two key areas. First, it has increasingly served to restrict the number of forced migrants able to reach UK borders, a policy introduced by most industrialized countries (Suhrke, 1997). Second, welfare entitlements have been gradually curtailed for those who do manage to gain access to the UK's asylum determination process.

Currently forced migrants living in the UK fall into four different categories: refugees, people with Exceptional Leave to Remain (ELR), those with temporary protection status and asylum seekers.[2] These categories are important because each confers, on individuals, different social and economic rights and different levels of security in the country of asylum and this in turn can affect settlement (Bloch, 2000a). Moreover, there are different strategies for reception and settlement, depending upon the status of the forced migrant on arrival to the UK.

### Refugees

Refugees are those who are recognized as such under Article 1 of the 1951 Geneva Convention relating to the Status of Refugees. There are two types of refugee: 'quota' refugees and 'spontaneous' refugees. Quota or programme refugees are those who are taken in a group

---

2. The term refugee will be used as a generic one to describe asylum seekers, people with ELR and those on temporary protection, unless the differentiation in status is relevant to the arguments.

under an organized programme and are accepted as refugees on arrival to the UK. Spontaneous refugees come to Britain and seek asylum. They are known as asylum seekers throughout the determination process (see below).

For those who come as quota refugees there is no permanent central programme in place for reception and settlement. Instead facilities are set up for each new group of programme or quota refugees. Programme refugees arriving in the 1970s and 1980s, such as Ugandan Asians, Vietnamese and Chileans, were initially placed in reception centres and then moved on to available accommodation around the country using a system of dispersal. Once refugees were housed, there were no specialist support services available in the dispersal areas (Duke *et al.*, 1999). The problems with the reception and resettlement of programme refugees as well as dispersal policies have been well documented (see Community Relations Commission, 1974; Joly, 1996; Jones, 1982; Robinson and Hale, 1989).

There is a hierarchy of rights associated with different statuses though only forced migrants who are naturalized have full citizenship rights. Refugees have most favoured alien status, which confers economic and social rights. Refugees recognized under the Geneva Convention are entitled to work legally, claim the same benefits as those available to UK and EU citizens, have access to education and they are entitled to immediate family reunion with spouses and children.

### Asylum seekers

An asylum seeker is a person who is seeking asylum on the basis of his or her claim to be a refugee. People who are waiting for the Home Office to consider their case are known as asylum seekers regardless of whether or not the claim is valid or will eventually be accepted as legitimate.

The majority of forced migrants come as spontaneous asylum seekers and as a result receive no formal and coordinated assistance. In the past policy has been based on two approaches: equal access to state provision and support for community self-help (Renton, 1993). Historically, much of the responsibility for meeting the reception and resettlement needs of refugees has fallen on community groups who work nationally and locally with refugees and asylum seekers (Renton, 1993). The government department responsible for immigration and asylum matters, the Home Office, has continuously provided an element of core funding for some nationally based provision, namely the Refugees Arrival Project, Refugee Action and the Refugee Council. However on a locality and/or community basis, there are no formal structures in place and the short-term nature of funding is a major obstacle for refugee organizations (Carey-Wood, 1997).

Asylum seekers are known to rely heavily on community organizations and they play a crucial role in the settlement of forced migrants (Carey-Wood *et al.*, 1995; Gold, 1992 ). Certainly this research shows that Somalis, Tamils and Congolese, most of whom arrived in the UK as spontaneous asylum seekers, relied heavily on community organizations for basic advice and information (see Chapter 9).

The Immigration and Asylum Act, 1999 has affected access to state support and has made it more difficult for asylum seekers to access community support by introducing a new dispersal programme. Destitute asylum seekers are excluded from the social security system and instead find themselves dependent on an assessment of their circumstances made by the National Asylum Support Service (NASS) who then determine eligibility for housing, supermarket vouchers, 'in-kind' provisions and a small cash stipend.

Asylum seekers have the fewest rights of all forced migrants. This group have no immediate statutory right to seek employment and cannot submit an application for discretionary permission to work, from the Home Secretary, until they have been living in the UK for six months. The process of obtaining permission to work is often a slow and protracted one (Carey-Wood *et al.*, 1995). Permission to work is generally limited to just the principle asylum applicant, which often excludes women from seeking employment. Asylum seekers are not eligible for family reunion and have to pay overseas fees for education. Moreover, because asylum seekers are not eligible for student loans, they are effectively excluded, except for the very wealthy, from participating in education.

### Exceptional Leave to Remain

Asylum seekers who are not recognized as refugees are not always expelled. In some cases they are given Exceptional Leave to Remain (ELR). ELR is given to asylum seekers who do not meet the Convention criteria but where there are humanitarian grounds for granting them leave to remain in the UK. People with ELR lack security of settlement because the Home Office can refuse them the right to remain. After four years people with ELR are entitled to apply for Indefinite Leave to Remain (ILR). Prior to July 1998, ELR was granted for one year after which it could be extended twice for three years each time. After seven years an application could be submitted for ILR.

Those with ELR have no family reunification rights for their first four years in the UK. After four years, by which time someone with ELR should have ILR, the Home Office will consider an application for family reunion although this usually means demonstrating the ability to support relatives without recourse to public funds. Such a policy is particularly problematic and effectively excludes those with ELR from family reunion due to the disproportionately high levels of unemployment experienced by forced migrants in the UK (Bloch, 2000b; Carey-Wood *et al.*, 1995). Other restrictions placed on those with ELR include paying overseas fees for study during the first three years of residence although those with ELR are entitled to social security benefits and to social housing.

### Temporary protection

More recently a new status, temporary protection or temporary refuge, has emerged in European countries of asylum. Temporary protection was first utilized in response to the displacement of 500,000 Bosnians to the EU in 1992–3 at the request of UNHCR. According to Koser and Black (1999), temporary protection was used as a mechanism for 'burden-sharing' and harmonization. Moreover, it was politically expedient because public support could be maintained by emphasizing the temporary nature of the status because this group had a need for protection even though they did not meet the criterion of the Convention. Temporary protection was used once again at the request of UNHCR in the case of the humanitarian evacuation of Kosovar Albanians (Guild, 2000).

Temporary protection is an adaptation of ELR but with some significant differences. First, those on temporary protection are entitled to immediate family reunion. Second, those on temporary protection are assisted on arrival through staffed reception centres while those on ELR who arrive as spontaneous asylum seekers have no formal and organized assistance on arrival (Bloch, 1999a). Third, temporary protection is given for a limited and pre-specified duration. In the case of Bosnians temporary protection was granted initially for six months then a year and in the case of Kosovars for one year in the first instance but there was no settlement schedule (van Selm-Thorburn, 1998). The terms of the temporary protection scheme operated with the Bosnians and Kosovars excluded the right to be considered for refugee status under the Geneva Convention (Guild, 2000). In the case of the Bosnians, the period of protection was extended but this has not happened with the Kosovars.

Table 1.1    Decisions on asylum applications: 1990–2000

| | Refugee status | | ELR* | | Refusal | |
| | (%) | (No) | (%) | (No) | (%) | (No) |
|---|---|---|---|---|---|---|
| 1990 | 23 | 920 | 60 | 2400 | 17 | 705 |
| 1991 | 10 | 505 | 44 | 2190 | 46 | 2325 |
| 1992 | 6 | 1115 | 80 | 15325 | 14 | 2675 |
| 1993 | 9 | 1590 | 64 | 11125 | 27 | 4705 |
| 1994 | 5 | 825 | 21 | 3660 | 74 | 12655 |
| 1995 | 5 | 1295 | 19 | 4419 | 76 | 17705 |
| 1996 | 6 | 2240 | 14 | 5055 | 80 | 28040 |
| 1997 | 13 | 3985 | 11 | 3115 | 76 | 22780 |
| 1998 | 17 | 5345 | 12 | 3910 | 71 | 17465 |
| 1999** | 36 | 7075 | 11 | 2110 | 54 | 10685 |
| 2000 | 15 | 10185 | 16 | 11365 | 69 | 48855 |

*This does not include the 2500 former Yugoslavs brought to the UK under temporary protection programme
**Numbers rounded up so the total percentage adds up to 101 per cent.
*Source*: Refugee Council (1998) *Asylum Statistics 1987–1997*, Home Office (1999) *Asylum Statistics United Kingdom 1998* and Home Office (2001) *Asylum Statistics: July 2001 United Kingdom*.

Table 1.1 shows the decisions on asylum applicants and the shift, during the 1990s, from granting ELR to the refusal of applications.

Given the different rights associated with different statuses, it is not surprising that immigration status affected settlement. The fieldwork for this study was carried out prior to the introduction of dispersal, but what it does show is that dispersal will be problematic because it takes away the opportunity to seek help and support from community organizations who have previously been the main suppliers of help for new arrivals who are trying to negotiate their way through a complex system.

## The case study and the research basis[3]

This book reports on a case study of refugees and asylum seekers living in the London Borough on Newham, an area in east London, at the end of the twentieth century (see the Appendix for a discussion of the methodology). Through the use of a case study, the book is able to analyse the experiences of refugees and asylum seekers within

---

3. For a full discussion of the research methodology see Bloch (1999b).

the context of the relevant theoretical debates and within the current policy context. Although the book reports on a case study, there are wider lessons to be learned about the direction of asylum policy and the impact of policy on refugee settlement. It is these broader concerns that will be addressed throughout the book.

## The London Borough of Newham

Newham is an area with high levels of migration and has a tradition of being a starting place for new migrants. In addition, Newham has one of the largest refugee populations of any local authority district and the diversity of the refugee population allows the variation in refugee experience by country of origin to be explored. Ethnic diversity is not a new feature of life in Newham. From as early as the seventeenth century, east London was the home of diverse migrant communities (Kushner, 1993). The arrival of Jewish migrants fleeing persecution from the Russian Empire between 1882 and 1905 meant that the Jewish community formed the largest minority group in the east end (Fishman, 1979). It also turned east London into a major centre of migrant settlement (Holmes, 1978).

East London has also housed a sizeable German population since the eighteenth century. German migrants were involved in the sugar baking industry and those arriving at the start of the twentieth century were actively recruited from Germany to work in the bottle works. In addition to the Germans, there were Lithuanians in the locality from the mid-nineteenth century as well as a constant flow of Irish people who came as seasonal workers.

Black and South Asian migration to Newham grew in the nineteenth century with the construction of the docks. By the 1930s, Canning Town (in Newham) had the largest black community in London. Bombs destroyed the area during the World War II and most of the black seafarers who were evacuated did not return (Newham History Workshop, 1986).

The East India Company, from the eighteenth century, recruited South Asians but there was an increased demand for lascars (seafarers) in the nineteenth century due to the Napoleonic wars, their relative cheapness to employ compared to European seafarers and their willingness to undertake the least desirable tasks. Some lascars either lost their ships when they became ill or jumped ship so small communities emerged in the dock areas (Visram, 1993).

The next period of South Asian migration to East London occurred in the 1950s due to the increased demand for labour and the upheavals that followed the partition of India in 1947. Most of the primary labour migrants were men from India and Pakistan. The numbers of women and children increased in the 1960s and 1970s as a result of family reunification. In the 1970s and 1980s people from Bangladesh arrived in east London, mostly in the neighbouring borough of Tower Hamlets, though there is also a sizeable Bangladeshi community in Newham.

### Newham's ethnic minority communities: demography and geography

Contemporary Newham has one of the largest ethnic minority and refugee populations of any local authority area in Britain (Bloch, 1994). Data from the 1991 Census show that Newham is the local authority area with the second largest proportion of people from ethnic minority groups (42.3 per cent) in Britain. Only Brent has a larger proportion of people from ethnic minority groups (44 per cent).

Table 1.2 shows the ethnic composition of Newham at the time of the 1991 Census and compares it with the population of Great Britain.

With the exception of white, Newham has above average proportions of every other ethnic group categorized in the 1991 Census. Migration patterns of different ethnic groups are reflected by an analysis of the country of birth question in the 1991 Census. Table 1.3 shows that people who described their ethnic group as Black Caribbean

Table 1.2   Resident population by ethnic group – Great Britain and Newham, 1991 Census

|  | *Per cent of total population of Great Britain* | *Per cent of Newham's population* |
|---|---|---|
| White | 94.5 | 57.7 |
| Black – Caribbean | 0.5 | 7.2 |
| Black – African | 0.4 | 5.6 |
| Black – Other | 0.3 | 1.2 |
| Indian | 1.5 | 13.0 |
| Pakistani | 0.9 | 5.9 |
| Bangladeshi | 0.3 | 3.8 |
| Chinese | 0.3 | 0.8 |
| Other Groups – Asian | 0.4 | 3.0 |
| Other Groups – Other | 0.5 | 1.4 |
| Total (number) | 54,889,000 | 212,171 |

Table 1.3   Proportion born in the UK by ethnic group, 1991 Census, Newham

| Ethnic Group | Percentage |
| --- | --- |
| Chinese | 27 |
| Black – African | 32 |
| Bangladeshi | 36 |
| Indian | 41 |
| Pakistani | 50 |
| Black– Caribbean | 55 |

were most likely to have been born in the UK reflecting the relative longevity of their migration to Britain. Conversely the relatively low proportions born in the UK of those who described their ethnic group as Bangladeshi or Black African reflects their more recent migration.

Ethnic minority communities tend to be residentially spatially clustered. What that means is that particular ethnic groups tend to be located within local authority areas. The most extreme example of this pattern is in the London Borough of Tower Hamlets where the Bangladeshi population account for 22.3 per cent of the total resident population in the borough (Teague, 1993).

Table 1.4 shows the ward distribution of different ethnic groups in Newham and demonstrates clearly the spatial concentration of ethnic groups within local authority ward areas.

The wards to the south of the borough – see Figure 1.2 – Beckton, Canning Town, Customhouse and Silvertown, Greatfield, Hudsons, Ordnance and South have much higher than average white populations than the borough average.

The wards to the North East have a higher than average proportion from ethnic minorities. In Kensington, Monega, St Stephens and Upton, more than two-thirds of the population described themselves as coming from an ethnic group other than white. Within Newham there is a spatial concentration of ethnic minority groups within wards.

### The case study groups

Three refugee communities resident in Newham were involved in the research: Somalis, Tamils from Sri Lanka and Congolese. The communities were selected on the basis of size, migration patterns and pre-existing links with the UK. Sixty interviews were carried out with

Table 1.4  The ethnic composition of ward areas in Newham, 1991 Census

| Ward | White | Black Caribbean | Black African | Black Other | Indian | Pakistani | Bangladeshi | Chinese | Other |
|---|---|---|---|---|---|---|---|---|---|
| Beckton | 84.5 | 5.8 | 6.2 | 1.4 | 0.5 | 0 | 0.1 | 0.5 | 1.0 |
| Bemersyde | 69.4 | 6.3 | 5.3 | 1.5 | 4.9 | 4.6 | 1.1 | 0.6 | 6.2 |
| Canning Town/ | | | | | | | | | |
| Grange | 75.0 | 6.8 | 5.6 | 1.8 | 2.0 | 1.9 | 1.6 | 1.6 | 3.6 |
| Castle | 53.2 | 6.8 | 4.7 | 2.1 | 13.3 | 9.4 | 3.2 | 0.7 | 6.6 |
| Central | 40.3 | 4.6 | 5.2 | 1.2 | 21.6 | 15.3 | 3.1 | 0.5 | 8.2 |
| Custom-house/ | | | | | | | | | |
| Silver-Town | 81.1 | 4.8 | 6.2 | 1.1 | 2.0 | 0.9 | 0.3 | 1.3 | 2.2 |
| Forest Gate | 60.2 | 12.4 | 6.4 | 2.6 | 7.4 | 4.6 | 3.1 | 0.7 | 2.7 |
| Greatfield | 80.3 | 4.0 | 2.9 | 0.9 | 5.6 | 3.0 | 0.9 | 0.4 | 2.0 |
| Hudsons | 79.0 | 5.3 | 5.5 | 0.6 | 2.5 | 2.2 | 1.7 | 0.7 | 2.6 |
| Kensington | 25.2 | 4.5 | 3.9 | 1.2 | 38.6 | 12.1 | 6.0 | 0.6 | 8.0 |
| Little Ilford | 51.2 | 9.5 | 6.4 | 1.6 | 12.8 | 5.4 | 8.5 | 0.3 | 4.3 |
| Manor Park | 45.7 | 8.8 | 4.4 | 1.7 | 18.3 | 7.1 | 10.2 | 0.4 | 3.4 |
| Monega | 26.5 | 8.4 | 5.1 | 1.2 | 31.6 | 12.1 | 10.2 | 0.5 | 4.5 |
| New Town | 62.6 | 10.7 | 7.6 | 2.5 | 5.9 | 3.0 | 1.8 | 1.0 | 4.0 |
| Ordnance | 77.4 | 7.2 | 7.7 | 1.5 | 1.8 | 1.5 | 0.3 | 0.5 | 2.1 |
| Park | 49.2 | 10.5 | 8.7 | 2.3 | 13.6 | 4.8 | 6.0 | 0.5 | 3.5 |
| Plaistow | 56.5 | 8.1 | 5.8 | 1.6 | 9.4 | 6.6 | 3.7 | 0.9 | 7.5 |
| Plashet | 48.5 | 8.0 | 6.4 | 1.8 | 18.6 | 7.5 | 5.0 | 0.4 | 3.7 |
| St. Stephens | 30.1 | 5.0 | 5.0 | 0.6 | 33.8 | 11.8 | 6.3 | 0.5 | 6.0 |
| South | 77.6 | 3.9 | 3.8 | 1.5 | 4.0 | 4.1 | 0.9 | 1.9 | 2.3 |
| Stratford | 63.8 | 9.9 | 7.9 | 2.9 | 6.4 | 1.7 | 1.4 | 1.8 | 4.1 |
| Upton | 27.7 | 9.2 | 6.0 | 1.4 | 31.7 | 10.0 | 8.5 | 0.4 | 4.1 |
| Wall End | 51.1 | 3.9 | 4.1 | 1.1 | 18.7 | 8.0 | 3.4 | 1.0 | 9.0 |
| West Ham | 64.3 | 10.9 | 6.2 | 2.9 | 5.7 | 1.6 | 0.8 | 1.7 | 5.8 |

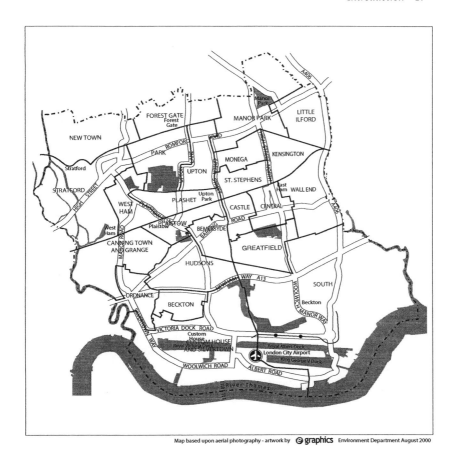

Map based upon aerial photography - artwork by ⊝ graphics Environment Department August 2000

*Figure 1.2*   London Borough of Newham.

members of each community and respondents were selected using snowball sampling techniques. It is impossible to be precise about the numbers of refugees living in any local authority area because of the lack of reliable data and the unsuitability of official data (Robinson, 1998). Refugees from all over the world live in Newham as demonstrated by an analysis of the country of birth data from the 1991 Census that show resident populations, in Newham, of people born in refugee producing countries including Sri Lanka, Turkey, Former Yugoslavia, Sierra Leone, Iran and Vietnam though the data are not disaggregated for all communities that include refugees.

Estimates about the numbers of refugees in the borough vary, though estimates by the local authority place the number of refugees at around 20,000, which represent around 9 per cent of the total population resident in the borough. Nonetheless, by triangulating multiple sources of data it was possible to estimate the sizes of different refugee communities in Newham.

Refugees from Somalia form the largest refugee community in Newham and estimates place the number of Somalis in the locality at between 6,000 and 8,000. Tamils from Sri Lanka are the second largest refugee community living in Newham and estimates range from just under 2,000, which were the number of people living in Newham who were born in Sri Lanka at the time of the 1991 Census, to a voluntary sector adviser's estimate of 10,000. Newham is home to the largest Congolese community in Britain. At the time of the fieldwork, it was estimated that there were between 2,000 and 2,500 Congolese in the borough (Bloch, 1996).

Quotas, for age, gender and length of residence, were specified for each community to ensure that some of the key experiences, which are known to affect settlement, were incorporated into the study. The quotas specified that, for each community, there had to be 30 interviews with men and 30 with women. Thirty interviews were to be carried out with people aged 34 and younger and 30 with people aged 35 and older. This was because previous research had found that refugees, aged 35 and older, experienced a much greater sense of loss than those aged 34 and younger (Chan and Lam, 1987 cited in Montgomery, 1996). Lastly quotas were set for length of residence and 30 interviews were to be carried out with people who had been in the UK since 1992 or earlier and 30 interviews with people who had arrived after 1992. The quotas were not met exactly due to the profiles of the different communities (see Appendix). However, there was sufficient diversity in the sample to ensure that the three case study communities enabled an analysis of the key theoretical concerns.

Due to limited information and problems accessing refugees for the purpose of social research, non-probability samples were used and so generalizations can not be made from the sample to the refugee population as a whole. Nevertheless, in the presentation of the data, Phi or Cramers V are used as a measure of association where 1 indicates complete association and 0 is no association. While the reliability of the statistical measures are not guaranteed, due to the limitations of the sample, they do provide an indication of the strength of the association between key variables and this offers a better understanding of the data.

## Content of the book

Chapter 2 reviews the history of migration to Britain and will show the links between migration, the economy and policy responses from the start of the twentieth century. It shows the consistency in the responses to migration in times of economic recession and where it is deemed to be politically expedient. Responses to migratory movements, both voluntary and forced, have been characterized by increasingly restrictive legislative responses in the areas of border controls and the social and economic rights conferred on migrants.

Chapter 3 focuses on domestic developments since the introduction of the Asylum and Immigration Appeals Act 1993 and European level agreements since the 1986 Single European Act. Most notable in the European context are measures to control external borders, to share information and the longer-term plan for the harmonization of reception standards for asylum seekers. It is this chapter that provides the current policy context for the case study material presented in chapters 6, 7, 8 and 9.

Chapters 4 and 5 provide the theoretical context to the book focusing on theories of migration and migrant settlement. In Chapter 4 the development of migration theory will be discussed and the unique situation of forced migrants within the literature will be highlighted. Material will be presented from the case study to show the migration experiences of refugees in Britain. Chapter 5 concentrates on refugee settlement, from a theoretical and a policy perspective.

Chapters 6, 7, 8 and 9 will present empirical data from the survey and the data will be discussed in the context of secondary data and theoretical sources. Chapter 6 will document the experiences and views of those who have participated in language classes, education and training in Britain as well as the ways in which provision could be improved.

Chapter 7 will examine economic participation and the main factors that affect the economic settlement of refugees. Access to the labour market is a crucial element in the settlement of refugees because it provides economic independence, enhances self-esteem and facilitates contacts with members of the host society. Data will show that refugees remain largely excluded from the labour market as well as statutory job-seeking services. The reasons for this segmentation will be looked at as well mechanisms that would help to improve participation.

Chapter 8 is concerned with the social settlement of refugees. More specifically it explores attitudes to Britain as home, as well as the social settlement of refugees in the London Borough of Newham. The data show that refugees remain largely excluded from social contacts with people from outside of their immediate group and most find it hard to make contacts with British people. Moreover, some sub-groups find it difficult to meet members of their own community and remain isolated and marginalized.

Chapter 9 will examine the social situation of refugees and will evaluate the role of the ethnic enclave or community in their settlement. The probable impact of dispersal on community activity and refugee settlement will also be considered. The data presented in Chapter 9 show that the community sector plays a crucial role in the settlement of refugees, not just for those who use the services of such organizations but also for those who volunteer.

Chapter 10 concludes and summarizes the main arguments put forward in the previous chapters and suggests theoretical developments and policy initiatives that would improve understanding of, and support for, the position of refugees and forced migrants in Britain.

# 2
# Migration to Britain and Policy Responses

According to the 1991 Census, 5.5 per cent of the population of Great Britain, or just over 3 million of the total population are from an ethnic group other than 'White'. Half of this total is accounted for by South Asians (Indians, Pakistanis and Bangladeshis). 'Black' ethnic groups (Black African, Black Caribbean and Black Other) make up 1.6 per cent of the total population while Chinese and other ethnic groups make up 1.2 per cent of the population (Teague, 1993).

Migration to Britain is often portrayed as a recent phenomenon emerging in the postwar period (1945 onwards) as a result of labour migration from the Caribbean and South Asia. While numbers of migrants undoubtedly increased, with the demand for labour in the postwar period, migration itself is not a new phenomenon. From as early as the twelfth century Britain contained a number of distinctive ethnic minority groups (Panayi, 1994). Migrants came to Britain due to economic and political push circumstances in their country of origin, pull factors in Britain and enabling factors such as kinship ties. This chapter will focus on the history of migration to Britain and policy responses to migration during the twentieth century. What will become evident is the way in which the economy, public opinion and political responses to migration and migrants are all linked.

## Early migrants

The first distinct minority ethnic group in Britain were Jews. Their numbers increased in the twelfth century as result of anti-Semitism in Spain and Italy. Initially the Jewish community was mostly located in London. By the end of the twelfth century Jews had taken up residence in about 70 locations around the country. Many were employed in the money lending business, as this was an occupation forbidden to gentiles for religious reasons. The Jews were subjected to discrimination throughout the thirteenth century: in 1218 they were compelled to wear badges which distinguished them as Jews, in 1245 an Act forbade them to settle in any new locations and in 1290 they were faced with expulsion (Merriman, 1993).

During the thirteenth and fourteenth centuries European merchants were a feature of life in London and included Flemish, Dutch, French, Italian, Spanish and Germans (Merriman, 1993). The German merchants dominated trade in London though their history is similar to that of Jews in medieval England. They were subjected to rising hostility that eventually led to their expulsion for seven years in 1598 (Panayi, 1994).

In the sixteenth century new minorities, who were the victims of religious persecution, began to enter Britain. These included Calvinists from Germany and France, as well as French Huguenots who moved to Britain after the St Bartholomew's Day massacre in 1572. Although Huguenot migration slowed down towards the end of the sixteenth century with the passing of the Edict of Nantes in 1598, that offered toleration for French Protestants, they were never entirely safe from persecution. Gradually their privileges were eroded and Charles II of England offered them asylum in 1681. When the Edict of Nantes was revoked in 1685 more Huguenots fled to England and the word 'refugee' from the French 'réfugié' entered into the English language (Merriman, 1993).

Also arriving in Britain in the sixteenth century were Africans – who were mostly brought to Britain as slaves – Irish, Italians, Germans and gypsy travellers. The presence of some of these new minority groups was consolidated during the next few centuries and created the foundations for the growth and establishment of diverse ethnic communities (Panayi, 1994).

## Migration: 1800 until 1914

During the nineteenth century most migrants to Britain were from Europe. In order to understand the reasons for migration, it is necessary to place it within the context of European economies during that period. The largest number of new immigrants came from Ireland, Germany and Russian Poland and there were similarities. A feature of all three countries during the nineteenth century was expanding populations that led to a pressure on resources. Furthermore, there were also changes in production away from labour intensive cottage industries towards greater industrialization that resulted in a lower demand for labour and an increase in the level of unemployment. Another influential factor leading to emigration was the change in land owner-ship. The population increase meant that land was divided up, leaving holdings that were too small to support families (Panayi, 1994). Thus, population growth, changes in agriculture and industrialization were the economic push factors for migrants. Britain was seen as a viable destination because it was the first industrial country and this resulted in a growing economy that was able to provide migrants with economic opportunities. Panayi (1994, p. 39) notes, however, that: 'The level of newcomers has fundamental connections with the short term condition of the British economy'.

The largest minority group in Britain during the nineteenth century was the Irish. Although Irish immigration can be traced back to medieval times, migration increased rapidly after the Act of Union (1800) which made Ireland part of Britain. Migration from Ireland increased again during the 1840s and 1850s as a result of the great famine (1845–50). Among Irish people, factors influencing migration were a combination of economic push factors as well as perceived opportunities in Britain that acted as a pull. In addition, there was chain migration facilitated by social networks (Holmes, 1988).

The 1841 Census identified 289,404 Irish born people resident in England and Wales. Their number had increased to 519,959 by the 1851 Census and to 601,634 by the 1861 Census as Table 2.1 shows. The main centre of the Irish community was London, where they

Table 2.1   Foreign born population of England and Wales, 1861 and 1901

| Birthplace | 1861 | 1901 |
|---|---|---|
| Ireland | 601,634 | 426,565 |
| France | 12,989 | 20,797 |
| Greece | 574 | 979 |
| Italy | 4,489 | 9,909 |
| Germany | 28,644 | 50,599 |
| Russia | 1,633 | 23,626 |
| Poland | 3,616 | 21,448 |
| China | 146 | 767 |
| United States | 7,686 | 19,740 |
| Total | 685,724 | 619,678 |

*Source*: Panayi (1994), p. 51.

made up 4.6 per cent of the total population in 1851. Most of the Irish migrants were casual workers and they tended to form a reserve supply of labour (Panayi, 1994). There was also a large Irish community in Scotland that peaked at 207,367 at the time of the 1851 Census (Holmes, 1988).

For most of the nineteenth century, the Germans formed the second largest minority group in Britain. The size of the German born population grew gradually (Holmes, 1991). German migration was characterized by a combination of economic and political factors. There were five main types of German migration to Britain in this period. First were those Germans who were pushed out of their country by population increases and a lack of economic opportunities in their homeland. This group tended to be poor and formed part of the working class on arrival in Britain. The second group comprised merchants and clerks from the middle classes who tended to leave Germany as a result of the lack of opportunities available in their homeland. The third strand were political refugees who made their way to Britain as it offered greater freedom than any other European country (Panayi, 1993a). The first cohort of these political refugees arrived in the 1830s, as they feared a clampdown on the liberal Young Germany movement by the German Confederation. The second wave of refugee migration occurred due to the failure of the 1848 revolution and the third wave of refugees came after anti-socialist laws were passed in 1878 (Panayi, 1994). The fourth dimension to German immigration was Jews who were either pushed out of Germany by anti-Semitism or pulled to Britain by economic motives. The fifth strand were gypsy travellers who arrived from Germany between 1904 and 1906. This group was largely forced migrants who had been expelled from Germany to Holland and then shipped from Holland to Britain (Holmes, 1988).

London was the major place of settlement for Germans with around 50 per cent of all Germans residing in the city. People from Germany remained the second largest migrant population, second only to the Irish community, until the latter part of the nineteenth century when Russian Poles, most of whom were Jews, formed the second largest group. Migrants from Russian Poland started to come to Britain in increasing numbers by the 1880s in response to Tsarist persecution (Panayi, 1993b). Between 1870 and 1914 approximately 120,000 Jewish people had settled in Britain and by 1914 the Jewish population had reached around 300,000.

The Jewish immigrants, at the end of the nineteenth century, tended to settle in and around the Whitechapel area of east London. Many

Jewish people worked as sweated labourers in the garment trade and they tended to work and live in the worst conditions (Kershen, 1993). Jewish migration was dictated by chain migration and a number of voluntary organizations like the Jewish Board of Guardians and The Poor Jews' Temporary Shelter were set up to help new arrivals.

Hostility towards the Jewish community was evident, as they were perceived to be taking away jobs and housing from the indigenous East Enders. Holmes (1988, p. 66) argues that responses to this group were: 'closely related to specific tensions located in the economic, social and political context of the late nineteenth and early twentieth centuries'

In fact it was in response to Jewish migration from Eastern Europe that asylum policy in Britain was first formalized with the 1905 Aliens Act (Cohen, 1994). The 1905 Aliens Act set limits on the numbers of migrants who could enter Britain and deportations increased. Moreover, entry could be refused if the migrant had no means of subsistence or they could be deported if they were receiving poor relief within one year of entering Britain (Miles and Clearly, 1993). This Act was significant because it was the first attempt, by a British government, to ensure that migrants would not be a burden on the state. It should be noted, however, that under this legislation no one could be refused entry to Britain if they were seeking to avoid persecution on either religious or political grounds.

The political expediency of the Act has been noted because it was introduced by a failing Conservative government in order to exploit anti-alien feeling (Layton-Henry, 1992). Certainly the Jewish population in the East End of London was subjected to hostility and much of the impetus for the 1905 Act came from the East End where Jewish migrants were seen as an economic and social threat (Holmes, 1988; Panayi, 1993b).

There were a number of other smaller migrant communities present in Britain during this period as Table 2.1 shows. Italians came to Britain as a result of economic problems in Italy and worked in service trades. There was also a Chinese community that came over to the port towns of London, Liverpool and Cardiff as seafarers, and then set up laundries. The Chinese community was very small and, at the time of the 1911 Census, it numbered only 1,319 (Holmes, 1991). There were also people from Africa living in Britain as students and seafarers, people from the Indian sub-continent were present as seafarers, performers, students and businessmen and people from the Caribbean were present as students. Thus, at the start of the twentieth century Britain was already multiethnic. This period of migration was significant for two reasons: first it brought with it an increase in the ethnic diversity of Britain and second, it marked the first ever legislation that limited the number of immigrants that could enter Britain, while those who could not support themselves could be deported. It was the first attempts of a British government to ensure that migrants would not be a burden on the state.

## Migration: 1914 until 1945

The introduction of the 1905 Aliens Act did not bring to a close the public debate on immigration. In fact more restrictive legislation was passed in August 1914 just 24 hours before Britain declared war on Germany. The Aliens Restrictions Act, 1914 gave the Home Secretary control over the entry, registration, movement and deportation of all aliens. The Act introduced the notion that an alien had no right to come to Britain or to remain but instead could only be received or remain if it was in the interests of the state (Dummett and Nicol, 1990).

It was the German-born residents of Britain who were in the forefront of the legislatures' minds with the introduction of the 1914 Act. There was public support for strong action demonstrated through violence and general hostility against Germans. Anti-German feeling continued throughout the war period (1914–18) (Holmes, 1991).

The period 1914 to 1945 was one that saw the arrival of refugee groups from Europe as shown in Table 2.2. The first refugees to arrive in Britain during this period were Belgians from mainland Europe. The majority arrived between August 1914 and the end of 1915 and for

Table 2.2　Main refugee groups arriving in the UK, 1870–1945

| Date | Group | Number |
|------|-------|--------|
| 1914–18 | Belgians | 250,000 |
| 1918–39 | Armenians | 200 |
| 1918–31 | White Russians | 15,000 |
| 1933–9 | Germans, Czechs and Austrians from Nazism | 55,000 |
| 1937 | Spanish | 4,000 |
| 1940–3 | Europeans | 60,000 |
| 1945 | Poles | 135,000 |

*Source*: Kushner and Knox (1999) Maps.

many the stay was brief (Holmes, 1988). By 1916, the numbers had reduced to 160,000 as some joined the allied forces while others returned to Europe (Kushner and Knox, 1999). The Belgians received a very positive response in Britain and much public and private support.

Other migrants arrived in Britain during the war or stayed after the war. Around 15,000 White Russians, who fled their home-land after the Bolsheviks came to power in October 1917 found their way to Britain (Holmes, 1988). World War I also resulted in an increase in Britain's black population as conscription created gaps in the labour market filled, to some extent, by black workers. In addition, black troops from the West Indies and troops from India fought as part of the war effort. In 1919, just after the end of the war the Aliens Restriction (Amendment) Act was passed. The new legislation imposed even more restrictive measures over the entry, employment and the deportation of aliens. Holmes (1991, p. 27) writes that: 'There is no doubt that the Act constitutes an important landmark in the State's control over alien immigration'. Indeed, the 1919 Aliens Act made it statutory for all aliens to register with the police and under the Act the deportation of Russian Polish Jews continued to take place.

In the immediate postwar period there were outbreaks of collective violence in cities around the country alongside racial tensions in Liverpool, Glasgow, London, Newport and Cardiff though it was evident that white people were the aggressors (Holmes, 1988). Holmes (1988) explains the complexity of the collective violence in terms of the competition for jobs, housing and the attempts by whites to reassert their dominance. An analysis of responses to later migratory movements shows little change in the discourse.

In the inter-war years (1919 to 1939) there were political and econ-omic developments in Europe. These included the rise of communism, the rise of nationalism and high levels of unemployment. Europe expe-rienced a large increase in the number of refugees who were fleeing either persecution or government ideologies they disagreed with (Zolberg *et al.*, 1989). This was coupled with high levels of unemploy-ment during the inter-war years that affected Europeans and potential non-European migrants. More legislation was introduced in response to the economic and political climate.

In 1920 a new Aliens Order was introduced and this was renewed annually until the 1971 Immigration Act superseded it. The Aliens Order placed further restrictions on immigration and gave the Home Secretary the power to control entry into the country and to exclude or deport any alien whose presence in Britain was not thought to be for the public good (Layton-Henry, 1992).

Due to the economic decline in the shipping industry and the competition for jobs among black and white seafarers, the Special Restrictions (Coloured Alien Seaman) Order was published in 1925. The order meant that black seamen had to prove they were British nationals before they could work. Those who could not provide evidence of nationality were not allowed to work and they were subject to immediate deportation without recourse to appeal.

The 1930s saw the increase in fascism in Europe notably in Italy, Spain and Germany and with this an increase in political refugees. In Britain fascist groups that had emerged in the 1920s achieved greater popularity in 1930s, a period that also coincided with the end of an international economic crisis. Anti-Semitism was rife and according to Holmes (1991, p. 34) had 'an influence on official policy in the inter-war years'. Between 1933 and November 1938, prior to the outbreak of World War II, 11,000 Jewish refugees entered Britain (Paul, 1997). The refugees were especially unpopular with the middle classes because many were professionals from Germany who were seen as a threat to employment prospects (Cohen, 1994).

The government operated a policy of internment during the early war years and it is thought that around 22,000 Germans and Austrians (including Jewish refugees) and 4,300 Italians were incarcerated during the period up to 1942 (Holmes, 1991). Thus the war years were not ones of tolerance. There was much anti-refugee feeling as well as racism against black and Asian workers and servicemen and this often manifested itself in violence (Holmes, 1988).

Anti-Semitism was to continue throughout the war years (1939–45) and was directed at British born Jewry as well as the refugees from Europe. A total of around 65,000 Jews settled in Britain in the period between 1933 and 1945. (Saggar, 1992). The reasons why the numbers were small were due to immigration controls and anti-Semitism. Saggar (1992, p. 29) argues that:

> despite overwhelming threat and reality of persecution faced by Jews and others, the legal framework governing British immigration control remained unchanged since the 1920 Order. This meant that those refugees lacking the obvious means to support themselves and their dependants were subject to refusal by the immigration authorities.

Even during this period of massive unrest and war in Europe there was a clear link between the British economy and responses to migrants. Panayi (1994, p.46) writes that:

> the entry of immigrants to Britain between 1915 and 1945 did not take place steadily but occurred in waves ... The health of the British economy played a very important role, because in periods of slump the government imposed stricter legislative controls, while at times of labour shortage it loosened its controls upon entry.

The link between the economy and attitudes to migration is a trend that continued throughout the twentieth century and is clearly demonstrated in relation to both voluntary and forced migrants in the post World War II period.

## Migration: 1945 until 1961

In the aftermath of the war there was a shortage of the labour necessary to rebuild Britain. The government was active in its recruitment of Irish workers and it is estimated that during the period of 1945 to 1951 between 70,000 and 100,000 Irish workers and their families settled in Britain (Solomos, 1993). In addition, the period after the war was most significant in terms of labour migration from the Caribbean and to a lesser extent South Asia. Europeans, who had been displaced during the war, as well as refugees from Eastern Europe also arrived in Britain in the period immediately after the war.

### Eastern European displaced persons and European Volunteer Workers

One of the consequences of the war was that millions of people had been displaced and it was recruitment of some of these displaced people that helped to alleviate some of the existing labour shortages. The government started the Displaced Persons Scheme in October 1946. The first phase of labour recruitment was 1,000 women, from the Baltic States of Estonia, Latvia and Lithuania to work in either tuberculosis sanatoria or as residential domestic workers. Soon after, 5,000 people were recruited to work as hospital domestic workers. This scheme was known as Balt Cygnet.

The second phase of labour recruitment, among displaced persons, was called Westward Ho! This scheme re-opened recruitment to people of all nationalities in the displaced persons camps. The people who migrated to Britain under this scheme were assigned employment on arrival. This scheme operated until 1949 when the more neutral sounding European Volunteer Worker (EVW) scheme was put in place (Kay and Miles, 1988). Between 1946 and 1949 Britain accepted more than 90,000 people from displaced persons camps in the British zones in Austria and Germany. Other displaced persons were then admitted as part of the EVW scheme making them the largest group of refugees to enter Britain (Cohen, 1994). In total 74,511 people, mostly from Estonia, Latvia, Lithuania, Poland and Yugoslavia, were recruited as part of the EVW scheme. In addition, some Ukrainian prisoners of war were also treated as EVW (Solomos, 1993). The EVW had their activities strictly contained. For example, they were assigned to a particular job on arrival to Britain and their leave to remain was dependent on them staying in that job. If they broke their conditions of recruitment they could be either prosecuted or deported (Layton-Henry, 1992). Indeed, according to Loescher (1993, p. 20): 'for the first two decades after World War II ... refugees provided much-needed labour for the expanding economies of the West'.

The government wanted to safeguard against unsuitable people, which meant that the EVW were brought over with very restrictive landing conditions, which affected both employment and settlement rights. The scheme created the idea that the recruits were labour migrants rather than refugees and as such were not being accepted for settlement. On arrival in Britain the EVW were allocated a job and they had to get permission to change jobs. These restrictions resulted in a concentration of EVW in particular industries. Seventy per cent of men worked in agriculture or coal mining while 95 per cent of women worked in either textiles or domestic work. According to Kay and Miles (1988, p. 231), the EVW scheme meant that:

> Refugees were selected and landed in Britain largely according to an explicit criterion of economic utility ... What mattered most to the British government was the capacity of the refugees to work, and hence the emphasis on their fitness, health and strength when selecting those allowed to enter Britain and the concern that deportation should remain an option for those who might prove unwilling or unable to play the economic role that was expected of them.

Because of the level of control that the government had over the EVW, they were preferred to colonial workers. The government was afraid that there might be disincentives for colonial workers to contribute to the economy as employment benefits were very high compared to wages in the West Indies (Layton-Henry, 1992). Moreover, the issue of assimilation was high on the political agenda and according to the Royal Commission on Population (1949):

> Immigration on a large scale into a fully established society like ours could only be welcomed without reserve if the immigrants were of good human stock [presumably European] and were not prevented by their religion or race from intermarrying with the host population and becoming merged with it (cited in Layton-Henry, 1992, p. 28).

## Migration from Commonwealth countries

Although there were government reservations concerning migrants from the Commonwealth, levels of unemployment were high in the Caribbean. This created the necessary push factors that complemented the demand for labour in Britain (Panayi, 1999). Moreover, the 1948 British Nationality Act ensured an open door policy for migrants from the Commonwealth. Under the 1948 Act British subjects had the right to enter, work and settle with their families in Britain and citizenship was granted to anyone who was born within the territories of the crown (the *jus soli* rule). Citizenship could also be acquired through descent (the *jus sanguinis* rule) (Juss, 1993).

The 1950s were the key decade for labour migration from the West Indies and, to a lesser extent, from the Indian sub-continent. Patterns of migration correlated strongly with demands for labour, especially among people from the West Indies (Peach, 1986). Also, employers in Britain, such as London Transport, recruited people directly from the Caribbean to take up specific jobs in Britain. Commonwealth migrants who came to the UK without the employee/employer link settled in areas where there were jobs and housing, particularly greater London, the West Midlands and the North West.

Commonwealth migrants tended to be employed in unskilled and semi-skilled occupations and social mobility and economic success were elusive. Layton-Henry (1992, p. 46) states that:

> Immigrant workers thus formed a replacement labour force, overwhelmingly occupying the unskilled, semi-skilled and skilled manual jobs vacated and rejected by the native workforce as they obtained better-paid and higher-status positions in the expanding economy.

Migration from the Indian sub-continent was correlated with labour demand although not as strongly as migration from the Caribbean for five reasons. First, there was a tradition of emigration from the Indian sub-continent to a number of different destinations of which Britain was only one. Second, people from the West Indies had fewer migration destinations, which were further reduced when the United States imposed restrictions in 1952 with the passing of the McCarran–Walter Act which virtually closed the door on Caribbean migration to the US (Cashmore and Troyna, 1990). Third, the 'beat the ban' rush, prior to the introduction of the Commonwealth Immigrants Act in 1962, was largely made up of dependants from the Caribbean (see below). In contrast, South Asian migration was in its early stages and so the expectation was not to stay and there were fewer existing residents who wanted to bring dependants over. Fourth, the spatial concentration of Asian minorities in geographical areas resulted in an internal ethnic economy that was outside the UK economy. Finally, chain migration was a dominant feature of migration from South Asia and according to Robinson (1980, p. 119): 'the close knit nature of the village-kin network, and the presence of numerous hierarchical obligations ensured that few Asians left India or Pakistan without a job arranged by an existing resident of the UK.'

The different migration patterns of primary labour migrants are illustrated in Table 2.3, most coming to Britain in the second half of the 1950s while migration from India and Pakistan increased dramatically in 1961.

Table 2.3   Estimated net immigration from the New Commonwealth, 1953–62

|        | West Indies | India  | Pakistan | Others | Total   |
|--------|-------------|--------|----------|--------|---------|
| 1953   | 2,000       |        |          |        | 2,000   |
| 1954   | 11,000      |        |          |        | 11,000  |
| 1955   | 27,500      | 5,800  | 1,850    | 7,500  | 42,650  |
| 1956   | 29,800      | 5,600  | 2,050    | 9,350  | 46,800  |
| 1957   | 23,000      | 6,600  | 5,200    | 7,600  | 42,400  |
| 1958   | 15,000      | 6,200  | 4,700    | 3,950  | 29,850  |
| 1959   | 16,400      | 2,950  | 850      | 1,400  | 21,600  |
| 1960   | 49,650      | 5,900  | 2,500    | −350   | 57,700  |
| 1961   | 66,300      | 23,750 | 25,100   | 21,250 | 136,400 |
| 1962[*] | 31,800     | 19,050 | 25,080   | 18,970 | 94,900  |

[*] First six months up to introduction of controls in 1962.
*Source*: Layton-Henry (1992), p. 13

Table 2.4   Main refugee groups arriving in the UK, 1946–61

| Date | Group | Number |
|------|-------|--------|
| 1947–9 | EVW from Eastern Europe | 84,000 |
| 1948 | Czechs | 2,000 |
| 1956 | Hungarians | 22,000 |

*Source*: Kushner and Knox (1999) Maps

Labour migration was not exclusively from the Caribbean and Indian sub-continent. The postwar period also saw the arrival of migrants from other Commonwealth countries like Malta and Cyprus. In 1951, the number of people resident in Britain from these countries was less than 25,000 but this had increased to 66,000 by 1961 (Castles and Kosack, 1985). During this period, refugees also arrived in the UK from Eastern Europe. Table 2.4 shows the main refugee groups arriving in Britain between 1945 and 1961.

Concerns about migration, or more specifically, over what was termed 'coloured immigration' in the 1950s placed the issue of immigration controls on the political agenda. As with earlier periods there was violence and racism against migrants. In 1958, urban uprisings in Nottingham and Notting Hill comprising attacks on blacks by whites were used as an opportunity to highlight problems associated with black immigration and provided the justification for the introduction of new legislation, the 1962 Commonwealth Immigrants Act.

## Controlling migration: 1962 until 1988

The Commonwealth Immigrants Act, 1962 sought to curb black immigration among Commonwealth citizens. The Act aimed to rationalize labour and reduce the migration for settlement of citizens from the Commonwealth and colonies by introducing a work voucher system. Three categories of people were identified: those with skills in demand, those with jobs to come to and those who would form part of an undifferentiated group whose numbers would be set in accordance with the demand for labour in the UK economy. The significance of the Act was that it differentiated, for the first time in law, between the rights of British subjects whose passports were issued in Britain and British subjects whose passports were issued by other Commonwealth countries (Spencer, 1997). Prior to the Act, there was a strong correlation between immigration and the needs of the economy, but the status quo was affected for the first time because paradoxically the Act led to a rush to 'beat the ban' resulting in an increase in immigration (Peach, 1986). In fact, beating the ban was a key factor in explaining the doubling of the Asian and Black population, living in Britain, between the middle of 1960 and the middle of 1962 (see Table 2.3) (Spencer, 1997). It was only in the years 1960, 1961 and 1962, which marked the period of debate through to the introduction of the Act, that net immigration was greater than the demand for labour (Peach, 1998).

The 1960s saw the start of restrictive immigration controls that have formed the basis of all subsequent legislation. The period between 1962 and 1988 was significant because it brought to a close virtually all labour migration, through the introduction of legislation. This period also saw the arrival of refugees and asylum seekers, in Britain, from all over the world. Up until the 1970s, the majority of refugees in Europe were from other European countries but the 1970s saw the emergence of refugees arriving in Europe in increasing numbers from crisis areas in Africa, Asia and Latin America. The end of colonization contributed, in part, to the change in refugee-producing nations. Political independence brought with it the creation of arbitrary borders that did not reflect populations and in some cases resulted in internal conflicts and disputes (Loescher 1993). This period also brought the debate around immigration into the electoral arena because it could be used to win popular votes. This was exemplified by the electoral success, in Smethwich, of the overtly racist and right wing Conservative candidate Peter Griffiths. As part of his campaign Griffiths used the slogan 'if you want a nigger for a neighbour vote labour', and this helped to win him the majority of the votes in what was considered a safe Labour seat (Goulbourne, 1998; Solomos, 1993).

Following the election victory of the Labour party in 1964, new measures to control immigration were quickly introduced. The impetus was the obvious popularity, among the electorate, for curtailing black and Asian migration (Spencer, 1997). In 1965, the White Paper *Immigration from the Commonwealth* announced further restrictions to immigration by abolishing the work category that included semi-skilled and unskilled workers and reducing the numbers who could come into Britain under the other two categories, those with jobs and those with skills that were in demand. Primary labour migration decreased but the number of people entering Britain did not really change due to the increase in the number of dependants joining people who were already living in Britain (Booth, 1992).

In 1968, the second Commonwealth Immigrants Act was rushed through Parliament in only three days, by the then Labour government, amidst fears of increasing numbers of East African Asians exercising their right as UK passport holders to come to Britain from Kenya after independence from colonial rule. East African Asians had been seeking refuge in Britain in the 1960s as a consequence of the post-independence Africanization policies adopted by Kenya, Uganda and Malawi. Between 1965 and 1968, 36,000 Asians came to Britain from Kenya (Robinson, 1986). Under the Act, all UK passport holders were subject to immigration control unless they had a parent or a grandparent who had been born, naturalized or adopted in the UK. Only those with close ancestral links could enter the UK. Many Asians could not establish such links and they were admitted at the discretion of the State who set a quota of 1,500 per annum. Spencer (1997, p. 142) notes that the Act was 'a straightforward device to deny rights to, amongst others, East African Asians without disenfranchising the numerous 'white' people of British origin settled outside Britain in the "old" dominions and in southern Rhodesia, Kenya or Argentina'. As a result of the Act, the British High Commission-issued passports of the East African Asians were no longer of any use to those wanting to gain entry to the UK (Spencer, 1997). Like earlier legislation the 1968 Act also coincided directly with a period of economic decline and most significantly in terms of the employment of people from minority ethnic groups, the onset of de-industrialization.

Even after the 1968 legislation, Asians continued to arrive, in Britain, from East Africa. Between 1969 and 1971 over 24,000 Asians left Uganda, mostly to come to Britain (Robinson, 1986). In 1971, when Idi Amin gained power in Uganda, Asians were ordered to leave and many came to Britain. In total around 155,000 East African Asians, mainly from Uganda, have settled in Britain. Between 1972 and 1973, 29,000 Ugandan Asians arrived as programme refugees.

The Ugandan Resettlement Board (URB) was set up to direct resettlement. The Board tried to disperse this cohort of refugees and delineated areas as red 'no-go' areas and green 'go' areas. When a city was declared 'red' the URB tried to discourage refugees from settling there. In spite of the URB's efforts, many chose to settle in areas with already established Asian communities and there was also much secondary migration especially to London and the Midlands. In fact, the government's policy of dispersal resulted in a more concentrated spatial distribution of East African Asians than had occurred naturally among Pakistanis and Bangladeshis (Robinson, 1986). The arrival of these refugees coincided with high unemployment and pressure on housing. The URB gave little attention to employment, a criticism that was later directed at the Vietnamese programme (see Joly, 1996) and among those who found work more than two-thirds were downwardly mobile (Kushner and Knox, 1999).

Other groups arrived as programme refugees. The Ugandan Asians were followed by 3,000 Chileans in 1973 and 19,000 Vietnamese, Laotians and Cambodians came to Britain as programme refugees between 1975 and 1990. The only European group to come as part of a programme were the 10,000 Greek Cypriots who came to Britain after the Turkish invasion of Cyprus in 1974. For those arriving as recognized or programme refugees in the 1970s and 1980s there was help with reorientation and adaptation. This period is noted for its utilization of dispersal and for the reliance on the voluntary sector (Joly, 1996; Kushner and Knox, 1999).

In addition to programme refugees, spontaneous asylum seekers also came to Britain from all over the world. The cultural and ethnic diversity of these refugees not only affected the responses of the countries of asylum but also affected the experiences of the refugees themselves. This is due to the general rule that the greater the differences in terms of racial, religious and cultural characteristics between refugees and the host population, the harder integration will be for new arrivals (Loescher, 1993).

Like the Ugandan Asians, the Vietnamese formed part of a programme that included dispersal. Groups of between four and ten families were dispersed from reception centres to locations around the country where there was available housing. In some areas there was little opportunity for economic resettlement. Once again, there was large-scale secondary migration to large urban centres with established Chinese communities (Robinson and Hale, 1989). Jones (1983) noted the difficulties faced by Vietnamese refugees in terms of language learning, employment and social relations with British people due to cultural differences.

Alongside refugee migration were the continued attempts, through legislation, to curb migration as well as overtly racist discourse most notably through the brief rise of Enoch Powell, as a public figure, following his 'river of blood' speech (Layton-Henry, 1992). Powell was criticized by members of the Labour government as well as his Conservative colleagues for the offensive content of his speech. Powell was sacked from the Conservative shadow cabinet, though he retained and acquired much support from constituency members and the public at large.

The Conservatives won the 1970 general election and soon after introduced the 1971 Immigration Act. The Act became law in 1973 and created an exclusionary aspect to British citizenship based on the concept of patrials and non-patrials (Goulbourne, 1998). The Act restricted the entrance to Britain of non-patrials, including UK passport holders. In effect, the legislation changed the status of New Commonwealth citizens to aliens by only allowing the right to abode of people who were either born in the UK or had parents born in the UK. The patriality clause created racially defined categories that excluded almost all non-white Commonwealth citizens from entry (Spencer, 1997). In addition, the Act also changed the status of employment vouchers to work permits that did not carry rights for permanent residency or entry for dependants. Layton-Henry (1992, p. 85) noted that the legislation was 'another major milestone in the process of erecting racist immigration controls'.

Although primary labour migration had virtually ended as a consequence of the 1971 Act, in the early 1980s Immigration Rules and the 1981 British Nationality Act were introduced to further restrict the entry of Black and Asian migrants to Britain (Spencer, 1997). This period saw the introduction of the 'Primary Purpose Rule' that forbade the entrance of spouses and betrothed persons who could not prove that the purpose of their marriage was settlement.

The 1981 British Nationality Act reduced rights to citizenship through the creation of three categories of United Kingdom and Commonwealth citizenship: British citizens, British Dependent Territories citizens and British Overseas citizens. Only those in the first category had any rights of settlement and abode in the UK. The category British Overseas citizens had the effect of excluding British citizens, of mostly Asian origin, from living in Britain and because of this the Act was criticized for reinforcing racial discrimination (Layton-Henry, 1984). Under the Act the immediate rights to citizenship, to those born in the UK, came to an end (*jus soli*). Only those who were able to satisfy the requirements of patriality were automatically entitled to citizenship. According to Paul (1997, p. 183):

> Thus after more than thirty years of placing limits on the practical rights of British subjects, London formally divided all British subjects into categories perceived to be appropriate to their level of 'real' Britishness ... It accepted a narrowly conceived domestic

community of Britishness based firmly within Britain and rejected the broader political community based within the wider empire/commonwealth.

The final piece of immigration control in the 1980s was the Immigration Act, 1988. This Act introduced significant changes relating to entry into Britain and around the notion of recourse to public funds. Under the Act, the spouse and children of Commonwealth citizens settled before 1973 were no longer entitled to the automatic right of entry. It was this Act that brought about an end to nearly all migration from Commonwealth countries. The Act also introduced the criterion that families of those already living in Britain were only entitled to enter the UK if the family will be maintained without recourse to public funds. This was a further extension of the link between welfare and immigration first established in UK law as early as 1905 with the Aliens Act. Thus successive pieces of legislation have brought primary labour migration to Britain to a virtual end.

## Demography and geography of ethnic groups at the end of the twentieth century

The 1991 Census data show that at the end of the twentieth century Britain is a multiethnic country. The profile of Britain's ethnic minority population changed dramatically in the postwar period with the increase in labour migration from former British colonies. In 1951 there were 218,000 people of New Commonwealth origin living in Britain and this had increased to over three million in 1991. While Britain is statistically ethnically diverse, the distribution of ethnic minorities tends to be highly concentrated in certain urban areas while other areas remain largely homogeneous and white.

The main concentration of ethnic minorities is in Greater London. In fact 44.6 per cent of all people from ethnic minority groups living in Britain are resident in Greater London (Owen, 1994). Table 2.5 shows that eight of the ten local authority areas with the highest proportion of ethnic minority residents in England are in Greater London. Only Leicester and Slough are outside London.

Outside London there are concentrations of ethnic minorities in the 'mill towns' of Lancashire, greater Manchester and Yorkshire, the Midlands, the University towns of Oxford and Cambridge and towns in the north of the south east region, namely Luton, Peterborough and Northampton (Owen, 1994). Some of the localities with the main

Table 2.5    The ten local authority areas with the highest proportion of ethnic minority residents in England, 1991 Census

| Rank | Local Authority | Percentage of ethnic minority residents |
|------|-----------------|------------------------------------------|
| 1 | Brent | 44.8 |
| 2 | Newham | 42.3 |
| 3 | Tower Hamlets | 35.6 |
| 4 | Hackney | 33.6 |
| 5 | Ealing | 32.3 |
| 6 | Lambeth | 30.3 |
| 7 | Haringey | 29.0 |
| 8 | Leicester | 28.5 |
| 9 | Slough | 27.7 |
| 10 | Harrow | 26.2 |

concentrations of an ethnic group include Leicester where 22.3 per cent of the population described their ethnic group as Indian while 22.3 per cent of the population of Tower Hamlets, in east London were Bangladeshi. In Hackney 22 per cent of the population described themselves coming from one of the 'Black' ethnic groups and 9.9 per cent of the populations of Bradford were of Pakistani origin (Teague, 1993).

Residential segregation takes place for a number of reasons. First, migrant workers usually start in low paid work and are sending home remittances so they seek out cheap housing. Second, people migrated to areas where there was employment and so this reinforced the pattern of clustering. Third, social networks and the pattern of chain migration facilitated the pattern of ethnic clustering. In addition to the social and economic factors that lead to clustering, migrants are also forced out of areas due to racism. It was the recognition of racism that resulted in the introduction of the first race relations legislation in 1965.

## Race relations

From the early 1960s, as we have seen, immigration control became politically expedient and was used as a mechanism for gaining the support of the electorate by both political parties when in government. One of the main arguments used by successive governments for immigration control is that it is a necessary precondition of good race relations (Spencer, 1998). Immigration controls have not been introduced in isolation; they have been accompanied by race relations legislation. Race Relations Acts have entered the statute book in 1965, 1968, 1976 and as recently as 2000.

The Race Relations Act 1965, set up the Race Relations Board to deal with cases of discrimination. It also made it unlawful to discriminate in public places or on public transport. Outside the remit of the Act was discrimination in key areas of life such as housing and employment. Even though the Act was limited, it was significant in that it acknowledged the fact that racial discrimination existed and that it was an undesirable aspect of British society (Goulbourne, 1998).

Between 1965 and 1968, when the second Race Relations Act was introduced, Roy Jenkins, the then Home Secretary set out his vision for society, which was an integrated multiracial society characterized by equal opportunity (Goulbourne, 1998). To this end, other policy initiatives came on stream during this period notably Section 11 Funding, which was introduced as part of the Local Government Act 1966. The scheme was set up to divert funds to local communities. The significance of the scheme was that it diverted local funding to specific provisions for Black and Asian people within local government spending. This preceded the introduction of the Urban Programme, under the 1969 Local Government Act, and was concerned with regeneration of deprived areas (see Chapter 6). Due to the omissions and lack of impact of the 1965 Race Relations Act (see Daniel, 1968) new legislation was implemented in 1968. The 1968 Act outlawed discrimination in employment, housing, the provision of goods and services and in advertisements. Under the Act the Community Relations Commission was set up to promote harmonious race relations at the grass roots level.

Further legislation was introduced in 1976 when it was realized that earlier legislation was having little impact on race relations. The 1976 Act extended and strengthened existing policies rather than initiating new ones. The most important development in the 1976 legislation was that it included racial disadvantage brought about by systematic racism. It made it illegal to discriminate on basis of 'colour, race, nationality or ethnic or national origin' or to segregate people on racial grounds. The 1976 Act also resulted in the reorganization of the Race Relations Board and the Community Relations Commission into the Commission for Racial Equality (CRE) and new procedures for handling complaints about discrimination. Complaints procedures included direct access to industrial tribunals in the case of employment (Solomos, 1993). A significant feature of the 1976 Act is that it distinguishes between direct and indirect discrimination and between discrimination and victimization although there are exemptions including employment and housing.

Between 1985 and 1991 the CRE made a series of recommendations for changing and improving the law. The context is the clear inequality that exists in the areas of employment, education, housing, health and the criminal justice system. The CRE also called for clearer provisions in the area of indirect discrimination. One of the major criticisms of race relations legislation was the exclusion, from its jurisdiction, of public bodies such as the police, the criminal justice system and immigration officials. In February 1999, the Stephen Lawrence Inquiry Report into the investigation of the racist murder of Stephen Lawrence in South London was published (Macpherson, 1999). One of its key recommendations was that:

> the full force of the race relations legislation should apply to all police officers and that chief officers of police should be made vicariously liable for the acts and omissions of their officers relevant to that legislation (Recommendation 11).

One of the consequences of the Inquiry was that the then Home Secretary, Jack Straw, committed himself to introducing legislation that would bring all the functions of all public bodies, not just the police, within the scope of race relations legislation. In 2000 the Race Relations (Amendment) Act entered the statute books and under the Act public bodies are no longer exempt from the legislation. However, an amendment to the race relations legislation does not prevent racist attacks and discrimination from taking place all over Britain.

## Summary

This chapter has shown the longevity of migration to the UK, the introduction of increasingly restrictive immigration controls, the demography and geography of ethnic minority communities in Britain at the end of the twentieth century and the development of race relations legislation.

Immigration controls began at the turn of the century in response to large scale Jewish migration, but it was not until the 1960s that Britain set out to prevent the migration of nationals from Commonwealth countries through the racialization of immigration controls. Policies and attitudes towards refugees and asylum seekers also varied during this period though they were free to enter the UK until the 1968 Act, which was in direct response to the situation in East Africa. Refugees who entered the UK in the postwar period under the European Volunteer Workers scheme were selected for their economic utility and were preferred to the colonial workers because the terms of their residence were strictly controlled. However, workers from the former colonies were also recruited in an effort to rebuild Britain after the war. The government intervened with restrictive legislation in 1962. There was a strong correlation between the economic needs of the country and the number of migrants entering Britain.

From 1962 until 1988, successive pieces of legislation changed the citizenship rights of former colonial subjects and brought to an end almost all primary migration. Throughout the 1990s, successive Conservative and Labour governments, with the aim of curtailing the numbers of spontaneous asylum seekers arriving in the UK, have introduced new immigration legislation. The Labour government has just introduced the Race Relation (Amendment) Act though this has been alongside more restrictive immigration control.

Chapter 3 will explore asylum policies in the 1990s. It will also examine the development of European policy, which is becoming increasingly more significant at the nation state level.

# 3
# Current UK and European Policy

Asylum policy in Britain and Europe has been affected by the increase in the diversity of refugees and asylum seekers arriving in Europe coupled with increasing numbers. It is these developments, alongside economic variations and public opinion, that have led to European countries of asylum, including the UK, introducing restrictive new immigration controls.

Alongside national legislation, the European harmonization project has gathered pace and is set not only to affect border controls but also the reception and resettlement of forced migrants to Europe. Patterns of migration across Europe have changed and even countries that were previously countries of emigration, for instance Greece and Italy, have found themselves countries of immigration (Sitaropoulos, 2000; Vincenzi, 2000). Policy initiatives have been in response to such changes.

In this chapter, refugee migration to Britain will be documented followed by developments in UK asylum policy and the introduction of European-level agreements for the handling of border controls and asylum applications. The European dimension is becoming increasingly influential as countries are, according to Schuster (2000, pp. 120–1), 'approaching and striving for this common policy ... Harmonisation remains an ideal to which all these countries are committed.'

## Refugee migration at the end of the twentieth century

Throughout the 1980s and 1990s diversity of origin was a key characteristic of asylum seekers to Britain. Alongside this was the increasing numbers of spontaneous asylum seekers. Though the majority of

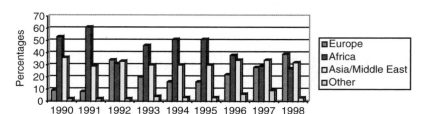

Source: Refugee Council (1998) and Home Office (1999a)
*Figure 3.1*   Principal asylum applicants by area of origin, 1990–98.

asylum seekers during the 1980s and 1990s arrived spontaneously most recently there have been quotas accepted on Temporary Protection from the Former Yugoslavia (2,500) and from Kosovo (4,000) (Bloch, 1999a; Cohen, 1994).

Figure 3.1 and Table 3.1 clearly demonstrate not only the diversity of origin of asylum seekers to the UK but also the way in which asylum applicants reflect areas and regions of crisis. For instance, the proportion of asylum seekers who arrived in Britain from Europe increased in 1992 as a direct consequence of the conflict in Bosnia. Table 3.1 shows that the three case study communities – refugees from Somalia, Sri Lanka and the DRC – were key countries in terms of the origins of asylum seekers in the 1990s.

The data in Table 3.2 show numbers of asylum applicants arriving in Britain. With the exception of 1992, 1993 and 1996 the rest of the 1990s has shown a year-on-year increase in the numbers of asylum seekers arriving.

Table 3.1 shows that throughout the 1990s, asylum seekers arrived in the UK in large numbers from Sri Lanka, Somalia and Turkey. The largest number of asylum seekers arriving in Britain, in the 1990s, came from the former Yugoslavia.

## Policy responses to refugees at the end of the twentieth century

In response to increasing numbers of asylum seekers arriving in Europe in the 1980s, Britain and other European countries began to introduce more restrictive asylum regimes. Moreover, the curtailment of voluntary migration brought about by earlier legislation, meant that refugees and asylum seekers have become the largest single category of people coming to the UK after transit passengers and visitors (Home Office, 2000).

Table 3.1   Countries with the most asylum applicants to the UK, 1990–9

| | | | | | Number of applicants | | | | | |
|---|---|---|---|---|---|---|---|---|---|---|
| | 1990 | 1991 | 1992 | 1993 | 1994 | 1995 | 1996 | 1997 | 1998 | 1999 |
| Sri Lanka | 3,300 | 3,765 | 2,085 | 1,965 | 2,350 | 2,070 | | 1,830 | 3,505 | 5,130 |
| *Former Yugoslavia | | | 5,635 | 1,830 | | | 2,245 | | 7,980 | 14,375 |
| Ghana | | 2,405 | 1,600 | 1,785 | 2,035 | 1,915 | | | | |
| Nigeria | | | | 1,665 | 4,340 | 5,825 | | | | |
| Turkey | 2,110 | 1,865 | | 1,480 | 2,045 | | | | 2,015 | 2,850 |
| Somalia | 2,250 | | 1,575 | 1,465 | 1,840 | 3,465 | 2,730 | | 4,685 | 7,500 |
| India | | | | | 2,030 | 3,255 | | | | |
| Pakistan | | | | | | 2,915 | | 1,616 | | |
| Former USSR | | 3,245 | 1,700 | | | | 2,015 | | 2,820 | 4,110 |
| Zaire/ Democratic Republic of Congo | 2,590 | 7,010 | | | | | | | | |
| Ethiopia | 2,340 | | | | | | | | | |
| Afghanistan | | | | | | | | | 2,395 | 3,985 |
| Angola | 1685 | 5,780 | | | | | | | | |
| China | | | | | | | | 1,945 | | |

* Does not include programme refugees from Bosnian or Kosovo
*Source:* Refugee Council (1998), http://www.unhcr.ch/statist/0002euro and
http://www.homeoffice.gov.uk/rds/areas/immipf.htm

Table 3.2   Asylum applications, 1988–99

| Year | Number | Percentage change from previous year |
|------|--------|--------------------------------------|
| 1988 | 3,998 | −6 |
| 1989 | 11,640 | +191 |
| 1990 | 26,205 | +125 |
| 1991 | 44,840 | +71 |
| 1992 | 24,605 | −45 |
| 1993 | 22,370 | −9 |
| 1994 | 32,830 | +47 |
| 1995 | 43,965 | +34 |
| 1996 | 29,640 | −33 |
| 1997 | 32,500 | +10 |
| 1998 | 46,010 | +42 |
| 1999 | 71,100 | +55 |
| 2000 | 76,040 | +6.5 |

*Source*: Refugee Council (1998) and Home Office (2000)

As a result, asylum seekers have become the focus of new immigration legislation and immigration rules.

Successive governments have attempted to reduce the number of asylum seekers gaining access to the UK through the introduction of visa restrictions on the nationals of asylum producing countries. Visa requirements were imposed on nationals from Sri Lanka in 1985 and in 1989, at the time when Kurds were claiming asylum, the government imposed visa requirements on Turkish nationals (Cohen, 1994).

In addition to the new visa requirements, the Immigration (Carrier's Liability) Act, 1987 was introduced amidst fears of the numbers of people entering Britain, some with false documentation. Under this Act, fines of £1,000 were imposed on carrier companies that brought passengers, with false or without the necessary documents and visas, into the UK. Carrier's liability has since been extended. The fines were doubled to £2,000 in 1991 and in 2000 trucking companies were also included under the terms of Carrier's Liability. This Act was significant because it introduced a new approach to immigration control that imposed responsibilities on other bodies to prevent and control immigration. Other deterrents have also been introduced including the use of detention and the curtailment of the welfare entitlements available to asylum seekers waiting for their cases to be determined (Bloch, 2000c). Welfare is perceived as a pull factor by some states even though the argument is without empirical justification (Bloch and Schuster, 2002 forthcoming; Thränhardt, 1999).

## Detention

The use of detention has increased in Britain. In the early 1990s around 200 asylum seekers were detained at any one time but numbers increased with the opening of more dedicated detention centres. In October 1996, there were 864 asylum seekers in detention of which 343 were in ordinary prisons (Liebaut and Hughes, 1997). By July 1998 as many as 800 asylum seekers were detained at any one time and by July 2000 the number had increased to 1,037. Of those detained, 37 per cent are in immigration detention centres and 63 per cent are in prison establishments (National Coalition of Anti-Deportation Campaigns, 2000). The average time spent in detention is 65 days although some asylum seekers are detained for much longer periods of time (UNHCR, 2000a).

Asylum seekers are detained under immigration law and they can be detained for any length of time and for any reason. Detention is often used by immigration officials at the beginning of the asylum process in order to prevent asylum seekers absconding and to facilitate speedy deportation. One of the concerns about detention is that it is being used as a deterrent to other asylum seekers from a particular country of origin (Morrison, 1998).

As the system stands, asylum seekers can apply for bail if they have been detained for more than six days and they can also apply for bail pending the hearing of an appeal against a negative decision. However the conditions attached to getting bail, such as the posting of financial bonds, make it difficult to get. A centre was opened in March 2000 for asylum seekers whose claims are considered to be 'manifestly unfounded'. Asylum seekers are detained in the centre for one week while their claim is processed in an accelerated procedure. Many are then moved to detention centres or prisons prior to removal. The government is also using detention more at the other end of the asylum process – prior to the removal of asylum seekers from the country following a negative decision.

## Immigration legislation in the 1990s

### Asylum and Immigration Appeals Act, 1993

The first piece of legislation introduced into British law, designed specifically to target asylum seekers, was the 1993 Asylum and

Immigration Appeals Act (Schuster and Solomos, 1999). The 1993 Act was justified as a mechanism for speeding up asylum applications although in reality what it did was introduce new harsh measures designed to act as a deterrent (Macdonald, 1993). Fingerprinting was introduced for asylum seekers. The practice of returning asylum seekers to a third country if they had passed through a safe third country on route to the UK was introduced. In addition, asylum seekers' rights to social housing were reduced and asylum seekers who had received a negative decision on their case were given only 48 hours in which to lodge an appeal.

In addition, carrier's liability was extended so that airlines have to demand transit visas to prevent people disembarking in the UK and claiming asylum. Fines were increased for carriers bringing people into the UK without the correct documentation (Cohen, 1994; Kushner and Knox, 1999). Not surprisingly, there was a correlation between the extension of visa controls and the subsequent increase in the number of asylum seekers using false documentation (Guild, 2000).

## Asylum and Immigration Act, 1996

In November 1995, just two years after the introduction of the 1993 Act, a new Asylum and Immigration Bill was introduced into Parliament. The Bill was justified by the then Home Secretary Michael Howard who stated that the UK

> is a far too attractive destination for bogus asylum seekers and other illegal immigrants. The reason is simple: it is far easier to obtain access to jobs and benefits here than almost anywhere else (*Hansard* 20/11/1995, 338).

The argument put forward by the government in support of the Bill was that 'bogus' asylum seekers came to Britain because of economic opportunities rather than persecution. The Bill became the 1996 Asylum and Immigration Act. The Act introduced new regulations around social security by differentiating between asylum seekers who applied at the port of entry, who were seen as genuine, and those who applied in-country who were labelled as bogus. Under the legislation, port applicants were still entitled to 90 per cent of the social security benefit income support while those who applied for asylum in country were no longer eligible for cash benefits or homeless persons assistance and instead had to rely on very limited in-kind support from local authorities. In-kind support was often in the form of vouchers and food handouts. Local authorities had a statutory duty to provide for destitute single asylum seekers under the 1948 National Assistance Act while local authorities under the provisions of the 1989 Children Act supported asylum-seeking families.

Dividing asylum applicants into those who applied at the port of entry and those who applied in country was a problem given that there is little correlation between place of application and the outcome of the determination process. In 1997, a greater proportion of cases given refugee status applied in country than at the port (Refugee Council, 1998).

The 1996 Act also included a clause relating to employment whereby any employer who took on someone without the appropriate documentation was subject to a penalty fine. According to Morris (1997, p. 255):

> internal policing will tend to focus suspicion on the 'visibly different' minorities and have the effect of eroding their legitimate rights, affecting both employment opportunities and access to services ... the requirement of employers to police the legality of their workers ... common elsewhere in Europe and known to discriminate against legally present minorities, has been introduced in Britain by the 1996 Asylum and Immigration Act.

Research carried out by the Refugee Council (1999) found that employers were less likely to employ asylum seekers and refugees due to the extra burden of checking documentation.

Another measure introduced under the 1996 Act was a 'White List' of countries that were judged to be safe. Applicants from countries on the 'White List' were to be fast-tracked through the appeals process as the underlying assumption was that their claims were unfounded.

Housing provision was also affected by the 1993 and 1996 legislation. Prior to the 1993 Act, asylum seekers were entitled to local authority housing and to nominations for housing association accommodation. The statutory duty of local authorities to provide social housing for all in priority need was curtailed and replaced by a complex system of exclusion and eligibility. Zetter and Pearl (1999, p. 240) note that the impact of the policy change 'is to create a distinction between refugees and asylum seekers so far as housing and housing benefits are concerned'. While refugees and those with ELR qualify for local authority housing virtually all asylum seekers are excluded.

Prior to the implementation of the Immigration and Asylum Act, 1999, in April 2000, London boroughs were supporting around 80,000 asylum seekers (Audit Commission, 2000a). A survey carried out by the Audit Commission (2000b) found that more than one-third of asylum-seeking families had been housed in bed and breakfast accommodation, hostels or hotel annexes and the largest proportion (48 per cent) were in private rented housing. Of the single asylum seekers receiving support under the 1948 National Assistance Act the largest proportion (44 per cent) were in private rented property and just under one third were in bed and breakfast accommodation or hostels. The consequence of placing asylum seekers in temporary and often unsuitable accommodation is that the sense of social exclusion is increased and settlement is undermined (Zetter and Pearl, 1999).

## Immigration and Asylum Act, 1999

The 1999 Act follows its predecessors by adopting a dual strategy of further restrictions to the UK as an asylum destination and the curtailment of welfare provision. To reduce the number of asylum seekers gaining access to Britain's borders a number of pre-entry controls have been introduced or reinforced. The number of Airline Liaison Officers deployed at airports in asylum producing countries has been increased as it was found to be effective in reducing the number of asylum seekers. In addition, carrier's liability has been extended to include trucking companies. Under the expanded carrier's liability, trucking companies are fined if they are found to be transporting clandestine entrants. The impetus for including trucking companies has been the increasing number of migrants who are being smuggled overland across borders.

The Act also created a new support system for asylum seekers that lies outside other statutory assistance schemes. Under the provisions of the Act all asylum seekers are excluded from the social security system and those entitled to support are assessed for vouchers administered by a new agency, the National Asylum Support Service (NASS).

Asylum seekers receive around 70 per cent of the welfare support received by British citizens of which £10 is in cash and the remainder in vouchers. Vouchers are redeemable at specified supermarkets and retail outlets, although change is not given to asylum seekers for purchases of less than the value of the vouchers and retailers keep the profit as an incentive to participate in the scheme.

The 1999 Act has also changed the housing provision available to those seeking asylum by introducing compulsory dispersal, on a no choice basis, to accommodation around the country for anyone who is recognized as destitute, after an assessment by NASS. There are stringent regulations attached to the provision of housing with regard to being absent from their designated accommodation that make it extremely difficult for asylum seekers to leave their dispersal area.

Asylum seekers who are dispersed under NASS are supposed to be assisted in accessing services by the housing providers who are contracted to 'facilitate' such access. However, the way in which access to services is facilitated varies between housing providers. Some housing providers employ an asylum support worker who helps new arrivals to access services, learn about the local area and the way in which the support system works. Other providers, in contrast, act like estate agents providing only housing or minimal support such as a list of names and numbers to new arrivals who are then left to try and negotiate their way through the system. On receipt of a positive decision from the Immigration and Nationality Department an asylum seeker has just 14 days to move out of NASS accommodation. If they are deemed to have 'priority need' they are then entitled to benefits and are eligible for local authority housing (Audit Commission, 2000b). The new system has effectively created a tier of provision exclusively for asylum seekers that separates them from mainstream support.

### The policy of dispersal

Dispersal policies have been justified by the government as a means of burden sharing due to the propensity of asylum seekers to remain in London and the South East of England. According to the then Home secretary Jack Straw:

> The pressure on housing and other services both from asylum seekers and others housed by local authorities in those areas is intense and unsustainable. It results in problems for London local authorities, and indeed for Kent local authorities, in discharging their duties towards local homeless households under homelessness legislation. Asylum seekers themselves often end up in very poor conditions. No one ... believes that such concentration of asylum seekers in one part of the country is sensible or defensible (*Hansard*, 9 November 1999, cited in Boswell, 2001)

Cluster areas have been set up using a regional consortia approach in partnership with the London Government Association who has responsibility for the management of dispersal on a local level.

Eight regional consortia have been set up in England. The areas are: North West, Yorkshire and Humberside, West Midlands, East Midlands, South West, South Central, North East and Eastern England. By dispersing asylum seekers to local authority areas around the country a holding operation has emerged for the duration of the asylum determination process. Refugee Council and Refugee Action have set up one-stop shops in the regions but most of their work is carried out in the regional centres. Those outside the centres do not have ease of access to the one-stop shops. Given the size of the regions, the costs of travel and the lack of cash benefits, it is clear that gaining access to such services will prove difficult for asylum seekers.

Dispersal is not a new phenomenon in Britain. In Chapter 2 it was noted that it had been a strategy adopted for the resettlement of both Ugandan Asians and Vietnamese refugees in the 1970s and 1980s. More recently it has been used in the temporary settlement of Kosovar Albanians. As with the cohorts of Ugandan Asians and Vietnamese, a pattern of secondary migration began to emerge with Kosovar Albanians very soon after their arrival and dispersal in Britain (Bloch, 1999a). The same pattern is emerging with current asylum seekers who arrive spontaneously and are dispersed by NASS. Table 3.3 shows the number of asylum seekers dispersed to the regions.

Table 3.3    Asylum seekers and their dependents allocated support by the National Asylum Support Service (NASS) until the end of May 2001

| Region | Allocated accommodation | Allocated voucher only |
|---|---|---|
| East Midlands | 1,550 | 280 |
| East of England | 220 | 1,050 |
| London | 650 | 11,040 |
| North East | 4,730 | 40 |
| North West | 5,950 | 270 |
| Northern Ireland | 70 | 10 |
| Scotland | 3,480 | 170 |
| South Central (including Kent and Sussex) | 370 | 2,040 |
| South West | 500 | 230 |
| Wales | 180 | 90 |
| West Midlands | 3,300 | 270 |
| Yorkshire and Humberside | 6,160 | 130 |
| Total | 27,160 | 15,620 |

Data does not include cases where support has been terminated
*Source*: Research Development and Statistics Directorate, Home Office.

According to data from the Refugee Council around 60 per cent of those dispersed as part of the interim scheme that preceded the full introduction of the new system returned to London. Moreover, 50 per cent have opted for the support package without housing, placing pressure on family, friends and community organizations to provide accommodation. Even though the justification for dispersal was to relieve pressure on London and the South East of England, the amount of secondary migration means that this is not in fact happening.

The main reasons for secondary migration are clear. On arrival in exile asylum seekers and refugees seek out social and community networks for support. Social networks are very important in the short-term adaptation process (Koser, 1997) and in some instances provide not only social support but also employment opportunities (Robinson, 1993a). Those living in dispersal areas can find themselves very isolated especially as dispersal is often housing rather than needs led. Some find themselves in largely white indigenous areas and this has effectively removed any access to community activity and support, help with language and translation as well as cultural needs like community food and places of worship (Zetter and Pearl, 2000).

Evidence from interviews with representatives from the Refugee Council[1] in July 2000, a few months after the implementation of dispersal for port applicants, suggested that there are a number of key areas that are proving problematic with the new asylum support system. First there are difficulties with the administration of vouchers. Outside the larger urban areas some supermarkets have not been informed about how to use the vouchers and are refusing to accept them. Moreover, in some cases the housing providers are not telling asylum seekers which supermarkets they can use and how to get to them which is causing problems. Also housing is a particularly problematic area. The whole process of housing allocation, especially the role of the housing providers is ad hoc and variable. The role of the housing provider needs to be clarified and enforced. In addition, the policy of no choice dispersal is leaving some asylum seekers in inappropriate and unsuitable housing in areas that have not been properly assessed. As a result, some single people are in housing with double beds and have been forced to share beds with strangers while others have been left isolated in white homogeneous areas where they

---

1. Exploratory interview carried out with two project workers and two development workers in one of the regions.

are increasingly vulnerable to racist attacks and racist abuse. Part of the reason for this is the new visibility of asylum seekers residing in predominantly white areas, but also the new system of vouchers makes asylum seekers instantly identifiable in local supermarkets and shops. Increasingly there are reports of the murder of asylum seekers in unprovoked racist attacks. For example, a young Turkish asylum seeker was killed in the Sighthill area of Glasgow in Scotland in August 2001, an area where there had already been 70 racist attacks on asylum seekers in the past 14 months. Other countries that operate dispersal policies, such as Germany, have also experienced violence towards asylum seekers in the dispersal areas (Schönwälder, 1999).

Third, the new system is evolving gradually. Asylum seekers are arriving in areas where there is little or no preparation for them or any understanding of their needs. Moreover, some asylum seekers are in areas where there are no interpretation services, legal advice or refugee community organizations to assist new arrivals. Because of this the system has been criticized by voluntary organizations (Boswell, 2001). Indeed, in the words of one project worker: ... 'the new system is very bureaucratic and lacks compassion. It's a system that's not meant to be easy for the asylum seeker ... it's meant to be a deterrent.'

The 1990s saw the introduction, into the statute book, of three new pieces of primary legislation. However, the strategies adopted in Britain, to deter and contain asylum seekers in not unique, it is part of a European wide trend that has seen similar measures introduced in many nation states (Schuster, 2000).

## The EU context

In addition to national restrictions on immigration, the Single European Act (SEA), 1986 which allowed freedom of movement within the European Union (EU) from 1993, led to a series of Europe-wide policy measures aimed at curbing migration from outside the European Union (King, 1993). The unification of European asylum policy was instigated at a time when there was an increase in asylum seekers coming to Europe, which coincided with an economic recession (Joly, 1996). Europe on the one hand has adopted a liberal approach to internal migration while on the other hand has imposed new controls and restrictions on people coming into Europe who are not citizens of an EU country (Convey and Kupiszewski, 1995).

The harmonization of European asylum and immigration policy has been a gradual and ongoing process and there are now plans to

Table 3.4    Number of asylum applications to countries of the EU by year of application, 1988–99

| Year | Number |
|------|--------|
| 1988 | 210,600 |
| 1989 | 288,100 |
| 1990 | 400,200 |
| 1991 | 512,700 |
| 1992 | 672,500 |
| 1993 | 515,900 |
| 1994 | 309,900 |
| 1995 | 131,400 |
| 1996 | 260,000 |
| 1997 | 252,000 |
| 1998 | 297,000 |
| 1999 | 387,330 |

*Source*: http://www.unhcr.ch/statist/9901asy/text.htm

harmonize standards for the protection and treatment of asylum seekers in European countries of asylum as well. The context for harmonization was first concerns that the SEA would lead to an increase in the numbers of migrants arriving from outside the EU. Second, the increase in the number of asylum seekers arriving in Western Europe, many of whom originate from conflicts in South Eastern Europe. Table 3.4 shows the numbers of asylum seekers to countries of the European Union. The numbers peaked in 1992 as a direct consequence of events in the former Yugoslavia.

There are differences in the numbers of asylum seekers arriving in individual European countries. Throughout the 1990s Germany has received more asylum applicants than any other European country. Table 3.5 shows the ten EU countries with the greatest number of asylum applicants in the 1990s.

Most refugees and asylum seekers from outside of Europe do not in fact seek asylum in European countries but in neighbouring countries in their region of origin. The events in the former Yugoslavia in the 1990s has resulted in a massive increase in the numbers of refugees and asylum seekers in Europe. Table 3.6 shows the numbers of refugees and asylum seekers by region in 1999.

In the UK asylum applications reflect global conflicts. For instance, in 1998 the number of applicants from the Federal Republic of Yugoslavia (FRY) was 7,395, an increase of 5,530 from 1997 (Home Office, 1999a). Kosovo, Montenegro and Serbia are included in the

Table 3.5    Ten European countries with the most asylum applicants, 1990–9

| Country of asylum | Total number of applicants |
|---|---|
| Germany | 1,879,590 |
| United Kingdom | 374,140 |
| The Netherlands | 321,540 |
| France | 296,850 |
| Sweden | 245,540 |
| Belgium | 180,400 |
| Austria | 129,710 |
| Denmark | 112,480 |
| Italy | 89,530 |
| Spain | 83,560 |

*Source*: http://www.unhcr.ch/statist/99oview/toc.htm

Table 3.6    Indicative numbers of refugees and asylum seekers by region, 1999

| Region of asylum/residence | Refugees | Asylum seekers | Total |
|---|---|---|---|
| Africa | 3,523,250 | 61,110 | 3,584,360 |
| Asia | 4,781,750 | 24,750 | 4,806,500 |
| Europe | 2,608,380 | 473,060 | 3,081,440 |
| Latin America/ Caribbean | 61,200 | 1,510 | 62,710 |
| Northern America | 636,300 | 605,630 | 1,241,930 |
| Oceania | 64,500 | 15,540 | 80,040 |
| Total | 11,675,380 | 1,181,600 | 12,856,980 |

*Source*: http://www.unhcr.ch/statist/99oview/tab207.pdf

FRY. In 1999, with the increased conflict in Kosovo, the number of applicants from the FRY rose to 14,180.

### Harmonization of asylum policy

Since 1985, there have been a number of agreements between member and non-member states of the European Union concerning immigration control, the exchange of information and countries responsible for examining individual asylum applications. The first international agreement was the Schengen Agreement drawn up in 1985. The original signatories of the Schengen Agreement were Germany, France, Belgium, the Netherlands and Luxembourg. In 1990, the Schengen Agreement was ratified as a Convention. With the exception of the UK and Ireland, all member states of the EU have subsequently signed the

Schengen Convention and two non-member states, Norway and Iceland, are also signatories.

Schengen was the first major step towards lifting internal European Union (EU) border controls for EU citizens. The agreement to dispense with internal border controls within the core group was not implemented until 1995 and then delayed until 1996 mainly due to French concerns over security issues. Alongside the lifting of internal borders was also the development of closer police and customs cooperation to monitor the movements of non-EU citizens and a computerized system for the exchange of personal data (Schengen Information System and European Automated Fingerprinting Regulation System). In addition, Schengen was also crucial to the development of an EU immigration and asylum policy (Geddes, 2000). Strategies included the harmonization of visa policies and conditions for entry as well as improved cooperation between states. It also included an agreement over state responsibility for the examination of an asylum application to prevent multiple applications being made by any individual (Joly, 1996).

In addition to the Schengen Convention, there have also been two other conventions concerned with similar issues: the Dublin Convention and the Draft Convention on the Crossing of External Borders. The remit of the Dublin Convention was wider than that of Schengen because it was EU wide rather than limited to the Schengen countries (Uçarer, 1997). The Dublin Convention went through a drawn out process of ratification and was only ratified in May 1997 when it was signed by Ireland (Levy, 1999).

The Dublin Convention, like Schengen, was concerned with providing arrangements for dealing with asylum applications to ensure that asylum seekers submitted only one application (Geddes, 2000). However, the premise upon which this policy is based is that an application made in any state of the EU will have the same outcome. That is to say that the procedures for determining an application are the same but this is not the reality (Guild, 1996). As Rogers (1992, p. 1124) notes: 'whether or not bona fide refugees receive official recognition may in some instances depend more on the particular host country in which they arrive rather than on the strength of their cases.'

There are many factors that affect the determination process, in addition to the facts of the case. These include relations between sending and receiving countries that take the form of diplomatic ties, imperial-colonial relations and trade links.

The Draft Convention on the Crossing of External Borders was agreed in 1991 but has not been ratified due a dispute between the UK and Spain over the status of Gibraltar. The purpose of the Convention is to strengthen the control of the outer borders of the EU. The Convention contains sections on carrier's liability; common visa policies and plans to create a database on unwanted third country nationals. In 1992, two additional resolutions, concerned with immigration, were passed. The first, the London Resolution, focused on safe third countries. Safe third countries are those that are passed through on the way to an EU country and are deemed to be safe for refugees and asylum seekers because they comply with the Geneva Convention. An asylum seeker can therefore be returned to a safe third country without their case being reviewed.

The second resolution in 1992 was concerned with 'manifestly unfounded applications'. Member states can fast-track applications in instances where it is deemed not to meet the requirements of the 1951 Geneva Convention or the 1967 Protocol. Moreover, applications can be fast-tracked if there is no substance to the claim or it is based on deception or abuse of the asylum system (Rasmussen, 1996). Such abuses may include the use of forged or false documents or false representations about the claim (Bloch *et al.*, 2000b).

In 1995 the resolution on minimum guarantees for asylum procedures and the resolution on burden sharing with regard to the admission and residence of displaced persons on a temporary basis were introduced. The resolution on minimum guarantees for asylum procedures covers rights in the appeal and review processes, mechanisms for handling unfounded cases and guarantees for women and children that vary in different countries of asylum. The resolution on burden sharing is concerned with taking into account contributions of member states in crisis resolution and the factors that affect the capacity for reception. Joly *et al.* (1997, p. 26) notes that it will be difficult to implement though 'it establishes the long-term position of the EU on temporary protection and is clearly designed for any possible future crises'. Although these Resolutions relate to asylum seekers and refugees, and seek to harmonize the response to asylum seekers on an EU level, they are not binding on the member states.

In 1997, the Treaty of Amsterdam was signed and, under the Treaty, most of the policy making relating to refugees and asylum seekers was moved from the inter-governmental Third Pillar to the communitarian First Pillar of the EU. Under the Treaty of Amsterdam, immigration, asylum and issues of migrant citizenship are very high on the EU policy agenda. The Treaty sets out to establish minimum standards for the treatment and protection of asylum seekers in EU states and is also concerned with the formulation of a pan-European migration policy. Such concerns were echoed in 1999 in Tampere, Finland, at the meeting of the European Council on the Establishment of an Area of Freedom, Security and Justice.

As things stand now, however, the concrete policy developments have been in the areas of border control, responsibility for individual applications and the exchange of information. The treatment of asylum seekers in any European country of asylum and the way in which any individual case is determined remains the domain of each nation state. The consequence is diversity among nation states though the overall trend of restrictionism and limited – or in some cases no social assistance – is to be found across Europe.

**Provisions for asylum seekers in European countries**

Some countries with long histories of immigration have had asylum policies in place for sometime while others who are historically countries of emigration, such as Greece and Italy, are just beginning to implement polices. Of significance in the seven EU states examined by Schuster (2000) is that the development of policy is reactive rather than developmental.

After implementing tighter border controls, access to welfare has become the second strategy used to limit the numbers of asylum seekers arriving in any host country. There is much disparity in the social assistance packages offered to asylum seekers in European countries as Table 3.7 shows.

One thing that emerges from a comparison of provisions for asylum seekers in Western Europe in 1997 (Liebaut and Hughes) and 2000 (Liebaut with Blichfeldt) is that in some countries the situation for asylum seekers has worsened. The only country where asylum seekers can apply immediately for a temporary work permit is Greece. Greece is also the only country without any statutory provision for asylum seekers so if asylum seekers without independent means were not allowed to work they would have to rely on charity or undocumented illegal work. Portugal is also notably harsh as those under accelerated procedures are excluded from social assistance and the labour market.

In addition, some countries, notably Ireland, Germany and Britain, operate compulsory dispersal to centres and localities around the country on a 'no choice' basis. Most countries operate some kind of reception centre provision of allocated accommodation for asylum seekers though the level of restriction and amount of choice varies.

Table 3.7   Monthly income of asylum seekers in European countries

| Country | Monthly allowance for single adult in Euros | Eligibility to work |
|---------|---------------------------------------------|---------------------|
| Austria | Those under 'federal care' (around 30% of asylum seekers) allowed pocket money of EUR 38.5. | Can apply for permit but few given permission to work |
| Belgium | Those outside of centres entitled to EUR 518. | Depends on a request for a permit from a prospective employer |
| Denmark | Those in reception/accommodation centres get EUR 304.2 for clothing, food and pocket money. Those outside centres get no financial support. | Not entitled to work |
| Finland | Living allowance – excluding accommodation – EUR 292.5. | After 3 months can apply for a work permit relating to a specific job. Permit only granted if the job cannot be filled by national or resident. |
| France | One off allowance of EUR 304.9 on arrival. Those in centres with full board get EUR 91.4 while those outside centres get EUR 274.4. | Not entitled to work |
| Germany | EUR 41 pocket money and in-kind support for those in centres. Those outside receive vouchers or currency. | After 12 months can apply for a work permit. |
| Greece | None – though vulnerable asylum seekers may receive assistance from NGOs. | Can be granted temporary work permit. |
| Ireland | Asylum seekers without income entitled to EUR 391.7. In addition, a rent allowance of EUR 377 many be granted. | Those who have been in Ireland since at least 26 July 1998 are allowed to work. |
| Italy | Those without support entitled to EUR 17.5 per Day for 45 days (i.e. EUR 525 for a 30 day month) | Not entitled to work |

Table 3.7   Monthly income of asylum seekers in European countries (*continued*)

| Country | Monthly allowance for single adult in Euros | Eligibility to work |
|---|---|---|
| Netherlands | Varies according to the extent of meal provision. If all meals provided asylum seekers receive EUR 68.1 and if no meals are provided it is EUR 167.6. | Can work for a maximum of 12 weeks a year but only in agricultural/season work. |
| Portugal | Admitted asylum seekers given EUR 140 for four months. Those under accelerated procedures receive no support. | After 6 months can apply for a work permit. |
| Spain | Those in centres receive pocket money of EUR 41, others receive EUR 242 for six months though it may be extended for 2 additional periods of 3 months. | After 6 months can apply for a work permit. |
| Sweden | EUR 255.6 for those in centres where they prepare their own meals and EUR 86.1 in centres where meals are provided. | After 6 months can apply for a work permit. |
| United Kingdom | Destitute asylum seekers entitled to EUR 72.9 cash alongside in-kind support and supermarket vouchers. | After 6 months can apply for a work permit. |

*Source:* Adapted from Liebaut with Blichfeldt (2000). Morris, L. (2001) 'Stratified rights and the management of migration: National distinctiveness in Europe,' *European Societies*, pp. 387–411

One of the concerns about a unified EU approach to asylum is that countries will opt for the lowest common denominator. Schuster (2000) notes that a unified asylum policy is likely to merely develop the trend of restrictionism across EU states. Moreover, Schuster (2000) maintains that unified policy is likely to continue the effective segregation of asylum seekers in areas where housing is cheap and available, and continue to limit their resources, often in kind, to spend on basics and only in designated shops.

## Summary

This chapter has shown both the increasing diversity and numbers of asylum seekers arriving in Britain at the end of the twentieth century. In response to increasing numbers the UK and European asylum regimes are becoming more restrictive. The legislation in the UK, for instance, has changed the status of asylum seekers from people who could access social security, housing benefits and social housing to a group who are completely outside the mainstream support system. Under the current system, asylum seekers who manage to gain access to the asylum determination process in the UK, are effectively marginalized and isolated through the new support system and compulsory dispersal.

Though successive pieces of legislation have been debated and introduced at times when there have been increases in the numbers of asylum seekers, the evidence shows that there is little or no correlation between new legislation and changes in patterns of asylum seekers. Much more relevant are conflicts that produce asylum seekers. The result of strategies aimed at curtailing the number of asylum seekers arriving in Britain has been an increase in the use of illegal routes including false documentation and the use of smugglers.

The same trend has been evident elsewhere in Europe where a more harmonized approach has emphasized border controls and the nations responsible for the determination of an individual case. Although the ratification of conventions has been slow, the intentions of policy developments are clear. Open internal borders have resulted in the closure of external borders.

New policies, notably temporary protection introduced at the time of the Bosnian crisis, were implemented to ensure 'burden sharing' and to make asylum seekers less unattractive to nationals of European states. This was because it was a short-term solution to a crisis rather than a long-term commitment to the settlement of refugees from the Former Yugoslavia. The same strategy was adopted in the Kosovar case in 1999.

The issue of asylum and the lack of support for asylum seekers are a European phenomenon. Coupled with this is the lack of social assistance provided for asylum seekers and some other forced migrants in European countries. This chapter has shown that provisions for asylum seekers are very minimal and in the case of Greece non-existent. It is evident that the trend across Europe is to prevent asylum seekers from settling as, in most cases, they are excluded from basic welfare, freedom of movement (through the use of reception centres, dispersal and detention) and they have pitifully few opportunities for economic settlement.

In Chapter 4, theories of migration will be examined and their usefulness in understanding refugee migration to Britain at the end of the twentieth century.

# 4
# Theories of Refugee Migration and Migration to Britain

Migration refers to the movement of people and in the context of this work, the concern is international migration, which is the movement of people across international borders. International migration is complex and can involve a number of interacting variables both at the individual level and the structural level. In Europe structural barriers, manifested through increased immigration controls, have gathered pace over the past few decades. These barriers affect access to countries of asylum and the actual migration process itself. Restrictions mean that it is more difficult to enter Europe legally as an asylum seeker. The consequence of border controls and visa restrictions has been the growth in the use of illegal migration routes facilitated by smugglers and traffickers. This necessarily limits the choices available to any potential migrant.

This chapter reviews the development of migration theory and its current application for refugees and asylum seekers. The circumstances surrounding any migratory movement are unique and complex, which makes it difficult for any theory to generalize or predict refugee movements.

Migration theories derive from a number of academic disciplines including sociology, geography, politics, law and economics. Three of the main approaches used in debates about migration are the neo-classical economic equilibrium perspective, the historical-structuralist approach and migration systems theory (Castles and Miller, 1998).

This chapter will first provide an overview of the main theoretical approaches to migration. Second it explores the ways in which the migration experiences of voluntary and forced migrants may differ. Finally, it presents evidence from the case study of refugees and asylum seekers in Newham as a mechanism for exploring the salience of the theoretical paradigms of migration among refugees in Britain.

## Theories of migration

### Neo-classical economic equilibrium perspective

Neo-classical economic theories of migration can be traced back to the work of a geographer, Ravenstein, in the 1880s (Ravenstein, 1885). Such theories argue that workers respond to wage differentials across space and move from low-wage to higher-wage localities. Ravenstein formulated a number of laws to explain migratory movements based predominately on an analysis of English Census data from 1871 and 1881. The main points of Ravenstein's laws were:

- The majority of migrants go only a short distance.
- The major direction is from agricultural areas to centres of commerce and industry.
- Women tend to dominate short journey migrants while men are more likely to travel overseas.
- Migration increases as industry and commerce develop and as transportation improves.
- Migrants going long distances tend to go to one of the great centres of trade and industry.
- The major causes of migration are economic.

Although Ravenstein tried to formulate a model to explain migratory movements, his propositions have been criticized because they neither tested actual movements empirically nor linked movements to factors outside those influencing the individual (Castles and Miller, 1998). Nevertheless, his work has remained important within the push–pull paradigm (Böcker and Havinga, 1997). Migration is often explained in terms of push–pull factors (Castles and Miller, 1998). The term push–pull is used because migration is seen as a combination of push and pull factors that result in the decision to migrate. Push factors are usually negative and include conflict, political instability and social inequality. Pull factors, those that attract people to a particular receiving country, include employment possibilities and freer communities in the country of destination (Loescher, 1993). Push–pull theories have been criticized for their parsimony as they are not able to explain actual movements of people nor are they able to predict the factors that will affect future migratory flows (Boyd, 1989; Kunz, 1973). In addition, economically based theories of migration presume that individual migrants are able to make free choices in order to maximize their well being and that the consequence of this free choice is market equilibrium. They fail to take account of structural factors that prevent the free movement of people such as border controls and fail to consider the situation of the millions of refugees and displaced people around the world (Davis, 1989).

### Historical-structuralist approach

The historical-structuralist approach had its origins in Marxist political economy that emphasizes the unequal distribution of economic and political power in the global economy (Castles and Miller, 1998). The function of migration is to mobilize cheap labour for capital. Thus the early push–pull thesis was superseded by more structural approaches that consider the role of capitalism and the state (Zolberg, 1989). The historical-structuralist approaches have been criticized. According to Castles and Miller (1998, p. 23):

> 'The historical-structural approach often saw the interests of capital as all-determining, and paid inadequate attention to the motivations and actions of the individuals and groups concerned'.

Such approaches also ignore the fact that not all migrants are workers and even when they are, they are various other things as well including members of ethnic and religious groups (Davis, 1989). Moreover, the migration process is not based solely on individual choice in response to market equilibrium. Instead policies exist, notably immigration controls that constrain individual choices. Zolberg (1989, p. 406) notes:

> The observation is applicable to refugees as well as to economic migrations. Regardless of what violence people may be subjected to in the country of origin, this produces a flow of refugees only if people have a place to go.

Migration is in fact more regionalized than it is globalized (Collinson, 1999). The massive number of internally displaced people – estimated by the UNHCR to be between 20 and 25 million – can be in part attributed to structural barriers.

Moreover, the vast majority of the world's refugees remain in their region of origin seeking refuge in a neighbouring country. Table 4.1

Table 4.1    Origin of major refugee populations and main countries of asylum, 31 December 1999

| Country of origin[1] | Total number | Proportion in each of the main countries of asylum (%) |
|---|---|---|
| Afghanistan | 2,601,400 | Iran: 51<br>Pakistan: 46 |
| Iraq | 639,300 | Iran, Islamic Rep.: 80 |
| Burundi | 524,700 | Tanzania: 95 |
| Sierra Leone | 487,200 | Guinea: 76<br>Liberia: 20 |
| Sudan | 474,700 | Uganda: 42<br>Ethiopia: 15<br>DRC: 14<br>Kenya: 14 |
| Somalia | 486,200 | Ethiopia: 36<br>Kenya: 28<br>Yemen: 11 |
| Bosnia-Herzegovina | 472,700 | Yugoslavia Fed. Rep.: 42<br>Austria: 14[*]<br>Sweden:11[*]<br>Germany: 11[*] |
| Angola | 349,600 | Zambia: 47<br>DRC: 43 |
| Eritrea | 345,500 | Sudan: 99 |
| Croatia | 342,400 | Yugoslavia Fed. Rep.: 87<br>Bosnia-Herzegovina: 12 |

[1] An estimated 3.5 Palestinian refugees are covered by a separate mandate of the UN Relief and Works Agency for Palestine Refugees (UNRWA) and are not included in this table.
[*] Number of refugees estimated by UNCHR, based on the arrival of refugees and/or recognition rates of asylum seekers as refugees over the last 10 years. Estimates exclude resettled refugees.
*Source*: UNCHR (2000) Annex 6, pps. 316–318

shows the country of origin and the main countries of asylum for the main refugee populations around the world. It is clear that only a small proportion of refugees ever leave their region of origin.

The emphasis of the historical-structuralist approach on the mobilization for capital neither explains the complexity of migration nor does it provide a theoretical basis for understanding refugee movements. More recently, a migration systems theory has emerged out of economic and structuralist theories that places emphasis on the interaction between a number of social, economic and political variables (Castles and Miller, 1998).

## Migration systems approach

Migration systems theory applies to both transnational relations and social network theory. In terms of transnational relations, the links between the sending and the receiving countries, with historical links between the two countries, are of primary importance and provide the 'historical-political' factors for migration (Böcker and Havinga, 1997). Prior links between the sending and the receiving countries may take the form of trade links, cultural ties, political links and imperial–colonial relations. Transnationalism is not only concerned with the movement of people. It also includes engagement in economic, social, cultural and political activities across national borders. Such activities can take place on an individual basis or through institutional channels (Al-Ali *et al.*, 2001). The extent to which migrants engage in transnational activities will vary according to a number of factors, which include economic circumstances and the circumstances of the migration. Portes (1998, p. 464) notes that:

> When migration is massive and motivated by political convulsions at home, it is likely that immigrants remain morally tied to kin and communities left behind and, hence, are more likely to engage in a variety of activities to bridge the gap and sustain a common bond … On the contrary, where migration is a more individualised process, grounded on personal and family decisions, transnational activities are more selective and, at times, exceptional, lacking the normative component attached to them among participants in a political diaspora.

In terms of migratory movements the links between the sending and the receiving countries is often apparent especially in the case of labour migrants. Chapter 2 showed the large-scale labour migration to Britain from former Commonwealth countries in the postwar period. The reasons for this included economic opportunities but also the pre-existing links between the sending countries and Britain. Such patterns of migration have been replicated elsewhere in Europe notably France and the Netherlands (Baldwin-Edwards and Schain, 1994; Castles and Miller, 1998).

There are a number of reasons why migrants are attracted to the former 'mother' country. First, there are the historical ties that mean there is a degree of familiarity with the migration destination. Second, language is a very important consideration because the language of the former colonizers is in some instances widely spoken. Third, migration networks and therefore community networks have emerged over time and these are important not only because they facilitate migration but they also have an important role in the economic and social settlement of new arrivals (Anwar, 1985; Robinson, 1993a; Shaw, 1988). Fourth, flight routes influence the pattern of migratory flows and there is a greater availability of connections between former colonies and the former imperial rulers. Finally, in the case of postwar labour migration to the UK, the absence of entry restrictions and therefore structural barriers was also an important factor.

The situation of asylum seekers can be more complex than that of voluntary migrants. Nevertheless, research carried out by Havinga and Böcker (1999) found that the single most important predictor of the country of destination, for asylum seekers, was colonial links between the sending and receiving countries. The majority of those seeking asylum in Western Europe were from the former colonies of the country of asylum although there were exceptions to the pattern.

In a study of Iranians in the Netherlands, Koser (1997) found that immigration rules and perceptions of these rules were most influential in determining the migration destination. More recently with the increased restrictions on entry to Europe, traffickers and smugglers as well as travel agents play an important part in the migratory process (Koser, 1997; Morrison, 1998). In reality what this means is that asylum seekers have little control over their country of asylum and so the variables that would be important, in theory, have increasingly become less important due to structural barriers and the resultant dependence on organized traffickers.

The key feature of the systems approach to migration is that it is concerned with the interaction between a number of different elements that affect the migration (Salt, 1987). Faist (2000) constructs a model that categorizes different micro, macro and meso types of migration as a starting point for understanding the processes involved in migratory movements (see Table 4.2).

Micro structures refer to the degree of liberty a potential migrant has in exercising choice. Macro structures refer to the level of nation-states (i.e. the sending and receiving countries) and the world level. The meso level is concerned with social and symbolic ties and the social capital that is fundamental in enabling migration to be the consequence of such ties. The meso level analysis forms the link between the micro and the macro levels and is a key feature in the systems approach to migration.

Table 4.2   Three stylized levels of migration analysis

| MICRO<br>*Values or desires and*<br>*expectancies* | MESO<br>*Collectives and social*<br>*networks* | MACRO<br>*Macro-level*<br>*opportunity structures* |
|---|---|---|
| *Individual value and*<br>*expectancies*<br>• improving and<br>  securing survival,<br>  wealth, status,<br>  comfort, stimulation,<br>  autonomy, affiliation,<br>  and morality | *Social ties*<br>• strong ties families and<br>  households<br>• weak ties networks<br>  of potential movers,<br>  brokers and stayers<br>*Symbolic ties*<br>• kin, ethnic, national,<br>  political, and religious<br>  organizations<br>• symbolic<br>  communities<br>*Content of ties –*<br>*transactions*<br>• obligations, reciprocity,<br>  and solidarity<br>• information, control,<br>  and access to resources<br>  of others | *Economics*<br>• income and<br>  unemployment<br>  differentials<br>*Politics*<br>• regulation of spatial<br>  mobility through<br>  nation-states and<br>  international regimes<br>• political repression,<br>  ethnic, national, and<br>  religious conflicts<br>  cultural setting<br>• dominant norms and<br>  discourses<br>*Demography and geography*<br>• population growth<br>• availability of arable<br>  land<br>• level of technology |

*Source*: Faist (2000, p. 31)

## Refugees: a unique type of migrant

Since the 1970s with the increase in south to north migration and the re-emergence of east to west migration in the 1990s, many western countries have been struggling to understand the differences between refugees and migrant workers (Cohen, 1994). This concern also corresponded with the oil crisis in the 1970s that resulted in restrictions being placed on labour migration to Western Europe.

In order to try and understand the differences between types of migrants Collinson (1993) devised a matrix. The matrix revolves around two key concepts: political versus economic migrants and voluntary versus involuntary migrants. Migration that is strongly economic and voluntary would be that of a migrant worker. For migration that is political and voluntary Collinson (1993) cites the example of Jews to Israel. Migration that is political and involuntary represents classic refugee flows and migration that is economic and involuntary would be refugees from famine and ecological disaster (Richmond, 1994). The distinctions are not always clear and further distinctions can be incorporated such as seasonal and permanent migrant worker and legal and illegal migrant.

In a more recent analysis of migration, Collinson (1999) identified three types of migration: global migration, liberalized commercial and worker migration and transnational migration. Global migration is linked to globalization because it has been created by new global structures in the world political economy and therefore differs from earlier types of international migration. It is the highly skilled personnel within the global economy who make up migrants in this category and they are not constrained by border controls. Liberalized commercial and worker migration are a function of economic and other ties between states that enable movement across borders. Examples of such arrangements would be those between EU member states and the North American Free Trade Agreement. The final category identified by Collinson (1999) is transnational migration and this category comprises the largest numbers of migrants including refugee migration, family migration and most legal and undocumented workers. According to Collinson (1999, pp. 18–19):

> the pattern and conditions of movement of transnational migrants is largely defined by the nature and strength of controls imposed by states at their borders. And transnational migration flows typically follow distinct territorial patterns, e.g. between neighbouring countries, between countries with close historical (e.g. colonial), linguistic and religious links, and/or within particular regional migration systems.

Certainly this has been the case in the past though increased border controls have resulted in more undocumented migration and a rise in the role of smugglers and traffickers in the facilitation of this migration (see below).

One of the consequences of lack of opportunities to migrate has been the confusion between different types of migrant. European governments and media are increasingly labelling asylum seekers as welfare and/or economic migrants and doubting the legitimacy of asylum seekers and refugees (Bloch and Schuster, 2002). However, Loescher (1993) maintains that the key difference between refugees and other migrants is that refugees are involuntary migrants; they did not want to leave their country of origin and are pushed rather than pulled (Loescher, 1993). According to Kunz (1973, p. 130): 'It is the reluctance to uproot oneself, and the absence of positive original motivations to settle elsewhere, which characterises all refugee decisions and distinguishes the refugee from the voluntary migrants.' However, the confusion arises, in part, because refugee migration will reflect some of the patterns of voluntary migration. For instance, in the case of refugee movements there are also elements of chain migration (Kunz, 1973). That is the economic facilitation of migration by kinship groups and the social dimension of family reunion. Thus, for voluntary migrants, chain migration may assist in decision making about possible destinations but crucially, in the case of forced migrants, flight has already been determined by the need to leave a situation.

Kunz (1973) proposes a kinetic model in which refugee movement falls into two distinct types: acute refugee movements and anticipatory refugee movements. Acute refugee movements, in contrast to anticipatory movements, arise from great political changes or from military activity. Refugees who flee under these circumstances do not have time for preparation. They are pushed out and their main goal is to arrive in a safe place. Thus the push factor is the overwhelming element that results in acute refugee migration.

Anticipatory refugees prepare to leave their homeland and they migrate before the situation prevents an orderly departure. It is these types of refugees that are sometimes mistaken for voluntary economic migrants and that is why knowledge of the historical background is vital. However, Kunz (1973, p. 132) argues that ultimately the pull factor has little part to play in the movement of anticipatory refugees.

> Anticipatory movements ... follow a *'push-permit'* model. The person under apprehension of future calamities determinedly seeks out a possible country of settlement ... he [sic] may have his preferences, the degree of the perceived 'push' and the availability of a landing permit, and not the desire to live in a particular country determines his choice.

Richmond (1993) contests Kunz's (1973) analysis of refugee migration and devised a model of migration that ranges from proactive on one end of the continuum to reactive at the other end arguing that all reactive migration is refugee migration. Through a typology of reactive migration Richmond maintains that the key determinants of reactive migration are political, economic, social, environmental and bio-psychological though there is no single determinant, instead the propensity to migrate is a result of the interaction between these factors.

When considering forced migration, however, Zolberg (1989) recognized the importance of structural, critical, global and historical factors due to the way in which all migration flows depend on the interaction of a whole range of variables. Zolberg *et al.* (1989) identified three types of refugee – activists, targeted and victims – and the factor that underpins all three is the threat of violence. Global issues come into play when people are facing violent situations. However, even in refugee producing situations, migration does not always occur due to structural factors present in both the sending and the receiving countries that can prevent migration occurring. As Richmond (1993, p. 15) notes:

> States continue to pursue polices which they regard as in their own collective self-interest, including the protection of their economic system and the standard of living of their own citizens ... uncontrolled immigration, including the admission of large numbers of refugees, is seen as potentially threatening to these standards.

One of the ways in which states protect their interests are through border controls, the consequence of which, as stated earlier is the increase in trafficking and smuggling and the use of agents.

## Trafficking and smuggling

The terms trafficking and smuggling are often used interchangeably and were defined by the United Nations General Assembly in 1999 in the following ways. *Trafficking in persons* means the recruitment, transportation, transfer, harbouring or receipt of persons, either by the threat or use of abduction, force, fraud, deception or coercion, or by the giving or receiving of unlawful payments or benefits to achieve the consent of a person having the control over another person (cited Morrison, 2000, p. 11). *Smuggling of migrants* shall mean the intentional procurement for profit for illegal entry of a person into and/or illegal residence in a State of which the person is not a national or permanent resident (cited Morrison, 2000, p. 11).

Using the above definitions, Morrison (2000) notes that smuggling better represents the experiences of refugees than does trafficking. Gaining entry to Europe legally has become increasingly difficult over the past few decades and so refugees are forced into using illegal means including smugglers and traffickers (Morrison, 2000). Moreover, Morrison (2000) emphasizes the way in which border controls and anti-trafficking agendas in Europe undermine the principles of the right to claim asylum and of *non-refoulement*. The smuggling and trafficking of people is seen by governments as one of the major components of transnational organized crime and is one of the factors that led to the inclusion of road haulage companies into the Carrier's Liability legislation.

Though there are problems with the reliability of the data used to assess the extent of smuggling it is suggested that the majority of asylum seekers arriving in Central and Western Europe may have been smuggled or trafficked (Morrison, 2000). Research carried out by Koser (1997) comprising interviews with 32 Iranian asylum seekers in the Netherlands found that the use of smugglers was extensive. Twenty-nine respondents had been assisted by smugglers who had helped asylum seekers to escape from Iran, to travel across Europe and to enter the Netherlands.

One of the consequences of the use of smugglers is a change in the geography of migration. New patterns of migration have emerged where some asylum seekers arrive in countries where there they have no pre-existing links or social and kinship networks (Koser, 1996). The expectation is that social networks will evolve around these new arrivals and so new communities will form.

Certainly empirical evidence from the case study of Newham reflects the same findings as other research: that is the lack of choice exercised by asylum seekers about their destination. In the next section of this chapter the migration experiences and attitudes to Britain, as an asylum destination, among the three case study communities will be explored.

## Refugee migration to Britain

### Seeking asylum in Britain

Of the 180 refugees interviewed, nearly everyone (93 per cent) had come to Britain directly from his or her country of origin. Most of those who arrived from a third country were Congolese. Interviews with key informants from the Congolese community in Britain suggest that those who did not come directly from their country of origin had fled to a neighbouring African country first. From there were able to organize their departure to the UK, often through the help of an agent. Only a small proportion, 8 per cent, came to Britain initially to study, visit family or have a holiday rather than to seek asylum. Those who came to Britain for reasons other than asylum found themselves unable to return home due to changing circumstances in their country of origin, which prohibited this.

The grounds for seeking asylum varied by country of origin. Nearly all the Congolese (nine in ten) were seeking asylum on the basis of their political opinion. Among Somalis the main reason was membership of a particular social group (nine in ten) while more than nine in ten Tamils were seeking asylum on the basis of race. Just over half of those seeking asylum in Britain arrived in the country alone (54 per cent). Men were more likely than women to arrive in Britain without anyone else. Somali women were the group most likely to arrive with someone else, a spouse and/or a child or children.

### Reasons for coming to Britain

The theoretical literature suggests that the reasons for coming to Britain would combine a number of inter-related factors including social and kinship networks. Among refugees in this study, more than two-thirds came to Britain because they had no choice over their destination. Instead some depended on agents who arranged their flight.

Figure 4.1 shows that for most, the choice of destination is not a rational one based on the relative merits of different countries. This was especially the case among Congolese respondents who were more likely to have come to Britain because they had no choice than others.

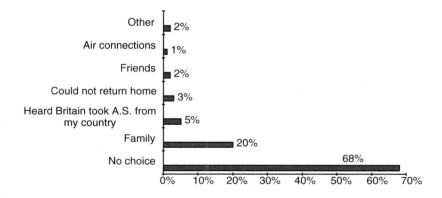

Base number = 177
*Source*: Bloch (1999c, p. 118)
*Figure 4.1*   Reason why Britain was country of asylum.

Others have noted such findings. Havinga and Böcker (1999, p. 49) conclude that: 'The country of destination is often accidental. In quite a number of cases, moreover, someone else makes the decision.'

However, just under a third did choose to come to Britain. Figure 4.1 shows that family ties was the reason for coming to Britain among a fifth of respondents and many of those were Somali women who came on family reunion. For most of these women, the basis of their asylum claim was also family reunion. Thus among Somali women there was evidence of chain migration: that is social and kinship networks influencing the migration.

### Preferred asylum destination

Respondents were also asked whether they would have preferred a different asylum destination and 44 per cent said that they would. Those who came to Britain due to family connections (Somalis) were much more positive about Britain as their asylum destination than those who came to Britain because they had no choice (Congolese) (Cramers V: 0.371). More than half (56 per cent) of those who had no choice said that they would have preferred a different asylum destination compared to a fifth who came to Britain due to family ties. Thus, among those who would have preferred a different destination larger proportions were Congolese (48 per cent) than were Tamil (35 per cent) or Somali (17 per cent).

One variable that is not explored in the literature but emerges as an important aspect in the analysis of forced migrants in Britain is the effect of immigration status on attitudes to settlement but also on experiences due to the differential rights associated with different statuses. There was a large variation in status by community. Nearly all the Congolese respondents were on temporary admission (i.e. asylum seekers waiting for their claim to be determined). Most of those with refugee status were Somalis. Both Tamils and Somalis had ELR but no Congolese had this status. Thus, most Congolese had no security of status while Somalis followed by Tamils were the most secure.

The asylum determination process can be and often is a lengthy one. This means that asylum seekers remain excluded from social and economic citizenship rights for years. Moreover, the implication, as we shall see, is that they are unable to get on with their lives in exile while they are waiting for their cases to be determined. At the end of 2000 there were 66,195 asylum seekers in Britain who were waiting for an initial decision on their case, a decrease of 35 per cent compared to 101,475 at the end of 1999 (Refugee Council, 2001) though many had

Table 4.3    Immigration status by length of residence in Britain

| Immigration status | <1 year (%) | 1–3 years (%) | 3–5 years (%) | >5 years (%) | Total number |
|---|---|---|---|---|---|
| Refugee status | 9 | 8 | 31 | 27 | 38 |
| ELR | 9 | 26 | 26 | 49 | 62 |
| Asylum seeker | 83 | 53 | 34 | 19 | 67 |
| Appeal | – | 13 | 9 | 5 | 12 |
| Total number | 23 | 38 | 35 | 83 | 179 |

*Source*: Bloch (2000a, p. 85)

been waiting since before 1996. Table 4.3 shows the immigration status of respondents in this study by length of residence in Britain.

The significance of immigration status is that it affects attitudes towards Britain as an asylum destination. Those with refugee status (22 per cent) and those on ELR (38 per cent) were less likely to have preferred a different asylum destination than were asylum seekers (57 per cent) and those who were appealing against a Home Office decision on their case (83 per cent). Among those would have preferred a different destination Canada was the most popular choice as Table 4.4 shows.

The preferred destinations of Congolese refugees include ex-colonial countries (France and Belgium) and Canada and Switzerland, where French is one of the official spoken languages. This reinforces the importance of pre-existing links and language in relation to asylum seeker's preferences. However, it is notable that a fifth of those who would have preferred a different destination stated that they would like to go anywhere that takes asylum seekers and is safe rather than a country destination.

To gain a clearer understanding of the different preferences of asylum seekers, had they been in a position of choice, respondents who would have preferred a different asylum destination were asked why that was the case. Table 4.5 shows that the reasons given by respondents reflect perceptions of immigration policies and attitudes towards refugees and asylum seekers in other countries.

Clearly asylum seekers wanted to be in a country with a more open immigration policy and one that better understood their situation. The importance of asylum policy has been noted by others (see Koser, 1997). However there were other factors that were not structural that

Table 4.4    Preferred asylum destination, by country of origin

|  | Somalia | Sri Lanka | DRC | Total number |
|---|---|---|---|---|
| Canada | 3 | 6 | 12 | 21 |
| Anywhere that takes asylum seekers and is safe | – | 5 | 11 | 16 |
| USA | 4 | – | 8 | 12 |
| Australia | 1 | 3 | 5 | 9 |
| Other European countries | 7 | – | – | 7 |
| France | – | – | 7 | 7 |
| Any French speaking country | – | – | 7 | 7 |
| Germany | – | 5 | 1 | 6 |
| Belgium | – | – | 6 | 6 |
| Singapore | – | 5 | – | 5 |
| India | – | 5 | – | 5 |
| Norway | – | 2 | – | 2 |
| Switzerland | – | – | 2 | 2 |
| North America | 1 | – | 1 | 2 |
| Japan | – | 1 | 1 | 2 |
| Italy | – | 1 | – | 1 |
| Asian countries | – | 1 | – | 1 |
| Total number* | 16 | 34 | 61 | 111 |

* Some respondents gave more than one reason so the total adds up to more than the base number (79)
*Source*: Bloch (1999c, p. 120)

Table 4.5    Reasons for preferred asylum destination by country of origin

|  | Somalia | Sri Lanka | Congo | Total |
|---|---|---|---|---|
| Immigration policy/more open | 6 | 5 | 11 | 22 |
| Understanding/sympathetic/ welcoming To refugees | 3 | 3 | 16 | 22 |
| Language (French) | – | – | 15 | 15 |
| Whoever accepts refugees | – | 3 | 10 | 13 |
| Opportunities for refugees | 3 | 4 | 3 | 10 |
| Family | – | 7 | – | 7 |
| Climate | – | 7 | – | 7 |
| Historic ties | – | – | 2 | 2 |
| Other | 1 | 1 | 1 | 3 |
| Column total | 13 | 30 | 58 | 101* |

* Some respondents gave more than one reason so the total adds up to more than the base number (79).
*Source*: Bloch (2000a, p. 83)

were important to asylum seekers such as language and kinship ties. Language was especially important among Congolese, while family was more important for Tamils. Tamils were the only group that mentioned kinship networks as the reason for their preference.

## Summary

In this chapter theories of migration were examined along with migration to Britain and attitudes towards migration among refugees in Newham. Refugee migration can be either acute or anticipatory in nature but the key factor in refugee migration is that refugees do not choose to migrate but are forced to leave their homeland. The very fact that the migration is forced or involuntary rather than voluntary makes this group of migrants and their relationship to the host society qualitatively different from that of voluntary migrants.

The migration of refugees is influenced by a number of micro and macro factors. These include social networks and the policies of the potential receiving countries. Certainly policy, in the form of structural barriers, has become a major factor affecting migration due to the increased role of smugglers and agents. Refugees who came to Britain because they had kinship ties were more likely than others to be happy with Britain as their country of asylum than were others. Among those who would have preferred a different asylum destination, language was a major factor. Most important however, were perceptions about immigration policy and a wish to be in a country that was more understanding, sympathetic or welcoming to refugees. It can be argued, therefore, that for many refugees the theoretical paradigms of migration do not in fact represent the reality of their experience. While for some the concerns are around language and kinship networks, for most it is perceptions about asylum policy and the desire to be in a country that is more open and accepting of refugees than is Britain.

# 5
## Theories of Migrant Settlement

Previous research suggests that the settlement of refugees and asylum seekers in the country of asylum will depend on four key factors. First, are the policies of the country of asylum including the legal system, citizenship rights conferred on individuals through their immigration status in the country of asylum (Cohen, 1994; Robinson, 1986) and strategies of migrant incorporation such as differential exclusion and multiculturalism (Castles, 1995). Second, the presence or absence of social networks affects settlement (Robinson, 1993a). Third are the characteristics of individual migrants including language skills, education and employment. Economic participation is one of the key indicators of settlement. Fourth are the circumstances of the migration itself and linked to this are attitudes and aspirations about the migration (Al-Rasheed, 1994; Kunz, 1981). This chapter explores the factors that affect migrant settlement.

### Theories of migrant settlement

Early research and theoretical developments in the area of migrant settlement originated with the work of the Chicago School in North America. Park (1950) was concerned with the process of assimilation that he argued would be the eventual outcome of the 'race-relations cycle' of host society member and migrant interaction. However, Park's work did not dissect the concept of assimilation and this was not done until the work of Gordon (1964) (Alba and Nee, 1997).

Gordon (1964) presented seven dimensions or stages in the assimilation process: cultural, structural, marital, identificational, attitude receptional (absence of prejudice), behavioural receptional (absence of discrimination) and civil (absence of power or value conflict). Gordon (1964) maintained that the adoption of the cultural pattern of the host society, or acculturation, comes first though it does not necessarily mean progression to the second stage of the assimilation process. However, once a migrant has achieved structural assimilation then the other stages in the process would necessarily follow. Structural assimilation is defined by Gordon (1964, p, 80) as 'entrance of the minority group into the social cliques, clubs, and institutions of the core society'.

Gordon's work is criticized because it assumes a two-group framework of American society and fails to account for the diversity in society and the relationships between different ethnic minorities (Alba and Nee, 1997). Theories of assimilation have been criticized because they fail to recognize the way in which minority cultures influence 'mainstream' Anglo-American life and the way in which different groups interact and adopt traits of each other. Such influence in most obvious in the areas of food and music though Alba and Nee (1997) allude to the way in which Irish and Italian family relations and responsibilities have become part of the dominant culture.

Moreover, this linear model of assimilation has been criticized because it assumes that the shared goal of both the society and the individual migrant was assimilation. When assimilation did not occur, it was assumed that this happened because migrants were unable to assimilate, were reluctant to give up their traditional values or because the host community was unable to accept them due to their differences (Portes and Manning, 1986).

Later work such as that carried out by Glazer and Moynihan (1970) highlighted the importance of the aspirations of the migrants themselves in the settlement process. There was no longer the assumption that the aim of migrants was to assimilate, as in earlier work, but instead the recognition that some migrant groups did not assimilate out of choice.

Berry (1980), who devised a model of migrant adaptation, uses the term adaptation generically to refer to the process and outcome of acculturation. What distinguishes assimilation from acculturation is that the former is unidirectional while the later can be a two way process involving a cultural exchange. Berry (1988) maintains that alongside adaptation there are different ways in which an individual and/or groups may acculturate in a plural society. Using Berry's (1988) model, there are four possible acculturation outcomes: assimilation, integration, separation and marginalization.

Using this model, assimilation implies that societies are homogeneous and that migrants leave their cultural identities behind and replace them with those of the dominant society. However, assimilation is not a very realistic assumption because every group of new arrivals brings with it their own distinct culture. Moreover, both migration and culture are fluid and evolving phenomena.

Integration is usually seen as a positive outcome because it enables the retention of identity alongside the capacity to access aspects of the dominant culture thus preventing exclusion. Valtonen (1998, p. 41) maintains that integration implies 'the full and unimpeded participation in society and the access and openness of institutions to all members of society'.

Separated groups preserve their own identity and culture but are restricted because they do not gain access to wider society. When separation is a state imposed by others it is known as segregation. The final possible outcome is marginalization and this occurs when a group loses its own identity and culture without becoming part of the wider society.

More recently a body of work has emerged that explores the concept of 'segmented assimilation' (Zhou, 1997). Segmented assimilation refers to the different patterns of adaptation that occur among second generation migrants and three possible outcomes are identified. First is growing acculturation and integration, second is poverty and assimilation into the underclass and third is economic advancement but with the preservation of the community values and solidarity (Portes, 1995). The explanation for differential outcomes lies not in individual or structural determinants but, as Zhou (1997, p. 984) notes, 'on the interaction between the two'. While the theory of segmented assimilation is most concerned with the outcomes of second generation migrants, some of the issues faced by the first generation may be similar while others may differ.

Gans (1997, p. 879) notes that in North America, ethnic minority people cannot assimilate unless they are given 'permission to enter the "American" group or institution' and there are often legal barriers as well as discrimination impeding assimilation. Thus the policies of the host society and the attitudes of members of the dominant culture to the adaptation of migrants are important in determining outcomes.

## Policies of receiving countries

Castles (1995) presents four different ways in which host societies respond to the migration and settlement of migrants. The four models are total exclusion, differential exclusion, assimilation and pluralism. Total exclusion is an approach that has not been successful in any highly developed country. Differential exclusion is the inclusion of migrants in some aspects of society, usually the labour market, but the exclusion of migrants in other areas such as welfare or voting rights. Castles (1995, p. 294) writes that:

> In such situations, immigrants become ethnic minorities, which are part of civil society (as workers, consumers, parents etc.) but are excluded from full participation in economic, social, cultural and political relations.

An example of a country which operates a policy of differential exclusion is Germany with its guest worker scheme where the children born to migrant workers in Germany are not German citizens (Weiner, 1996). Although the children of migrant workers born in Germany have some social and cultural rights their political rights are virtually non-existent. They can acquire political rights through naturalization but this is a difficult process.

Inclusion and access to all the social and economic facets of society are prerequisites for structural assimilation so laws that differentiate between groups would reinforce segregation by putting up barriers, which prevent people from gaining access to institutions and services (Robinson, 1986; Thomas, 1992). In Britain, for instance, laws that impede equal access to welfare and employment would reinforce segregation and inhibit structural assimilation.

The third model identified by Castles (1995) is the assimilationist model where the process of settlement is one sided: migrants are meant to give up their own cultural identity in order to adapt to the new society. Certainly this has been the French model and this policy was the dominant one in the UK until the late 1970s as well. Since the late 1970s, there has been a shift in the UK. Castles (1995, p. 30) maintains that 'the socio-economic marginalisation of immigrants and the growth of racism have led to a contradiction between assimilationist policies and social reality'. The result has been a more pluralist approach, which is Castle's final model. Pluralism or multiculturalism (the two terms contain subtle differences but are often used interchangeably) has been a key dimension of policy since the late 1970s although within political debates the term has evoked a number of views regarding its meaning and practice. Multiculturalism can include public policy aimed at minorities, distinctive institutional arrangements and/or tolerance and respect for 'exotic otherness' (Vertovec, 1996, p. 50).

Multiculturalism according to the *Harper Collins Dictionary of Sociology* (1991) is 'the acknowledgement and promotion of cultural pluralism as a feature of many societies ... multiculturalism celebrates and seeks to protect cultural variety, for example, minority languages. At the same time it focuses on the often unequal relationship of minority to mainstream cultures' (cited in Wieviorka, 1998, p. 881). In order for the multiculturalist approach to work, it is necessary for the government to intervene with legislation to ensure that barriers to participation can be overcome. A political science approach to multiculturalism would analyse the concept from the vantage of institutional and political forms (Wieviorka, 1998). Multiculturalism does not simply emerge instead it is dependent on state policy. To this end Weiner (1996, p. 55) defines multiculturalism as 'a set of state policies aimed at enabling, even encouraging, migrant communities to maintain their own language, culture, identity, and especially their history, and to act as a cohesive political force'.

Multicultural policies do not necessarily mean equality as they do not produce economic and political equals among different groups and so hierarchical relationships between different groups still exist (Marcuse, 1996). Thus, even in the absence of legal barriers, discrimination between different cultural groups often leads to inequality. Rex (1996, p. 8) notes that debate about multiculturalism actually 'conceals a policy of ghettoising immigrants'.

Castles (1995) concludes that Britain is somewhere in between an assimilationist and pluralist model. However, the situation for forced migrants, especially asylum seekers, is different. Laws do not exist to assist their participation in the social and economic institutions of society. Instead, laws exist that contribute towards their exclusion, the impact of which impedes settlement.

## Citizenship

Citizenship is a universal feature of modern society and every state defines what it means by citizenship. In purely territorial terms, closure is operationalized at the point of entry through border controls but also through exclusion from certain rights within countries. The practice of closure varies but the ability of nation states to control which people cross its borders is fundamental. Citizenship is important, according to Brubaker (1992, p. 181) because it:

confers not only political rights but the unconditional right to enter and reside in the country, complete access to the labour market, and eligibility for the full range of welfare benefits. In a world structured by enormous and increasing inequalities ... the rights conferred by citizenship decisively shape life chances.

The concept of citizenship, and its different facets, is debated in the social science literature (see for example Andrews, 1991; Bulmer and Rees, 1996; Kymlicka, 1995; Twine, 1994; Walzer, 1983). Citizenship defines both rights and the set of institutions that define and guarantee rights. The starting point has been Marshall's (1950) identification of three dimensions of citizenship: political, civil and social. Citing Marshall's work, Bulmer and Rees (1995, p. 5) define the three dimensions of citizenship.

The civil element is composed of the rights necessary for individual freedom ... liberty of the person, freedom of speech, thought and faith ... and the right to justice ... By political element I mean the right to participate in an exercise of political power, as a member of a body invested with political authority or as an elector of such a body ... By the social element I mean the whole range from the right to a modicum of economic welfare and security to the right to share to the full in social heritage and to live the life of a civilised being according to the standards prevailing in the society.

Marshall identifies the different institutions associated with the three dimensions of citizenship. The courts are associated with civil citizenship, Parliament and local elective bodies are associated with political citizenship and educational and social services are linked to social citizenship. Marshall's work has been criticized for its lack of relevance to contemporary society. Most notably his work does not deal with the issue of migration, it is too Anglocentric and it does not refer to the situation of women in relation to issues of citizenship (Bulmer and Rees, 1996; Close, 1995). Nevertheless, Marshall's work forms an important starting point for debates around citizenship and its associated rights.

The situation of forced migrants, with regards to basic civil, political and social citizenship is very precarious. According to Castles and Davidson (2000, pp. 105–6) civil rights include:

- protection from unlawful acts by the state, such as imprisonment or forced labour;

- equality before the law; and
- the prohibition of discrimination on grounds of gender, origins, race, language or belief.

In the UK, the civil rights of asylum seekers fall well short of those specified above. First, a system of detention exists for some asylum seekers and it is becoming more widely used. In terms of equality before the law, there is clearly inequality in the rights of different ethnic groups in the UK. This is exemplified through the disproportionately high numbers of people of African-Caribbean origin who are subjected to stop and search by the police and are sentenced to custodial sentences when compared to their white counterparts (Fitzgerald, 1999; Home Office, 1999b).

Third, there is the very salient issue of discrimination. Although Britain does have race relations legislation (1965, 1968, 1976 and 2000), there is still widespread racism operating within all spheres of society. Castles and Davidson (2000) note the dual problem of racist violence and inadequate institutional responses. Such racism was most recently exposed by a report of an inquiry into the murder of black teenager Stephen Lawrence (Macpherson, 1999). With regards to asylum seekers, one of the major concerns is that they are becoming frequent victims of racist violence. Certainly dispersal to regions, some of which are ethnically homogeneous, is a factor in this increase in violence.

Political citizenship, according to Marshall (1950) entails both voting rights and rights to participation in the political process. It also entails freedom of assembly and freedom of information (Castles and Davidson, 2000). Minorities without formal citizenship rights face greater barriers to the political system than do others (Statham, 1999). In the UK, naturalized citizens have full political rights as well as Irish citizens. Thus, many ethnic minority people remain excluded from the policy-making processes that help to alleviate inequality.

Five types of activity and institutions have been identified that enable ethnic minority people to express their interests in the policy making process to representatives of state institutions (Miller, 1989). First, is homeland organizations, second consultative bodies, third unions or work place councils, fourth political parties and fifthly through confrontational activities such as demonstrations and strikes. For refugees, homeland organizations exist but as we shall see the high levels of unemployment preclude workplace activity while the lack of representation of ethnic minorities in political parties has been well documented (Saggar, 1998). Refugees are on occasions involved in consultation, but the mode of this activity will depend on national regimes (Soysal, 1994) and are often more limited to the 'main' ethnic minority associations representing the larger communities (Vertovec, 1999).

If inclusion in policy and political decision making depends on homeland organizations there are clearly implications for asylum seekers under dispersal. It is only in areas of concentration of a particular group that associations, some with political remits, are able to form. Dispersal will limit such ethnic association and therefore hinder opportunities for activism and participation (Zetter and Pearl, 2000).

The final component of citizenship is social citizenship of which one key element is the right to welfare (Twine, 1994) while another is the right to work. Van Steenbergen (1994) notes that it is through labour market participation, that people who are excluded and marginalized from society can be integrated.

UK policy in the 1990s has gradually eroded the rights of asylum seekers to social welfare and hindered access to the labour market. This means that asylum seekers are not able to participate in society or live according to the standards of the society. Walker and Walker (1997) argue that it is important to separate material exclusion, that is a function of poverty, with social exclusion that implies a lack of access to society. Walker and Walker (1997, p. 8) make the distinction between poverty and social exclusion:

> regarding *poverty* as a lack of material resources, especially income, necessary to participate in British society and *social exclusion* as a more comprehensive formulation which refers to the dynamic process of being shut out, fully or partially, from any social, economic, political and cultural systems which determine the social integration of a person in society. Social exclusion may, therefore, be seen as the denial (or non-realisation) of the civil, political and social rights of citizenship.

Using this approach it is clear that asylum seekers are socially excluded through the denial of citizenship rights. The impact of this exclusion will be explored through the presentation of the research findings.

For migrants, it is not the precise content of citizenship but instead how it can be obtained so that equal status under the law can be ensured that is of primary concern (Castles and Miller, 1998). The prevalent situation, in the UK and other European countries, is one of different categories of people with different citizenship rights. Cohen (1994) divides people into three categories. The first category, citizens, includes nationals, convention refugees and repatriates. The second category, denizens, includes dual nationals, recognized asylum applicants and expatriates. The third category, helots, is the group with the least rights of all. Helots include seasonal and temporary workers, asylum seekers and illegal entrants. Meehan (1993) also separates people out according to their status, but her categorization differs from that of Cohen. She identifies four categories: citizens, denizins, helots and subjects and states (p. 18) that:

> A denizin is a lawfully resident alien with the same primary rights of political participation as a native or naturalised citizen. A helot is also a resident alien with legal status but enjoying only some of the rights of citizenship ... A subject may be of the same nationality as a citizen ... but ... the subject has no rights to participate in law-making.

Citizenship is important because anything less than full citizenship will impede settlement (Weiner, 1996). This is because the host society does not see the migrant as part of the society and grants only a restricted number of rights, while the migrant cannot properly adapt because there is always a sense of insecurity attached to their position in the society. In the context of forced migration to Britain, asylum seekers have the least rights and are excluded from basic political, civil and social citizenship. As we shall see, lack of rights affects integration and in some instances attitudes towards settlement in Britain.

## Social networks

In relation to migratory movements we have seen that social networks facilitate and maintain the flow of migrants from a sending to a receiving country. However, such networks also have an impact on the settlement of new arrivals because they affect both social and economic life (Desbarats, 1986; Robinson, 1993a; Thomas, 1992). Many voluntary migrants arrive in the new country through the route of chain migration and find accommodation and work through the ethnic enclave (Anwar, 1985; Shaw, 1988). As a result, the ethnic enclave is often associated with its economic and entrepreneurial function. If the aims and objectives of the migrant are compatible with acculturation, then the enclave will be temporary in so much as it provides a springboard from which migrants can make contacts with members of the host society (Robinson, 1986).

The ethnic enclave does not always fulfil an economic function. Some migrants might find themselves employed in the secondary rather than the primary labour market. The secondary labour market is the part of the dual labour market which is associated with the poorly paid unskilled jobs which are often taken by members of the most disadvantaged groups such as women and the newest migrant communities (Portes and Manning, 1986). The primary labour market is that part of the labour market associated with higher paid jobs offering progression and development.

Because the migration experience of refugees often differs from that of other migrants, some refugees arrive in the host society without previous contacts and in some instances, especially among new migrant groups, an ethnic enclave does not exist. As a result, refugees do not necessarily find themselves employed in an ethnic enclave, rather they may find employment in other sectors of the economy. According to Portes and Manning (1986, p. 64): 'Political refugees ... can select or be channelled in many different directions, including self-employment, access to primary labour markets, or confinement to secondary sector occupations.' For an ethnic enclave to provide economic opportunities for members of a particular community, there are certain prerequisites. First, there have to be large enough numbers in the community. Second, there has to be enough available labour and third, there has to be enough capital to start up businesses within which to employ members of the community (Portes and Manning, 1986). These preconditions do not always exist and in some instances, where an ethnic enclave exists, it provides a social rather than an economic function. In fact, Gold (1992) goes so far as to define an enclave in terms of the spatial concentration of a minority ethnic community in one geographical location rather than in economic terms.

Gold (1992) concludes that there are three factors that will affect the adaptation of refugees: collectivism, background and the larger structure. Collectivism refers to ethnic solidarity that provides social, economic and informational resources. Background refers to the ethnic diversity within communities and the presence of diversity results in the fragmentation of communities. The larger structure refers to macro and micro economic influences. On the micro level, Gold writes that 'the availability of jobs and housing in communities of settlement is a central factor in determining refugee's adaptation.'

Prior to the implementation of the Immigration and Asylum Act 1999, asylum seekers arriving in the UK were generally able to settle where they chose. Many arrivals elected to live in areas of London where they already had social networks or where there was an established community from their country of origin or ethnic group. Where communities congregate, community-based activities often emerge providing an economic and social role but also an advice and advocacy service. The rationale of dispersal policy put forward in the White Paper *Fairer, Faster, Firmer – A modern approach to immigration and asylum* that preceded the 1999 Act was to 'relieve the burden of provision in London' (The Stationery Office, 1998, section 8.22). This is in spite of the fact that the problems associated with dispersal are already well documented based on previous evaluation of such strategies. After an analysis of the Vietnamese programme, Robinson (1993b) concluded that the central concept of dispersal is seen as misguided.

Criticisms made of the Vietnamese programme by Robinson (1993b) and others (Bell and Clinton, 1992; Joly, 1996) identified a number of factors that contributed to its failure. First, refugees were sent to areas of high unemployment. This meant that they had virtually no prospects of obtaining work. Second, local authorities were unable to provide appropriate support services to the small number of Vietnamese refugees living in their locality. Under the programme as few as between four and ten families were housed in any given locality. Third, refugees had insufficient access to training. Finally, refugees were separated from their community that meant they had no access to community support.

Certainly the system of dispersal introduced in the UK in 2000 will hinder the formation and development of community-specific organizations whose functions are diverse. Activities include the provision of information and advice, mediation between clients and other agencies, interpretation and translation, opportunities for social, political and cultural activities, the chance to meet and exchange news from home as well as education and training (Carey-Wood *et al.*, 1995; Duke *et al.*, 1999; Wahlbeck, 1997a). There are around 400 refugee community organizations in Britain and most of them are in London. The impact of dispersal on community development is likely to be another factor that hinders the settlement of forced migrants in Britain. Chapters 8 and 9 will demonstrate the importance of social networks and community activities in the social and economic lives of forced migrants.

## Economic integration

The importance of employment as a means through which the settlement of refugees can occur cannot be underestimated and has been highlighted by a number of studies (see for example Joly, 1996; Valtonen, 1994; 1998). Refugees who are working and economically independent adjust more easily to the host society than those who are unemployed or dependent on benefits for extended periods of time (Finnan, 1981). Employment is crucial for providing self-esteem and contact with others from outside of the community as well as offering a means through which refugees can meet their cultural obligations including support for the extended family (Valtonen, 1994; 1998).

Refugees remain the most underemployed group in Britain. Estimates and survey findings about the levels of unemployment among refugees vary though they all show the high levels of unemployment experienced by refugees and asylum seekers. A national survey of 263 refugees carried out by the Home Office found that as few as 14 per cent of refugees had been in employment for most of their time in Britain. At the time of the survey only 27 per cent of those considered economically active were in paid employment (Carey-Wood *et al.*, 1995). More recently, a study of 236 qualified and skilled refugees and asylum seekers found that 42 per cent of refugees and 68 per cent of asylum seekers were unemployed (Peabody Trust and London Research Centre, 1999). Refugees who were employed were more likely to be male than female, had been in Britain longer than those who were unemployed, spoke good English on arrival to Britain, felt settled in the community and were more likely to have secure immigration status. In addition, the Home Office study found that those in employment were more likely to be living in the South East of England than elsewhere. This variation is likely to be a consequence of local labour markets.

Refugee employment is characterized by occupational downgrading and clustering in secondary sector jobs, within a few industries, with poor terms and conditions of employment (Girbash, 1991). A similar pattern of refugee employment has been found in other countries. In Australia for example, a country made up of diverse communities, unemployment rates among refugees from Cambodia, Vietnam and the Middle East are three to four times higher than those for the population as a whole and there is little upward occupational mobility (Coughlan, 1998). Similarly in Finland, unemployment rates among refugees are three times higher than they are among the Finnish born population (Valtonen, 1999).

Research carried out by the Policy Studies Institute found patterns of employment and unemployment between different groups to be complex and diverse, no longer representing a Black/White divide (Modood, 1998; Modood and Bertoud, 1997). When the labour market experiences of men and women are combined, three broad groupings emerge. White, Chinese and African Asians were doing best, followed by Indian and African-Caribbean people while Bangladeshis and Pakistanis were doing least well in terms of levels of employment and earnings. However, refugees and asylum seekers collectively are faring less well in the labour market than others.

Reasons for diversity in the employment experiences of different ethnic groups are complex and varied. First, there is the issue of discrimination and the stereotyping of different ethnic groups. Indeed, one in five of those interviewed for the Policy Studies Institute, Fourth National Survey of ethnic minorities said that they had been refused a job on the grounds of race or religion and three-quarters had experienced this more than once (Modood and Bertoud, 1997). Research carried out by Brophy *et al.* (1998) found that refugees also encounter discrimination.

Second, there is the group history prior to migration and the resources on which they can draw including capital and education. For example, the economic success of East African Asians in Britain has been attributed to their educational background, fluency in English, and high social status in their country of origin (Robinson, 1993a).

Third, place of birth, time of arrival and length of residence are important explanatory variables. Those born in the UK who were working have been found to be more likely to have good earning prospects though they were also more likely to be unemployed than those born outside of the UK (Iganski and Payne, 1996, Leslie *et al.*, 1998). Country of birth has been found to be an important variable elsewhere. In Sweden, for example, the rate of unemployment among those born abroad is 20 per cent, compared with 7 per cent among the Swedish born population (Swedish Institute, 1999).

Time of arrival is also important because of the economic cycle that affects the availability of jobs and public attitudes towards migrants. Valtonen (1999) maintains that the differential employment outcomes among Vietnamese refugees at two points in time in Canada and one point in time in Finland can be attributed partly to the fact that the first cohort arriving in Canada did so during an economic boom and this improved their job prospects in the short and longer term. Length of time in a country is also important. Carey-Wood *et al.* (1995) found that there was a correlation between length of residence and labour market participation with the main increase in employment coming after six years.

Fourth, regional variations along with the decline in manufacturing affect levels of unemployment along with the fact that unemployment is hyper-cyclical: 'differences widen in times of recession where ethnic minorities are the first to be laid off' (Leslie *et al.*, 1998). Certainly dispersal will affect the employment prospects of asylum seekers who may find themselves in areas with high levels of unemployment and unable to move to seek employment without forfeiting their welfare benefits.

Fifth, refugees and other ethnic minority people can be 'functionally overqualified' for the labour market. According to Bravo (1993, p. 3): 'they are too well qualified for lower grade posts, have too little work or professional experience for higher-management posts, and feel that they are too far along in their career path to switch careers. Frequently their language skills are not commensurate with their qualifications.'

Moreover, qualifications obtained outside the UK are often not recognized as commensurate with their UK equivalents and in some instances skills and experiences gained overseas may not be transferable to the UK economy. However, there is much variation between different communities (Parkinson, 1998). The problems faced by asylum seekers may also be compounded by the fact that asylum seekers, on arrival to the UK, are not eligible to work. Research carried out in Australia (Wooden, 1991) noted that one of the reasons for the disproportionately high levels of unemployment among refugees was the scarring effect of the initial period of unemployment that refugees experience on arrival to the host society. In Australia the unemployment rates among refugees was 33.1 per cent compared to 12 per cent among other migrants (Wooden, 1991). Excluding cultural factors and the effects of an initial period of unemployment, Wooden offers two additional explanations for this discrepancy. First, discrimination on the part of employers, and second, differences in English language skills. In spite of an element of catching up, after an initial period of unemployment, Wooden concludes that refugees remain permanently disadvantaged in the labour market largely because of a lack of English language proficiency though the other factors contribute.

Sixth, there are questions around the aspirations for the migration. Do communities want to settle and take primary sector jobs or is the migration either in fact or perception a temporary sojourn? Where the migration is seen as temporary, it can result in an orientation towards people from the same community rather than the host society and this has implications for employment. With regard to refugees from Iraq, Al-Rasheed (1992, p. 543) states:

> This prohibits people from having access to local information networks regarding job opportunities. Lack of social relations with the host society also entails lack of knowledge about how the occupations are organized here, potential gaps in the market that might be exploited, and a general feel about how businesses work in this country.

Research carried out by Coughlan (1998) in Australia found that upward occupational mobility was associated with having friends from outside the community. It is not known whether this is a causal factor as friends can provide access to jobs in the wider community and therefore outside of the constraints of employment by co-ethnics or whether it is a result of occupational mobility.

Gender is a seventh area that emerges as an important explanatory variable in explaining labour market differentials. Refugee women may face particular difficulties gaining access to the labour market, especially as they are less likely to be proficient in English than their male counterparts. Research carried out by the Home Office found that 44 per cent of men said their English language was good compared to 28 per cent of women. On arrival to Britain a quarter of the men interviewed had no English language skills compared to a third of women (Carey-Wood *et al.*, 1995).

Bach and Carroll-Seguin (1986) carried out research into labour force participation among Southeast Asian refugees in the United States. They found that difficulties of gaining access to the labour market for women were compounded by lack of childcare provision, transportation difficulties and the impact of social isolation that results from staying at home and looking after children. However, some women prefer to care for their children and cultural norms can dictate that a women's status within her community is related to her childcare role and so there can be a reluctance to designate childcare responsibilities (Ryan, 1997).

Other research has noted that refugee women often need to acquire new skills in order to participate in the labour market (Buijs, 1993) although they may be excluded either from such opportunities or available provision may fail to recognize their diverse needs (Bloch *et al.*, 2000a).

Due to the difficulties in finding employment, an important area of absorption into the labour market for refugees is self-employment. Research has shown this to be the case among East African Asians and Armenians (Malik, 1990; Robinson, 1993; Srinivasan, 1992). In fact, analysis of the Labour Force Survey showed that with the exception of respondents of Chinese origin, East African Asians were more likely to be self-employed than were those from other ethnic groups. On average, nine per cent of the population are self-employed compared to 14 per cent of East African Asians (Jones, 1993).

The propensity for self-employment among Asians in England is a consequence of the interaction between culture and economics (Metcalf *et al.*, 1997). Among African Asians, the majority of whom would have come to England as refugees, there were two main reasons for entering self-employment. First, self-employment offered an 'escape' from poor employment prospects and racism in the labour market for the individual and for family members. Second, it provided standing within the family, which is culturally important among members of this community. One of the conclusions of the study was that self-employment was an option for first generation migrants due to the structural barriers they experienced, but their aspirations for their children were different. More than half said that they did not want their children to take over the business but would prefer them to gain employment in one of the professions. Thus, Metcalf *et al.* (1997) argue that self-employment is transitory for new migrants and acts as a 'springboard' for the success of future generations.

However, as stated earlier, setting up businesses especially ones that cater for particular ethnic groups depends on the presence of a large enough community for such a business to be viable (Valtonen, 1999). In addition, setting up a business requires the necessary capital or guarantees for a loan, both of which may be problematic for some refugees.

## Migration, aspirations and settlement: the links

One of the main criticisms of migration theorists, according to Joly (1996), is the lack of theoretical concern given to the links between the migration process and settlement. Indeed, she argues that Kunz (1981) is the only theorist to make the links between the cause of migration, the migration process and the ability of the refugee to settle and adapt to the host society.

Kunz (1981) develops his kinetic model of acute and anticipatory refugee movements (Kunz, 1973) by arguing that in any refugee wave, people are going to have different experiences and attitudes towards the host society. Attitudes will depend on their social relationships and their feelings about their homeland. According to Kunz (1981, p. 42), in the resettlement stage: 'many of the refugees' problems could be traced back to their emotional links with and dependence on their past, the refugees' marginality within or identification with their former home country is important.'

Kunz (1981) argues that refugees have three categories of identification with the country they are leaving and that this is regardless of whether they are anticipatory refugees or acute refugees. The three categories are: majority-identified refugees, events-alienated refugees and self-alienated refugees. Majority-identified refugees are those who believe that their views against events in their homeland are shared by the majority of their compatriots. As a result, they identify strongly with their homeland but not with the government.

Events-alienated refugees are those who are resentful towards their former compatriots as they have been marginalized by most of society, perhaps because they belong to a particular ethnic or cultural group like German Jews. These refugees rarely either hope or wish to return to their homeland. Refugees are more likely to settle in the host society in instances where they are unable to return home and therefore have no choice (Weiner, 1996).

The third category self-alienated refugees do not wish to identify with their homeland and their departure is a result of their alienation. It can, in some cases, be hard to ascertain whether someone in this category is a refugee or a voluntary migrant.

Kunz (1981) maintains that resettlement into the host society will be influenced by which of the three categories the refugee falls into. Kunz (1981) develops his theory on settlement into the host society and stresses the influence of what he terms as 'attitude towards flight and homeland'. He argues that there are two types of attitudes prevalent among refugee groups that will be determined by their attitude towards displacement. The first category is termed as reactive fate-groups and the second category is described as purpose groups. Purpose groups are disaggregated into 'self-fulfilling purpose groups' and 'groups of revolutionary activists'.

Reactive fate-groups are generally majority-identified refugees as they are characterized by being the victims of war, revolution and expulsion. Some events-alienated may fall into this category but they tend to form the minority. In contrast, refugees who fall into the purpose groups contain mostly refugees who are self-alienated. Self-alienated refugees, who leave for political, religious or ideological motives are more likely to continue their activism in the host society in an attempt to influence events in their homeland. This activism will impact on settlement into the host society as their focus is still largely on the homeland rather than adapting to the new society. Some majority-identified refugees will be actively involved in issues evolving from their homeland as they may feel a responsibility and guilt for obtaining freedom while others will try to assimilate into the host society in an effort to forget the past.

Research carried out by Al-Rasheed (1994), among Iraqi Arabs and Iraqi Assyrians, utilized Kunz's (1981) typology. The research found that that views about the homeland and aspirations about return migration or 'the myth of return' affected not only the relationship with Iraq but also with Britain as the host country. Iraqi Arabs saw their exile as temporary and as a result were orientated towards their homeland. In contrast, Iraqi Assyrians saw their migration as a permanent solution to their minority status in Iraq and as a result were much more orientated towards the UK than were Iraqi Arabs.

## Summary

Theoretically, the settlement outcomes of refugees are complex and depend on a number of often interrelated factors. Some of the factors that affect settlement are as a direct consequence of national policy or what Weiner (1996) terms as 'immigrant policies' while some are due to the characteristics of the refugees themselves. Immigrant policies are those which are associated with the receiving country and their attitudes towards the settlement of migrants. More specifically, it is concerned with the extent to which migrants are granted full citizenship rights and the attitudes of the host society towards the absorption of migrants.

In terms of the characteristics of individuals, a number of factors or indictors that affect settlement have been identified by previous work. These include, education, length of residence, area of settlement, ethnicity and family separation (see for example Kim and Hurhn, 1993; Robinson, 1986; Strand and Woodrow-Jones, 1985).

For assimilation to take place, there can be no legal restrictions, the aims and objectives of the migrant have to be compatible with both social and economic acculturation and members of the host society have to accept migrants as equals (Robinson, 1986). Research shows that over time, migrants tend to adopt some aspects of the life of the host society while maintaining aspects of their own ethnic culture (Modood *et al.*, 1994).

Clearly the migration and settlement experiences of communities and individuals can be very diverse. The following chapters present empirical data in an attempt to unravel some of these complexities that emerged among three refugee groups in the London Borough of Newham.

# 6
# Language, Education and Training

Proficiency in the language of the country of asylum is key to the successful settlement of refugees. Research has consistently identified English language as a key variable explaining different rates of employment, occupation mobility and wage levels among migrants (Robinson, 1993a; Schellekens, 2001; Wooden, 1991). In addition English language is important for facilitating social interaction with the wider community (Schellekens, 2001) and so those who have difficulty communicating in the language of the host society are more likely to be excluded (Bach and Carroll-Seguin, 1986; Thomas, 1991; Wooden, 1992).

In addition to language skills participation in education and training have been identified an important indictors of settlement. In recognition of and in response to the disadvantages experienced by people from ethnic minority groups, when compared to their white counterparts, the Urban Programme was initiated in the 1960s (Chelliah, 1995). Money has been allocated to local areas under different schemes though the focus has been on language, training and employment.

This chapter will first outline the Urban Programme and then examine language learning, education and the participation in training for work schemes among refugees in this study. Views about provision will also be addressed to see the extent to which they are meeting the needs of refugees. Also, the sorts of improvements that could be made to those schemes within the remit of the urban regeneration programme will be examined.

## The Urban Programme

From 1966 until 1996 money was allocated specifically to projects concerned with ethnic minorities under three schemes: Section 11, Ethnic
Minority Grant (EMG) and the Ethnic Minority Business Initiative
(EMBI). Section 11 funding was established under the Local
Government Act, 1966 and money was used for English language training, youth and community work, social services and training and
enterprise schemes. The aim of the scheme was to ensure that people
in Britain, regardless of their ethnic origin, were able to 'participate
freely and fully in the economic, social and public life of the nation'
(Home Office, cited Chelliah, 1995, p. 10). Funding for Section 11 projects expired in 1995 and the initiative has now been subsumed within
the Single Regeneration Budget (SRB). The Single Regeneration Budget
(SRB) was set up in 1994 and is administered centrally by the
Department of the Environment. It is the main source of funding for
regeneration nationally.

The EMG was introduced in 1990 and was based on the same broad
principles as Section 11. The aim was to assist ethnic minority people
in the areas of training, employment and enterprise. The EMBI was
established in 1985 and set out to encourage enterprise and provide
business development services to ethnic minorities. Both these
schemes have since been integrated into the SRB and there are no
longer any specific funds earmarked for ethnic minority projects.
Under the SRB, money is allocated to geographical areas and focuses
on economic and environmental regeneration rather than the social
and community needs of local residents who experience disadvantage.
Robson *et al.* (1994) noted that the consequence of the Urban
Programme is the increasing polarization between the most deprived
and least deprived areas.

Ethnic minorities lose out under the Urban Programme due
to funding procedures. First, most funding requires an element of
match funding from local partners. Groups working with ethnic
minorities, especially new refugee community organizations may not
have as many 'mainstream' contacts to collaborate with and there is
evidence to suggest that minority ethnic organizations may be
excluded from local partnership networks (Crook, 1995). Second,
newer organizations tend to lack information about the bidding
process and have insufficient understanding of the priorities of the
urban programme. Hausner (1992, p. 12) notes that: 'In the absence of
pro-active and strategic allocations, a competitive bidding system is

likely to benefit larger, white-led or 'ethnic-elder' voluntary organizations.' The implication of no longer targeting funds and the bidding
process means that the Urban Programme disadvantages newer community organizations including refugee groups who struggle to raise
the necessary funds to carry out their work (Carey-Wood, 1997).

In addition to the SRB there are also funds available under the Urban
Programme that aim to combat high levels of unemployment through
local regeneration and training. The two main domestic initiatives
have been City Pride and City Challenge. City Pride set out to bring
together the major players in regeneration and it operates in London,
Manchester and Birmingham. City Challenge is a larger scheme than
City Pride with a total of 31 such programmes one of which,
Stratford City Challenge, is based in Newham. The initiatives under
the City Challenge programme set out to help communities that have
difficulties assisting themselves (Pratt and Fearnley, 1996). Included
under the scheme were access to jobs for local people, and enabling
local people to play a more active role in community life (Jiwani, *et al.*,
1994). In spite of such a remit, none of the projects funded under the
'access for local jobs' initiatives in Stratford highlighted working with
refugees.

There are also European regeneration initiatives and Newham has
successfully bid for structural funds from the European Union, designated to regenerate areas in decline and has been the recipient of
European Social Fund money. Newham has been the recipient of
regeneration money because it is one of the most deprived areas in
Britain.

## Newham: the economic context

The Department of the Environment identified Newham, using its
local conditions index, as having the highest level of deprivation out
of the 366 local authority areas in Britain. One of the measures of
deprivation used is rates of unemployment in any locality. At the time
of the 1991 Census, Newham had the fifth highest levels of unemployment of all local authorities (Green, 1994). Rates of economic activity
vary between and within ethnic groups and between and within localities (Ho and Henderson, 1997; Modood and Bertoud, 1999; Sly *et al.*,
1999).

Patterns of unemployment in Newham among ethnic groups are
broadly similar to the national trend but levels of unemployment are
higher than the national average. One of the reasons for the high

levels of unemployment in Newham has been the decline in manufacturing and industry. The decline has not been counteracted with comparable expansions in other employment sectors leaving a reduction in the overall number of jobs available in the locality (Griffiths, 1994). Moreover, there is a skills deficit between residents in east London and the needs of the local economy. As a result, local residents are unable to gain access to high skill jobs and instead they are going to inward commuters (Whyatt, 1996).

The main areas of employment in Newham are public administration, education and health (26.5 per cent), distributions, hotels and restaurants (21.8 per cent) and banking, finance and insurance (17 per cent). At present the sectors where there is a demand include academic, cultural, construction, business and financial services (LETEC, 1996a).

The Urban Programme aims to reskill local communities, though training and capacity building, to enable access to high skill local jobs. In the rest of this chapter, language skills and participation in language learning, education and training will be explored. The relevance of training to the local economy will be examined and outcomes will be assessed.

## Language and literacy skills

### Language and literacy skills in the first language

Language and literacy skills in the first language vary by country of origin and gender. In some countries, including Somalia, women may have little or no formal education and very low levels of literacy in their first language. Adult literacy rates in Somalia, in 1995, were 16 per cent among women and 41 per cent among men. In the DRC 68 per cent of women were literate compared to 87 per cent of men. In Sri Lanka the proportions were 87 per cent among women and 93 per cent among men (Sivard, 1995).

In this study, 91 per cent of all respondents could read in their first language and 91 per cent of those who could read could do so fluently. Eighty-nine per cent were able to write in their first language of which 91 per cent could write fluently. Nearly all of those without first language literacy skills were Somali women. A comparison of the average levels of adult literacy in the three countries of origin with levels of first language literacy among refugees and asylum seekers shows that the latter group have comparatively high levels of literacy compared to the average in the country of origin.

In addition to first language skills, nearly half (49 per cent) of all respondents were multilingual, speaking one or more languages in addition to their first language and English. Congolese interviewees were the most multilingual with nine in ten speaking an additional language. The languages spoken most often were Kikongo, French, Tshiluba and Swahili. Three in ten Somalis and Tamils spoke a language in addition to their first language and English. Most Somalis who spoke another language spoke Arabic while Tamils tended to speak Sinhalese.

## English language and literacy skills on arrival to Britain

Language skills of the host country have been identified as the first stage in the acculturation process (Bun and Kiong, 1993; Robinson, 1986). Thus, arriving in the country of asylum with language skills can only help to facilitate inclusion. Desbarats (1986) found a correlation between language skills on arrival to the United States and settlement outcomes among Vietnamese refugees. People whose English language skills were most proficient on arrival were more economically successful and less dependent on their community for help finding employment than respondents who were less proficient in English on arrival. On arrival in Britain, 16 per cent spoke English fluently, 15 per cent spoke at the level of simple sentences, 21 per cent spoke a few words and 48 per cent had no spoken English. There were clear differences in terms of gender and country of origin. More than half of the women interviewed (57 per cent) spoke no English compared to 17 per cent of men. On arrival 59 per cent of Somalis spoke no English (mostly women), compared to 53 per cent among Congolese and only 32 per cent of Tamils. However, of those who did speak some English, only 2 per cent of Congolese spoke fluently compared to 22 per cent of Somalis and a quarter of Tamils. Thus on arrival to Britain, women and Congolese respondents were less likely to speak English than others.

Part of the explanation for the language differentials by country of origin is the differing colonial histories. Sri Lankans had a better knowledge of English than did others because many learned English in school. English was only taught in Somali schools until the early 1970s so those educated subsequently will not have learned English while Congolese who spoke a European language, as stated earlier, spoke French reflecting their colonial past.

## English language skills and language learning

Most people had attained greater proficiency in English since being in Britain though there differences between the sexes in the attainment of language skills. While 36 per cent of women spoke no English at all or only a few words of English the same was true for only 13 per cent of men. The differences by sex are largely explained by an examination of country of origin. Table 6.1 shows that the strength of association by sex, when controlling for country of origin, is very strong among Somali respondents.

Table 6.1   Level of spoken English by country of origin and sex

|  | Somalia | | Sri Lanka | | Congo | | Total % |
|  | Cramers V = 0.587 | | Cramers V = 0.129 | | Cramers V = 0.374 | | |
|  | Male | Female | Male | Female | Male | Female | |
|---|---|---|---|---|---|---|---|
| *Level of spoken English* | | | | | | | |
| None | 3 | 13 | 1 | 0 | 0 | 1 | 10 |
| Few words | 3 | 6 | 3 | 3 | 2 | 7 | 13 |
| Simple sentences | 8 | 10 | 16 | 14 | 16 | 14 | 44 |
| Fluently | 16 | 1 | 11 | 11 | 15 | 5 | 33 |
| *Total number* | 30 | 30 | 31 | 28 | 33 | 27 | 179 |

Base number = 179

The correlation between language, country of origin and sex was strongest among Somalis and weakest among Tamil respondents. Nearly all of those who did not speak any English at the time of the survey were Somali women. Most were also lone parents. Being a lone parent can make participation in English for Speakers of Other Languages (ESOL) more difficult due to family responsibilities and the lack of childcare provision for ESOL students.

In addition to less access, the isolation of some Somali women may be increased by cultural and religious constraints that, in some instances, make it difficult for Somali women to participate in ESOL classes and in social and cultural activities outside of the home (Duke, 1996a).

### Learning English as a second language: provision

There are many different types of language training available to Newham residents. English for Speakers of Other Languages (ESOL), is designed for people who live in the UK and want to learn English for the purpose of everyday communication, education, training or employment. According to the World University Service, ESOL is more of an access point than a stand-alone subject. Although other sorts of English language training, such as English as a Foreign Language (EFL) are available, nearly all refugees study ESOL.

ESOL training is available at a number of places in Newham although most courses are not aimed specifically at refugees. The only two refugee specific ESOL classes were those provided by the Community of Zairian Refugees in Great Britain (COREZAG) and the Somali Women's Development Project, both in collaboration with Newham Council's Community Education division. The courses offered by COREZAG are available to all refugees in the borough. The courses are offered at two levels and each course runs for four hours a week. The courses also include an information technology component. Newham Somali Women's Development Project provides ESOL for Somali women. The classes are for beginners and run in the early evening three times a week. An English woman assisted by a Somali woman interpreter does the ESOL teaching.

The other key providers of ESOL are the local college of further education (Newham College of Further Education) and NEWTEC. The ESOL courses offered at Newham College of Further Education also include a core curriculum of English, Mathematics and Information Technology (IT) and can be taken on a full-time or part-time basis. The courses are offered at three levels and each course lasts for a year. NEWTEC, offers a one-term beginners ESOL course to women. The course runs for six hours a week, spread over three mornings. NEWTEC, as well as other training providers in Newham, offer a range of different courses that include a language support component.

One of the problems faced by potential refugee ESOL providers is the operation of the European Social Fund (ESF). ESF grants operate with a time lag between the start of the course and the transfer of the funds. As a result, small groups are not generally in a position to provide ESOL and/or training because they do not have the resources to pay out money up front while waiting for the ESF money to come on stream. This difficulty is compounded by problems of access for minority groups as we have already seen.

### Attendance at English language courses

In the absence of formal reception and resettlement programmes for spontaneous asylum seekers, one of the ways in which new arrivals learn or improve their English language skills is through attendance at

Table 6.2   Level of spoken English on arrival to the UK by attendance at English language classes

|  | None<br>(%) | Few<br>words<br>(%) | Simple<br>sentences<br>(%) | Fluent<br>(%) | Total<br>(%) |
|---|---|---|---|---|---|
| Attendance at<br>English classes |  |  |  |  |  |
| Yes | 78 | 92 | 81 | 10 | 70 |
| No | 22 | 8 | 19 | 90 | 30 |
| Total number | 85 | 38 | 26 | 29 | 100 |

Base number = 178

ESOL classes. Most people (69 per cent) had attended an English language course since arriving in the UK. Of those who had attended an English language course, 46 per cent were attending at the time of the survey. All but two of the Congolese respondents had attended or were attending classes at the time of the survey, compared to six in 10 Tamils and half of the Somali respondents. Congolese were the most likely to have attended English language classes which reflects, in part, the fact that this group were less likely to speak English on arrival than were others. Table 6.2 shows the relationship between English on arrival to the UK and attendance at ESOL.

Some respondents who did not speak English on arrival to Britain had not attended English language classes. More than half of the respondents who did not speak any English on arrival to Britain and had not attended English language classes were Somali women and more than half were also lone parents. Among those attending English classes the reasons for studying varied. The majority (86 per cent) studied to communicate better in everyday life. People also studied to increase their chances of getting a job (67 per cent), to enter education (41 per cent), to go on a training course (34 per cent) and to meet new people (19 per cent).

There were differences in the reasons for studying English by community. Most notable was the number of respondents from DRC – more than a third – who had studied English because it gave them an opportunity to meet new people. This is probably explained by the fact that a larger proportion of Congolese than Somalis and Tamils arrived in Britain without social networks or an established community in exile and so ESOL classes offered an opportunity for social interactions.

There were also differences by sex. Women were more likely to be interested in learning English in order to go on a training course than men while men were more concerned with jobs and education than women.

Often ESOL is taught in conjunction with other subjects and more than half (54 per cent) of those respondents who had been involved in language learning had studied English with additional subjects. Maths and information technology were the subjects studied most often alongside English language.

### Finding out about ESOL and getting on a course

There are many different ways in which someone can find out about an English language course. More than a third of respondents found out about English language classes from a friend and around a quarter found out by reading a leaflet. Seventeen per cent were informed about ESOL by a community advisor, 10 per cent obtained their information from a newspaper, 9 per cent from a relative and the remaining few from other sources that included the library, a chance conversation with a student and through a training provider.

Ways of obtaining information about English language provision varied among the three communities. Congolese were most likely to find out about language provision by reading a leaflet or through a friend, while Somalis were most likely to get their information from a community group advisor. This showed the propensity for this group to rely on face-to-face oral information, which is not surprising, given their lower levels of literacy in the first language when compared to others. Tamils were just as likely to get their information from a newspaper or a friend.

Of those studying English at the time of the survey, under half (44 per cent) had been on a waiting list before starting their course. Just over a quarter (29 per cent) of those who had studied in the past had been on a waiting list and more than half had waited for six months or more for a place on a course. Given the importance of language learning for settlement, the delay in starting courses can only be a hindrance in the settlement process. Refugees and those with Temporary Protection Status, who arrive as part of a quota, receive English language training as part of their reception. Asylum seekers who arrive spontaneously are the most disadvantaged by language provision.

The number of hours studied each week varied from less than five to more than 21. Policy changes, introduced in September 1996, reduced

Table 6.3　Number of hours attending English language classes each week

|  | Percentages |
|---|---|
| Less than 5 | 13 |
| 5 but less than 10 | 25 |
| 10 but less than 16 | 20 |
| 16 but less than 21 | 28 |
| 21 or more | 14 |

Base number = 123

the number of hours in education per week for students to be considered full-time from 21 to 16 hours. Students taking full-time courses at further education colleges are not entitled to social security benefits (Refugee Council, 1996). Table 6.3 shows the number of contact hours students had each week, before the changes were introduced.

### Views about English language courses

All those with current and past experience of English language classes were asked their views about the courses in general. In terms of learning English, almost everyone (92 per cent) said that they found their English language course either very helpful or fairly helpful. In addition, students and ex-students were asked their views about six different aspects of the course: course content, teaching methods, awareness of the refugee experience, student support, size of class and information about progression routes for further study or employment. On the whole, students were satisfied with most aspects of the course. Table 6.4 shows that the areas where students were least satisfied were: awareness of the refugee experience, student support and information about progression routes for further study or employment. The pattern of responses among those who were studying at the time of the survey and those who had studied in the past were similar, so both groups of respondents have been aggregated in Table 6.4.

Lack of understanding about the refugee experience was the area where the greatest proportion expressed dissatisfaction. Service providers were aware of the difficulties that refugees faced when studying ESOL but struggled to meet their diverse needs. According to one service provider: 'It is very hard to meet the needs of refugees. One of the main problems is resourcing at admission, which means that students do not necessarily find themselves on the right courses and then end up dropping out.' One Somali man summed up the problem of

Table 6.4    Satisfaction with different aspects of English language provision

|  | Satisfied (%) | Neither satisfied nor dissatisfied (%) | Dissatisfied (%) | Total number[*] |
|---|---|---|---|---|
| Course content | 75 | 19 | 6 | 117 |
| Teaching methods | 72 | 16 | 12 | 121 |
| Awareness of refugee experience | 59 | 16 | 25 | 115 |
| Student support | 58 | 23 | 19 | 120 |
| Class sizes | 84 | 7 | 8 | 107 |
| Information about progression | 66 | 16 | 19 | 116 |

[*] The base numbers vary for each question, as there were a lot of 'Don't Knows' recorded for some of these questions.

being in the wrong level class when he gave the following explanation for leaving his English language course: 'I can't read, write or speak English and I can't read or write any other language including Somali language. I could not get a beginners class so it was difficult to understand.'

Other service providers highlighted personal and cultural factors as well as practical problems that can affect the course completion rates among people from refugee communities. Although there was awareness along service providers about some of the issues affecting refugees, providers emphasized the fact that they had insufficient resources to mitigate against some of the problems encountered.

Nearly a third of those who had studied English in the past did not complete their course. The reasons for non-completion were very varied, but they do help to point to some of the problems faced by refugees generally. Reasons for leaving included getting a job, needing time to look for a job, the course was not what they wanted or was not suitable for them, family commitments, housing, immigration, personal problems and for financial reasons including being unable to afford the cost of travel to college.

Reasons for leaving English language courses show a mix of personal and structural problems. Some people simply could not afford to carry on studying and needed to get paid work. This situation will worsen now that some asylum seekers are not entitled to social security benefits and the hours of attendance and eligibility have been reduced making it more difficult to participate in some ESOL classes at Further

Table 6.5    Ways of improving English language provision

|  | *Percentages* |
|---|---|
| Teachers from own community | 44 |
| Different level classes | 42 |
| More hours | 33 |
| Longer courses | 22 |
| Teachers from refugee communities | 12 |
| Refugee only classes | 6 |
| Women only classes | 6 |
| Shorter courses | 3 |
| Greater mix of students | 3 |
| Better text books | 2 |
| More practical teaching methods | 2 |
| More flexible times | 2 |
| More exercises/homework | 2 |
| Less hours | 2 |
| Men only classes | 2 |
| Other | 5* |

Base number = 125
* Other includes: nursery provision, British teachers, weekend classes, and information about progression to college or employment.

Education colleges. This will have major implications for the ability of refugees to settle and gain access to basic social and economic life within the host society (Joly, 1996).

Respondents who had participated in language learning were asked to state all the different ways they thought that English language provision could be improved for their community. Table 6.5 shows that the most favoured initiatives were teachers from the same community and different level classes. More hours and longer courses were also popular ways of improving English language provision.

Favoured initiatives varied by sex and country of origin. The priority for men were more teachers from the same community while women were most likely to say that longer courses and more hours would improve language learning. This reflects, to some extent, the fact that a higher proportion of women than men were studying English for less than five hours a week. Finally, equal numbers of men and women thought that different level classes would improve language provision.

## Education and qualifications

Levels of education and qualifications obtained by refugees, before arriving in the host society, are known to affect adaptation to the new society, including labour market participation (Bach and Carroll-Seguin, 1986). An examination of pre-migration characteristics shows that refugees were among the most educated from their country of origin and were, on average, more educated than others in UK.

### Education and qualifications on arrival to Britain

On arrival to Britain, refugees bring with them different educational backgrounds. Congolese were the most highly educated while Somalis were the least well educated of the three groups though there are clear differences by gender for all three communities as Figure 6.1 shows.

All of those without formal education were Somalis and most were Somali women. Among the Tamil community, slightly more women than men had studied at university level. In contrast, among Somalis and Congolese, there was a large disparity between men and women. Only one Somali woman had studied at university level compared to 11 Somali men while among Congolese 12 men had studied at university level compared to four women. Among Congolese respondents there was a gender disparity between further and secondary education. A much larger proportion of Congolese men had studied at the level of further education while women tended to have studied up to secondary school.

Correlated with education are qualifications. Refugees are, on the whole, very well qualified from their country of origin, 15 per cent had

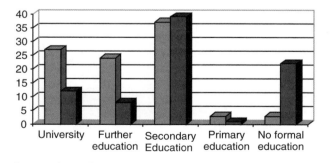

Base number = 176

*Figure 6.1*   Highest level of education by country of origin and sex.

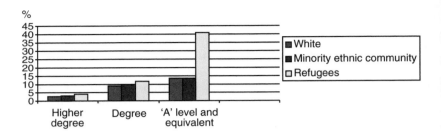

Source: Data for white and minority ethnic community populations from LETEC (1995)
*Figure 6.2* Highest academic qualifications.

either a degree or post-graduate qualification on arrival to Britain, a finding that mirrors the Home Office study (Carey-Wood *et al.*, 1995). In addition, 5 per cent of respondents were trained teachers.

There were differences between the communities. The majority of Congolese and Tamil respondents (nine in ten) had some kind of qualification but among Somalis the proportion was four in ten. Nearly all of those without formal qualifications were Somali women.

When the qualifications of refugees are compared to other minority groups and the majority white population in the east London area, it is clear that refugees are on average better qualified as Figure 6.2 shows.

Refugees and asylum seekers are, for the most part, unable to use their qualifications in Britain. Only 23 per cent of those with qualifications said that they were recognized in the UK and only 16 per cent of those with qualifications had tried to get them recognized and only one person was successful in getting a qualification obtained overseas recognized. The most frequently mentioned reason for not getting qualifications recognized was a lack of information.

### Study in Britain

At the time of the survey, 22 per cent of respondents were studying and 14 per cent, although not studying at the time of the survey, had studied since living in Britain. Whether or not a refugee has participated in adult education or training is one indicator of cultural adaptation (Desbarats, 1986). In order to examine the attributes of those who had participated in education in the past, or were participating in education at the time of the study, both categories of respondents were grouped together for the analysis.

A greater proportion of men than women had been involved in education in the UK (49 per cent and 20 per cent respectively). None of the women who had studied or were studying at the time of the survey were lone parents, which points to the difficulties that this group can face. Other factors that affected participation in higher education were immigration status, year of arrival to Britain, age, country of origin and main activity before coming to Britain.

A greater proportion of those with refugee status had been involved in education than others. Of those with refugee status, 45 per cent had been involved in education. This compares with 36 per cent of those with ELR, 33 per cent of those on temporary admission and 8 per cent of those who were appealing against a Home Office decision on their case.

There was also a correlation between participation in education and length of residence in Britain. Nearly two-thirds (63 per cent) of those who arrived in Britain before 1990 had studied compared to 31 per cent who arrived between 1990 and 1992, 24 per cent who came to Britain between 1993 and 1995 and 19 per cent who arrived after 1995.

Age was also influential in determining whether or not respondents had undertaken education since living in Britain. While 40 per cent of those aged 34 or younger had participated in education, only 22 per cent of those aged 35 or older had participated. Of those who had studied since living in Britain, 60 per cent were students in their country of origin and 27 per cent were working. Thus, older refugees and those who were already established in their careers were less likely to participate in education in Britain. That perhaps reflects less inclination to start over again. The importance of age as a factor affecting settlement has been noted by others (see Robinson, 1986; Stein; 1981).

More than half of the Tamil respondents had been involved in education, which is more than the other communities where the proportions were two in ten among Somalis and three in ten among Congolese. Even when length of residence was controlled for, country of origin was still an influential factor in accounting for participation in education. The situation of the Tamil community reflects the work carried out by Thomas (1992) who argues that the ethnic enclave can help in the transference and adjustment of minority ethnic groups into the host society. In Chapter 9, we shall see that Tamils are more involved in community-based activities than were people from the DRC and Somalia. This is because it can act as a springboard to contacts outside the ethnic enclave. Moreover, participation in education is seen as one mechanism for making contacts with members of the host society, an early stage in the settlement process (Robinson, 1986).

Among those who were studying at the time of the survey qualifications being studied for varied, but by far the most frequent was study at degree level: three in ten were working towards a degree. Congolese and Somalis were more likely to be working towards a degree than were Tamils. Only people who had been in the UK since 1992 or before were doing a degree at the time of the survey. This is easily explained by rules governing access to student grants. At the time of the study, the mandatory payment of fees and student grants were limited to people who had been resident in the UK for three years and the only exception to this was people with refugee status who are entitled to the same assistance as UK citizens.

Those who were not studying at the time of the survey, but had studied in the past, were more likely to have studied for and obtained a degree than anything else (nearly three in ten). However, refugees had obtained a diverse range of qualifications since coming to the UK that included: NVQ, GNVQ, CSE, GCSE and 'A' level qualifications.

People who were either studying at the time of the survey, or have studied in the past tended to have been educated in their country of origin. Pre-migration characteristics did therefore have an impact on participation. Four in ten of those who had attended university in their country of origin were studying or had studied in Britain. Half of those who had attended an institution of further education in their home-land were studying or had studied in Britain and four in ten of respondents who had studied up to secondary school level were studying or had studied in Britain. In contrast, only one respondent who was either educated up to primary level or had no education at all in their homeland was studying at the time of the survey and none had studied in Britain in the past. As with English language learning, there was a substantial rate of non-completion of courses. Fifteen per cent had started a course in Britain and not completed it. Tamil respondents were more likely than were others to have started a course and then not completed it. The proportions not completing a course were: three in ten among Tamil respondents, one in ten among respondents from DRC and less than one in ten among respondents from Somalia. The reason for not finishing a course, given most often, was finding it hard to concentrate and this was followed by child-care responsibilities. Other factors leading to non-completion were financial problems, the course was too difficult, not liking the course, health reasons, finding it hard to study in English, housing problems and experiencing discrimination on the course.

## Training

Training for work was provided in many locations around the borough and is one of the main strategies used to help long-term unemployed back into the labour market. Sixteen per cent of all respondents – that is 28 people – had participated in training for work courses in Britain. Of the 28 who had experience of training, 27 had done training in the past and one was doing a training course at the time of the research. Six people had done two training courses and so there was information about 34 courses in total.

People from DRC were more likely than others to have done a training for work course and accounted for more than half of those who had done training. Men were more likely to have done training than were women (seven in ten and three in ten respectively) and there was a relationship between length of time in the UK and participation in training. Of those who had participated in training, more than three-quarters had been living in Britain since before 1993 while less than two in ten had arrived in 1993 or later.

The types of courses taken by respondents were diverse. Table 6.6 lists the training courses taken by respondents and the number of respondents who had taken a particular type of course.

The vocational training and training for work that refugees in Newham had been involved in did not reflect the needs of the local economy. Indeed, many were being prepared for semi-skilled jobs rather than the better paid jobs in the growth areas of the East London economy.

Around two-thirds of the training courses included the provision of English language support. In some cases language support is crucial, as only half of those who have done training said that they were fluent in spoken English and less than two-thirds could understand English fluently at the time of the survey. Nearly everyone who either spoke a few words of English or simple sentences went on training courses that included an English language component.

Refugees may encounter difficulties coping with courses, especially where English is a problem. Given that funding for some courses is related to successful employment outcomes, some providers have intimated that it may influence who is accepted initially on courses and may disadvantage certain groups. According to one provider: 'The

Table 6.6    Training courses taken in Britain

|  | Frequencies |
|---|---|
| *IT/computer courses* | |
| Information technology | 3 |
| Computer software | 2 |
| PC user support | 1 |
| *Office/business skills* | |
| RSA II | 1 |
| Accountancy | 2 |
| Office skills | 1 |
| Touch typing | 1 |
| Clerical | 1 |
| Secretarial administration | 1 |
| Business administration | 1 |
| IT and business administration | 2 |
| *Service sector* | |
| Catering | 1 |
| Dressmaking | 3 |
| *Other* | |
| Welfare rights | 2 |
| Job interview techniques | 1 |
| Youth training | 1 |
| Care work | 2 |
| Immigration law | 1 |
| Language for work | 2 |
| Security work | 2 |
| Carpentry and joinery | 2 |
| Teacher training | 1 |
| Total number of courses taken | 34 |

output emphasis on courses may lead to discrimination in terms of taking refugees in the first place. They tend to take the best potential clients who are mainstream as they are the most likely to complete and be placed in jobs.' Nearly a quarter of all the courses that were started were not finished. The reasons for not finishing, where known, were as follows: got pregnant, child hospitalized, started course in a detention centre and got let out, did not like the course, wanted a course with a work placement and started own business. Some training providers argued that in order for refugees to successfully complete courses, training provision should incorporate advice provision and perhaps self-help discussion groups. Thus, some providers maintain that training needs to fulfil a social as well as an economic function if it is going to be successful.

Nearly everyone found their training course either very useful or fairly useful; only four said it was not very useful or useless. Of the four respondents who did not find the course useful, two referred to the course standard. One said the course was not useful because 'we hardly did any work I had not done before' and the other said that 'it was not up to standard'. Those who found the training fairly useful or very useful did so because, on the whole, they acquired new skills, although in many cases the acquisition of skills did not lead to employment.

There is a disparity in employment outcomes between ethnic minority trainees and their white counterparts (Moody, 2000; Rolfe *et al.*, 1996). This difference is ameliorated when local labour markets are taken into account due to the concentration of ethnic minority people in the most economically deprived areas (Moody, 2000).

There is little information about the training outcomes of refugees though among those in this research, there is little to suggest that training is providing access to the better paid jobs in the locality and in some instances access to the labour market. Exactly one-third of respondents who had done training courses in the past had never had a paid job in Britain; nearly a quarter had worked in the past but were currently unemployed while less than a fifth were working at the time of the survey. English language skills appear to be most influential. Only those who were either fluent in English or spoke simple sentences had obtained work while those who spoke a few words of English had been unable to find employment.

Table 6.7   Job outcome by white/non-white and whether English is first language

|  | Non-White English first language (%) | Non-White English not first language (%) | White All (%) |
|---|---|---|---|
| Got job | 38 | 22 | 65 |
| Did not get job | 62 | 78 | 35 |

*Source*: LEPU (1996)

The importance of language skills has also been found in work carried out by the Local Economy Planning Unit (LEPU) (LEPU, 1996). Table 6.7 shows that one of the main determining factors in terms of employment outcomes is English as a first language.

An examination of current and previous employment, among those who have worked in the past but were no longer working, shows that there is very little link between training and employment outcomes. For most, the type of training undertaken had little impact on future employment. Examples include one person who had trained in carpentry and joinery only to get a job for a couple of months as a kitchen porter. Another had done a course in dressmaking and then went on to get a temporary job as a cleaner while another had completed an IT course and was stocking shelves at a local supermarket.

Although there was little link between training and work outcomes, one thing that emerged was that a higher proportion of people who had done training for work courses had also participated in the labour market than those who had not done training for work. While half of those who had done training for work had been involved in the labour market, only 35 per cent of those who had not done any training had been involved in the labour market. Although the content of the training may not lead to training related work, there is evidence to suggest that the actual process of doing the training was useful in terms of future labour market participation.

Issues pertaining to training will be further explored in Chapter 7, particularly whether people wanted training and if so type of training they thought would be most helpful.

## Summary

Refugees arrive in Britain with varying levels of literacy, both in their first language and English. For most, language had improved but for Somali women there had been the least improvement and less participation in language learning than among others.

Since arriving in Britain, there had been a high level of participation in ESOL training and on the whole, respondents were satisfied with the language training they received. However, more than one in four of those who had participated in English language classes thought that language provision could be improved by the employment of teachers from their own community.

As with language classes, Somali women were the group least likely to participate in training and/or education. Participation was also related to English language proficiency, length of time in Britain and immigration status.

Those who had participated in training did not, for the most part, find employment that related to the training they had done. However, a higher proportion of those who had done training had worked compared with those who had never participated in training. Though training is meant to assist access to the labour market for disadvantaged groups, in the case of refugees there is little evidence to suggest that training outcomes are related to the nature of the training.

Chapter 7 will explore the labour market participation of refugees, methods of job seeking, and labour market aspirations and in light of the disproportionately high levels of unemployment among refugees, their views about barriers to employment.

# 7
# Labour Market Participation in Britain

Labour market participation is a strong indicator of the process of acculturation. Robinson (1986) argues that it is the second stage in the acculturation process; second to the acquisition of the language of the host society. Others, such as Schmitter Heilser (1992) maintain that incorporation into the labour market does not necessarily result in incorporation into other aspects of society. Nevertheless, the importance of employment cannot be underestimated. According to Knox (1997, p. 31):

> In many ways, for refugees, employment is the key to successful integration because it leads to interaction with British people, the chance to learn English, the ability to support oneself and rebuild a future, as well as a chance to regain self esteem and confidence.

Refugees bring with them diverse sets of skills and experiences though as we saw in Chapter 6, they tended to be among the more educated and literate in their countries of origin. However, what this chapter will show is that refugees are for the most part not using their skills in the UK and have lower levels of labour market participation than others.

## Ethnic minority employment

According to Ginsburg (1992), the labour market demonstrates the most basic operation of racial inequality. Black workers experience much higher levels of unemployment than their white counterparts and, when in paid employment, were more likely to be in occupations with low pay and low-status. Moreover, men and women from minority ethnic communities were more likely than white people to find their employment trends linked very closely to the economic cycle (Sly, 1996). This is not a new phenomenon; the economic slumps particularly the decline in manufacturing have had a disproportionate effect on black unemployment. This is because the employment of people from minority ethnic communities tends to be concentrated in the industrial sectors that have experienced major decline (Cross, 1992).

Nationally, around six per cent of all those of working age belong to a minority ethnic group. The unemployment rate for people from minority ethnic groups is just over double the rate of unemployment found among members of the white population: 18.7 per cent and 8.2 per cent respectively. There are large variations in the employment rates of people from different communities, although the overall rates of unemployment have changed little since 1984. The highest rates of unemployment are still found among those from the Pakistani, Bangladeshi and Black communities, especially those who describe their ethnic group as Black African, which will include people from refugee communities (Sly, 1996).

Throughout the east London area, the employment patterns found among different ethnic communities reflect the national trends. Table 7.1 shows the percentage of people from different communities in the LETEC area who are unemployed, by ethnic group. On average, therefore, the 46 per cent of refugees who were unemployed in Newham is a greater proportion than the proportion found among even the Bangladeshi community who experience the highest proportion of unemployment among non-refugee groups.

Table 7.1 shows that levels of unemployment in Newham were second only to those in Tower Hamlets. Nationally Newham has the second highest proportion of residents from ethnic groups, other than white, while Tower Hamlets has the highest proportion of residents who describe their ethnic group as Bangladeshi, a group with above average levels of unemployment. It is not surprising that levels of unemployment are higher in Newham and Tower Hamlets than in the other LETEC boroughs. Levels of unemployment in Newham and Tower Hamlets, among those who describe their ethnic group as white, were also higher than in other boroughs. This reflects the structure of the local economy and the closure of the docks and many of the manufacturing industries that were traditionally located in these two boroughs.

Table 7.1   Unemployment rate of ethnic communities in the boroughs covered by LETEC

| | White | African Car. | Indian | Pakistani | Bangladeshi | Chinese | Other Asian | Other | Total |
|---|---|---|---|---|---|---|---|---|---|
| Barking and Dagenham | 11.4 | 17.3 | 12.0 | 27.8 | 21.9 | 5.4 | 16.7 | 14.3 | 11.7 |
| Havering | 7.3 | 13.0 | 7.3 | 8.0 | 7.7 | 4.5 | 8.4 | 10.8 | 7.4 |
| Newham | 15.5 | 26.2 | 18.9 | 35.4 | 42.8 | 12.1 | 23.3 | 25.1 | 19.3 |
| Redbridge | 7.7 | 15.1 | 11.5 | 20.6 | 17.6 | 6.3 | 11.8 | 13.2 | 8.8 |
| Tower Hamlets | 17.1 | 26.6 | 18.7 | 31.6 | 47.3 | 24.2 | 30.8 | 27.6 | 21.8 |
| Waltham Forest | 10.2 | 18.9 | 15.2 | 29.1 | 33.3 | 13.3 | 21.9 | 18.9 | 12.5 |
| London East | 10.6 | 21.8 | 14.9 | 29.3 | 43.9 | 12.4 | 20.8 | 19.7 | 12.9 |

*Source:* 1991 Population Census

The most significant feature of employment patterns since 1984 has been the difference found between white women and women from minority ethnic communities. Between 1984 and 1995, the employment rate for white women increased from 59 per cent to 68 per cent while the proportion of working women from minority ethnic communities increased only marginally, from 44 per cent in 1984 to 46 per cent in 1994.

While nationally there has been an increase in women's labour market participation, in Newham the proportion of women working was fewer due mainly to the higher proportion of women from minority ethnic communities resident in the borough. In both Newham and Tower Hamlets, the proportion of economically inactive women was more than 40 per cent, which was 10 per cent more than the average for London. Also, part-time work among women in Newham and Tower Hamlets was noticeably lower than elsewhere, again reflecting the greater ethnic diversity of residents in these two boroughs. The main employment characteristics of men and women of working age, in Newham, are shown in Figure 7.1.

The change in economic structure, both nationally and in east London, has resulted in a decline in full-time employment and a corresponding increase in part-time employment. In the LETEC area, during the 1980s, there was a 20 per cent decrease in the number of men working full-time and in Newham the proportion was a quarter. By 1991, only 52 per cent of men of working age (16–64) were employed in full-time work, compared to a London average of 58 per cent.

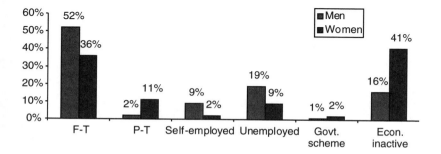

*Source*: Rix (1996)

*Figure 7.1*  Main employment characteristics of men (aged 16–64) and women (aged 16–59) in Newham, 1991.

Table 7.2   Total percentage unemployed in Newham by ethnic group and sex

|  | Male (%) | Female (%) | All (%) |
|---|---|---|---|
| White | 18.6 | 10.9 | 15.4 |
| Black Caribbean | 22.4 | 14.0 | 18.2 |
| Black African | 42.7 | 35.5 | 39.6 |
| Black (Other) | 25.8 | 19.8 | 22.9 |
| Indian | 18.5 | 19.5 | 18.9 |
| Pakistani | 35.0 | 36.9 | 35.4 |
| Bangladeshi | 41.3 | 48.5 | 42.8 |
| Chinese | 13.9 | 10.0 | 12.1 |
| Other Asian | 27.8 | 17.5 | 23.3 |
| Other | 26.8 | 22.4 | 25.1 |
| All (percentages) | 22.1 | 15.1 | 19.3 |

*Source:* 1991 Census [total population 212,170]

Table 7.2 shows that, with the exception of women from the Chinese community, women from all other minority ethnic groups experience higher levels of unemployment than do white women. It also shows that Indian, Pakistani and Bangladeshi women have higher unemployment rates than the men in these groups, reversing the general pattern.

## Refugee employment

Limited evidence from Britain and elsewhere points to the fact that refugees experience considerable occupational downgrading. Those who access the labour market often find themselves in jobs that are not commensurate with the qualifications and employment experience gained prior to arrival in Britain.

### Employment before coming to Britain

Before coming to Britain the majority of respondents (76 per cent) were either employed, self-employed or students. Seven per cent were unemployed and 15 per cent were looking after the home and family. Those who had been employed, before coming to Britain, were engaged in very diverse occupations. The main categories of previous employment were teachers, clerks, administrators and accountants though there were many other types of employment that included engineers, civil servants, farmers, business people, secretaries and

Table 7.3  Main activity before coming to Britain by country of origin and sex

| | Somali | | Tamil | | Congolese | | Total (%) |
| | *Male* | *Fem.* | *Male* | *Fem.* | *Male* | *Fem.* | |
|---|---|---|---|---|---|---|---|
| Student | 9 | 5 | 12 | 13 | 10 | 10 | 33 |
| Full-time employment | 14 | 1 | 12 | 9 | 14 | 7 | 32 |
| Home/family | 3 | 22 | 1 | 1 | – | – | 15 |
| Self-employed | 3 | – | 4 | 3 | 4 | 5 | 11 |
| Unemployed | 1 | 1 | 2 | 1 | 4 | 4 | 7 |
| Other | – | 1 | – | 1 | 1 | 1 | 2 |
| Total number | 30 | 30 | 31 | 28 | 33 | 27 | 179 |

shopkeepers. A fifth of those who were employed before coming to Britain had been working in their last job for 10 years or more.

There were differences by country of origin and gender. Most notable was the high proportion of Somali women who were looking after the home and family and the low number who were involved in education or employment as Table 7.3 shows.

### Employment in Britain

At the time of the survey only 14 per cent of respondents were working, either as employees or were self-employed. Respondents who were working, tended to be from Sri Lanka (18 out of 25) while respondents from Somalia were more likely to be looking after the home and family than were others. Of the 26 respondents looking after the home and family, 19 were from Somalia. People from DRC were more likely to be unemployed than were others. Of the 83 people who described themselves as unemployed, more than half (44) were from DRC compared to 20 Tamils and 19 Somalis. More men than women were in paid work (19 and six respectively) while more women than men were looking after the home and family (25 and one respectively).

Figure 7.2 compares the main activity of respondents before coming to Britain with their main activity at the time of the survey. The main difference in activity in the homeland compared to Britain was the reduction in the proportion of respondents who were working or students and the increase in the proportion that were unemployed. As many as 46 per cent of respondents described themselves as unemployed although there were very significant differences by community. As a group, however, refugees experience higher rates of unemployment than do others.

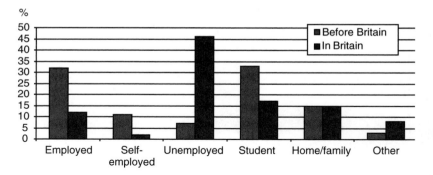

Base number (before): 180; base number (in Britain): 178
*Source*: Bloch (1996, p.44)
*Figure 7.2*   Main activity before coming to Britain and main activity in Britain.

Among refugees in this study, there were also differences in levels of unemployment by sex. More than half of the male respondents, 53 per cent, described themselves as unemployed compared to 39 per cent of female respondents – that is just higher than the proportion found among Pakistani and Bangladeshi women. Only Bangladeshi women have higher levels of unemployment, than is the average among refugee communities.

English language skills were key in determining labour market participation. Among those who were working, six in ten spoke English fluently and the rest spoke at the level of simple sentences. This reflects the findings of the Home Office study (Carey-Wood *et al.*, 1995), as well as research carried out in Australia, which demonstrated that language was a key component in labour market activity (Wooden, 1991).

Length of residence was also a key variable; a third of those who arrived in Britain before 1990 were working compared to one in ten among those who arrived after 1990 but before 1995. Less than one in ten of those who arrived in 1995 or later were working. Occupational downgrading was in evidence among those working. There is evidence from other research that suggests that refugees have to start over on arrival in the country of asylum (Valtonen, 1999). The sort of work that respondents were doing in the UK varied but was almost exclusively low-paid, low-skilled work with poor terms and conditions of employment. Among the minority who were working at the time of the survey, the largest number (nine respondents) were in shop or cashier work. Other work was factory work either as a machine operator or packing (four), administration (three) and security guard work (two).

In addition, the jobs that were just carried out by one respondent were sorting at the post office, a self-employed English language teacher, a self-employed printer, a community worker and a civil engineer. The level of work carried out did not reflect the skills and experience that refugees bring with them. Lack of diversity of employment among refugees has also been demonstrated by research carried out among Vietnamese refugees in Manchester where over half of those in employment were employed in the catering industry (Girbash, 1991).

People from minority ethnic communities, like refugees, tend to have their employment concentrated in the industries and sectors that are usually associated with low pay, low status, low skill and low levels of job security. White people are more likely to work in the private sector than are those from minority ethnic groups (62 per cent and 57 per cent respectively). Overall, around a quarter of white people and people from minority ethnic communities work in the public sector, although there are marked differences between communities. While a quarter of all people from ethnic minority groups are employed in the public sector there are large variations between groups. Forty-one per cent of Black people work in the public sector compared to 19 per cent of Indian people and 12 per cent of those who described their ethnic group as Bangladeshi or Pakistani. People of Pakistani and Bangladeshi origin are more likely to be self-employed (nearly a quarter) than are those who described their ethnic group as Indian (around one-fifth), white (15 per cent) and Black (7 per cent) (Sly, 1995; Twomey, 2001).

The employment characteristics of refugees differed from those of the community at large. Nearly everyone who was working was employed in the private sector (eight in ten) and nearly everyone was working full-time (eight in ten). Moreover, most people were working in Newham. Only two per cent of refugees in Newham were self-employed compared with a national average of 13 per cent and a Newham average of nine per cent among men and two per cent among women (Sly, 1995; Rix, 1996).

### Working hours and pay

Refugees in employment tended to work unsociable hours, that is, before 8.30 in the morning and after 6.30 at night (eight in ten). More than three-quarters also worked in the evening or at night and regularly at the weekends, that is two or more weekends in every month. Job turnover was high among refugees who tended not to have been in their current jobs for very long. Three in ten had been in their current job for less than a year, five in ten had been in their current job for one

Table 7.4    Number of hours worked by 'take' home pay

| Take home pay | 20 or fewer hours | 36 but less than 50 hours[*] | 50 hours or more | Total |
|---|---|---|---|---|
| Less than £50 | 1 | – | – | 1 |
| £50 but less than £75 | 2 | – | – | 2 |
| £75 but less than £100 | 1 | – | – | 1 |
| £100 but less than £125 | 1 | – | – | 1 |
| £125 but less than £150 | 1 | 5 | – | 6 |
| £150 but less than £200 | – | 3 | 5 | 8 |
| £200 but less than £250 | – | 1 | 2 | 3 |
| £250 but less than £300 | – | – | 1 | 1 |
| Total | 6 | 9 | 8 | 23 |

[*] No respondents worked between 20 and 36 hours.
*Source*: Bloch (1996, p. 48)

year but less than three years and only two in ten had been in their job for three years or longer. Refugees were also working in jobs, which, on the whole, showed little relation to their previous employment and did not utilize their skills and experience.

Respondents were asked how many hours a week they worked on average, and what their take home pay was per week, after any deductions for tax, National Insurance payments and pensions. The data in Table 7.4 shows that refugees were working very long hours for very low pay.

All the part-time workers worked for 20 hours a week or less each week and they all earned less than £200 a week. All of the full-time workers worked for 36 hours a week or more and most were paid less than £200 per week.

Refugees were earning less money than other ethnic groups in Newham. When the weekly rates of pay were transferred to hourly rates, most refugees earned less than £4 an hour. Table 7.5 shows that this was much less than the average hourly pay in Newham and across east London.

There are wage differentials among different ethnic groups. Data from the 1994 Labour Force Survey show that average hourly pay among those in full time work was £7.44 among the white population and £6.82 among ethnic minority communities. Table 7.6 shows that people from the Pakistani and Bangladeshi communities tend to be less well paid than people from other ethnic groups but still earn more than refugees.

Table 7.5    Average hourly earnings of the workforce, in pence

|  | 1990 | 1991 | 1992 | 1993 | 1994 | 1995 | Percentage change |
|---|---|---|---|---|---|---|---|
| Barking and Dagenham | 674 | 758 | 828 | 886 | 879 | 907 | 34.6 |
| Havering | 652 | 736 | 800 | 814 | 843 | 868 | 33.1 |
| Newham | 684 | 757 | 839 | 870 | 856 | 860 | 25.7 |
| Redbridge | 701 | 743 | 823 | 850 | 865 | 889 | 26.8 |
| Tower Hamlets | 865 | 980 | 1066 | 1168 | 1280 | 1257 | 45.3 |
| Waltham Forest | 606 | 712 | 755 | 711 | 785 | 830 | 40.0 |
| London East | 718 | 808 | 887 | 994 | 994 | 1005 | 40.0 |

*Source*: New Earnings Survey reported in LETEC (1996b).

Table 7.6    Average hourly earnings of full-time employees by ethnic group and sex

|  | All (£/hr) | Men (£/hr) | Women (£/hr) |
|---|---|---|---|
| All origins | 7.42 | 7.97 | 6.39 |
| White | 7.44 | 8.00 | 6.40 |
| Black | 6.92 | 7.03 | 6.77 |
| Indian | 6.70 | 7.29 | 5.77 |
| Pakistani/ Bangladeshi | 5.39 | 5.47 | 5.15 |

*Source*: Sly (1995)

## Barriers to employment

There was an awareness of a lack of utilization of pre-migration skills and nearly three-quarters of those who were working felt that there was another sort of job that would be more suitable for them than the one they were currently doing. The sorts of jobs that people felt would be more suitable were linked to their previous employment experience and skills and included: accountancy, civil engineering, finance/banking, mechanics, teaching, hairdressing, farming and clerical work. Refugees had spent varying amounts of time looking for what they considered to be a more suitable job but only a small proportion had either applied for other work and an even smaller proportion had reached the interview stage. One respondent noted that he was caught in a vicious circle because he was always asked for UK work experience but had been unable to gain access to such experience.

Table 7.7   Numbers of those working, stating different barriers as preventing them from getting a more suitable job

|                                    | All barriers | Main barrier |
| ---------------------------------- | ------------ | ------------ |
| *Barriers*                         |              |              |
| Racial discrimination              | 11           | 4            |
| Lack of experience                 | 9            | 2            |
| Discrimination against refugees    | 9            | 1            |
| Little work available              | 7            | 2            |
| English literacy skills            | 6            | 1            |
| Wages too low                      | 5            | –            |
| English language skills            | 3            | 2            |
| Relevant vocational skills         | 3            | –            |
| Lack of information                | 3            | –            |
| Child care problems                | 2            | 1            |
| Sex discrimination                 | 2            | –            |
| Lack of self-confidence            | 1            | 1            |
| Accent                             | 1            | 1            |
| Non-recognition of experience/     |              |              |
| Qualifications                     | 1            | 1            |
| Culture                            | 1            | –            |
| Total                              | 64           | 16           |

*Notes*: 1. * Respondents were asked to state all the barriers then the main barrier
2. Base number = 16

Those who were working were asked what they perceived to be the main barrier and all barriers to more suitable jobs. The responses, as Table 7.7 shows revolved mostly around racial discrimination and discrimination against refugees.

It is surprising that non-recognition of qualifications was not perceived as a greater barrier to labour market participation among refugees and asylum seekers.

## Past employment in Britain

Respondents who were not currently working were asked whether they had ever had a paid job in Britain: 25 per cent said that they had. The type of work that respondents had done in the past was similar to much of the work being carried out by those who were currently employed – that is low paid and unskilled shift work. Of those who had been employed in Britain in the past, 18 were from DRC, 15 were Tamils from Sri Lanka, five were from Somalia and most were men (seven in ten). The characteristics of those who had participated in the job market, with the exception of country of origin, were similar to those who were working at the time of the survey.

Those who had worked in Britain in the past, but were not working at the time of the survey, had a similar employment profile to those who were working when the fieldwork was carried out. There was an over representation of people in low-paid, low-skilled work and there was a notable lack of diversity. Nine respondents had worked in shops or as cashiers in their last job, eight as security guards, six as cleaners, five in factories, five in administration and two in kitchens.

A comparison of past employment in Britain, among those who were working before coming to Britain, shows the same lack of utilization of skills that was shown among those who were employed at the time of the survey. Past employment was characterized by diversity and many were in professional posts. In contrast in Britain, past employment had been largely unskilled. For example, civil servants and engineers in the country of origin were working as security guards in Britain while teachers had become clerical workers and cleaners.

Conditions of employment were generally poor combining unsociable hours, long hours, short-term employment and a lack of job security. Nearly half of those who had been employed in the past were in their last job for less than a year and for those in cleaning and security jobs it was a matter of weeks or months. Nearly three-quarters had worked unsociable hours, half in the evenings or at night and over half had worked regularly at the weekends (two weekends a month or more). The reasons why people had left their last job were varied as Table 7.8 shows.

Table 7.8   Reasons for leaving last job

|                                    | Number of respondents |
|------------------------------------|-----------------------|
| Redundant/job finished             | 11                    |
| Personal reasons                   | 7                     |
| Return to education                | 6                     |
| Look after home                    | 3                     |
| Low pay                            | 3                     |
| Ill health                         | 2                     |
| Unsociable hours                   | 1                     |
| Racism in workplace                | 1                     |
| Immigration restriction            | 1                     |
| Got sacked                         | 1                     |
| To look for full time job          | 1                     |
| Got arrested for working illegally | 1                     |
| Petrol garage business failed      | 1                     |
| Total                              | 39                    |

*Source*: Bloch (1996, p. 54)

Over half of those who left their last job because they were either made redundant or their job finished were from DRC. In many cases the reasons for leaving a job merely reflected the nature of refugee employment, which was sporadic work, with low pay and with poor terms and conditions of service. However, as many as two in ten had left their last job for personal reasons which suggests that refugees have serious problems to deal with which might affect their capacity to maintain employment.

## Labour market aspirations

More than half (51 per cent) of those who were not working said that they were looking for paid work. Among those not looking for paid work, the main reasons for not seeking employment were looking after the home and family (38 per cent), studying (31 per cent) followed by 14 per cent who did not have permission to work. Congolese tended not to be looking for work more than others due to a lack of permission to work. Seven out of ten of those without permission to work were from DRC and six of them had arrived in the UK a year or less before the survey was carried out.

Those who were looking for work were more often looking for low skill and often casual work. Jobs sought included cleaning, security, garment work, retail and the service industry and for some (two in ten) any job was being sought. A comparison of pre-migration employment and the sort of employment refugees were seeking at the time of the survey demonstrated that refugees were prepared to occupationally downgrade and had very low employment aspirations. Moreover, the areas where people were seeking employment were in no way commensurate with their qualifications. People with degrees were prepared to take 'any job' or specified shop work or clerical work. Those with 'A' levels or their equivalents were looking for work as security guards or 'any job' and teachers were seeking employment as clerical workers.

Interviews with refugees suggests that the reasons why people were going for low skill jobs was because new arrivals, based on the experiences they observed from those who had been resident longer, became aware that their only employment options were unskilled or low skilled jobs. Al-Rasheed (1992) notes however, that refugees may be unwilling to make too much of an economic investment in Britain because they see their sojourn as temporary rather than permanent.

## Unused skills and barriers to employment among those seeking work

Respondents were very aware of the lack of utilization of their skills and experiences. Of those looking for work, two thirds felt that they had skills that they had been unable to use in the labour market. Fifteen people had experience in retail and service industries and had been unable to use their skills in Britain. A further 13 had teaching skills, 11 respondents had clerical and office skills, nine had trade skills which included electricians, carpenters and mechanics, two were legally trained and five had other skills including accountancy, computing and civil engineering.

Everyone who was looking for work felt that they experienced barriers getting into the labour market. Figure 7.3 shows the barriers faced. The longer people had been in the country the more likely it was that they would specify discrimination, either racial or specifically against refugees, as the main barrier to employment. More recent arrivals were most likely to mention a lack of information. Although many of the barriers are structural, some could be alleviated with targeted resources in the areas of language skills, information, child-care and training in relevant vocational skills.

## Methods of job seeking

One of the factors that disadvantage refugees in the labour market is the cultural specificity of job seeking (Marshall, 1989; 1992). Methods of job seeking vary in different countries though for the majority of Somalis and Tamils employed before coming to Britain, responding to advertisements had been the main way of finding their last job. Among Congolese informal contacts were used more often including friends, family and recommendations from college or university lecturers. In contrast, people who were either working in Britain or who had worked in Britain in the past tended, for the most part, to find their jobs through friends. Among those who were working at the time of the survey or who had worked in the past, four in ten had found work through friends. Two in ten found work through advertisements, one in ten through private employment agencies and less than one in ten through the job centre, by contacting employers directly, through a community group or through a family member.

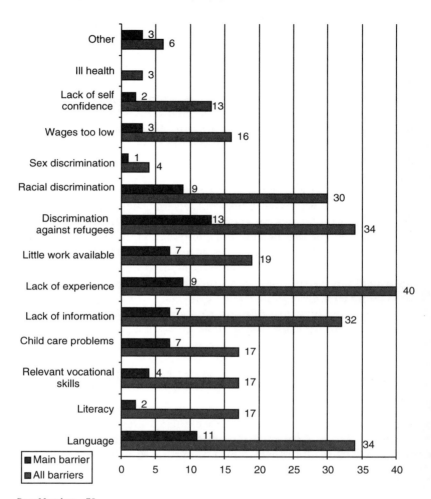

Base Number = 78
*Source*: Bloch (1996, p. 60)
*Figure 7.3*    Barriers to employment.

Methods of job seeking varied by community. However, the significant difference between finding employment in the country of origin and Britain was the dependence on informal contacts in Britain as opposed to advertisements. The importance of informal contacts, particularly with regard to the role of ethnic enclaves, has been noted by other research (Robinson, 1993a; Strand and Woodrow Jones, 1985).

In this study, English language skills were important. Those who spoke English at the level of simple sentences were most dependent on informal contacts for employment while those who spoke English fluently were more likely to find their job by responding to an advertisement.

Research among Sino-Vietnamese refugees in the United States found that economic self-sufficiency was dependent, in part, on English language skills on arrival (Desbarats, 1986). Moreover, those with high levels of English on arrival were more able to adapt economically and were less dependent on the ethnic community as a way of finding employment. This finding is replicated specifically among Tamils in Newham where all of those who spoke no English on arrival, but who were working at the time of the survey, had found their jobs through friends. Thus, the ethnic enclave was providing a stepping-stone for those members of the community who were not sufficiently acculturated in terms of language skills to seek employment through the statutory and formal mechanisms that exist.

### Sources of information and advice about job seeking

There were different sorts of help and assistance available for people seeking employment or careers advice in Newham. Newham Careers Service (NCS) provided advice on careers, employment and training. NCS had three staff that carried out adult guidance work and they also did outreach work at different centres around the borough. Three refugees in this study, who were working at the time of the survey, had heard of NCS although none of them had actually used the service. Twelve respondents (one-sixth) who were looking for work had heard of NCS and five had used the service. Three of the five who had used the service found it useful and two found it useless.

If someone was available for work and signing on then they were entitled to use the services provided by the Employment Services Job Centre. Most provision was aimed at the long-term unemployed – those unemployed for six months or more – and was only available to those who are legally entitled to work. The Job Centre offered a number of schemes designed to help people get into work. Respondents, who were either looking for work, or had been unemployed before they found their current job, were asked whether they had used any of the schemes. Those who had used any of the schemes were asked whether they found them helpful, neither helpful nor

Table 7.9    View about schemes designed to help people into work

|  | Helpful | Neither helpful nor unhelpful | Unhelpful | Total |
|---|---|---|---|---|
| Job club | 5 | 6 | 13 | 24 |
| Job interview guarantee | 3 | 2 | 7 | 12 |
| Job search seminars | 1 | 2 | 3 | 6 |
| 13 week review | – | 1 | 1 | 2 |
| Job review workshop | – | 1 | 2 | 3 |
| Restart interview | 1 | 2 | 4 | 7 |
| Employment on trial | 1 | 2 | 3 | 6 |
| Work trials | – | 1 | 2 | 3 |
| Jobplan workshop | – | 1 | 1 | 2 |
| Community action | 1 | 2 | 4 | 7 |
| 1-2-1- and workwise | – | 1 | 1 | 2 |
| Restart course | – | 2 | 1 | 3 |
| Job introduction scheme | – | 1 | – | 1 |
| Disability service | – | 2 | 1 | 3 |
| Access to work | – | 1 | 1 | 2 |
| Supported employment | – | 1 | – | 1 |
| Travel to interview scheme | – | 1 | – | 1 |
| Employed status training | 2 | 2 | 1 | 5 |
| Total number | 14 | 31 | 45 | 90 |

unhelpful or unhelpful. Table 7.9 shows the responses of those who had participated in schemes.

The Job Club and the Interview Guarantee Scheme were used most often, but on the whole, the schemes provided by the Job Centre are not meeting the needs of refugees as they were described as unhelpful more often that not. Indeed, one Tamil respondent summed up where she thought the schemes went wrong and what she perceived as the needs of refugees.

> I do not agree with most of the schemes run by the Job Centre because most of them insist on making CVs and I think this is a mere waste of time ... so people get fed up going to the Job Clubs, Restart workshops and seminars etc. The public fund is most of the time wasted running these schemes. Instead more hands-on work experience can be provided to unemployed people to get back to work.

Moreover, the usefulness of schemes for refugees can be questioned by the fact that only one respondent who was working had found a job

Table 7.10    Kind of help with job seeking thought to be most useful

|  | *Times cited* |
|---|---|
| General information about job seeking | 44 |
| Where to find vacancies | 44 |
| Advice about interview techniques | 26 |
| Help with applications | 23 |
| How to approach employers | 20 |
| English language training | 19 |
| English literacy training | 9 |
| Help with child care | 8 |
| Other | 4 |

*Base number = 60*

through the Job Club. Respondents who were looking for work were asked whether they would like any help and advice; three-quarters said that they would. The type of help and advice wanted was varied as Table 7.10 shows.

Help with where to find job vacancies and general information about job seeking was mentioned by nearly three-quarters of those who wanted help finding employment. There were some differences in the sort of help that respondents felt would be useful by country of origin, sex, length of residence and English language skills.

Congolese who said that they would like advice and help with job seeking, favoured help with general information about job seeking (nine in ten), information about where to find job vacancies (nine in ten) and advice on interview techniques (six in ten). Tamils favoured help with job applications (seven in ten), English language training (five in ten) and help with child-care (four in ten). Somalis mentioned information about job seeking (six in ten), where to find job vacancies (six in ten) help with job applications (four in ten) and English language training (four in ten) most often.

More recent arrivals wanted more general help than those who had been living in Britain for longer. People who spoke English less well tended to want more help in all areas than those who spoke English fluently. The only instance where this pattern was reversed was help with finding job vacancies.

Women were more likely than men to want general information about job seeking: nine in ten and seven in ten respectively. Women were also more likely than men to want help with how to approach employers: five in ten and three in ten respectively. Finally, three in ten women said that they would like help with childcare.

## Areas where training was wanted

The majority of respondents (62 per cent) said that there was training that they would like to do. People from DRC were most likely to say that they would like to go on a training course. Eight in ten Congolese said that they wanted training compared to six in ten Somalis and less than six in ten Tamils. A higher proportion of women than men said they would like training (69 per cent and 60 per cent respectively).

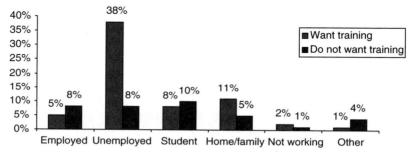

Base number = 172

*Figure 7.4*   Whether wants training by employment status.

Figure 7.4 shows that of all those who wanted training at the time of the survey, the largest proportion were unemployed (38 per cent) followed by 11 per cent who were looking after the home and family. People who were working were still interested in training, employed people made up 5 per cent of all those who wanted training.

The sort of training that people wanted was very diverse. Table 7.11 shows that clerical, office and business administration was the area where training was wanted most often.

Some differences in the type of training wanted emerged by country of origin and sex. Respondents from DRC were most interested in training in the areas of clerical, office and business administration (nearly three in ten) information technology (two in ten), retail and service (two in ten) than in other types of training. Also, Congolese made up all six of those who wanted training in building and design, all eight of those who wanted training in child minding and both the people who wanted training in engineering.

People from the Tamil community expressed more interest in training in the areas of retail and service (three in ten), clerical, office and business administration (three in ten), information technology

Table 7.11    Numbers wanting different types of training

|                                                | *Frequencies*[*] |
| ---------------------------------------------- | ---------------- |
| Clerical/office and business administration    | 24               |
| Information technology                          | 20               |
| Retail/service sector                          | 19               |
| Anything useful                                | 13               |
| Language                                       | 8                |
| Child minding                                  | 8                |
| Teaching                                       | 8                |
| Mechanical/electrical                          | 8                |
| Sewing/dressmaking                             | 8                |
| Law                                            | 2                |
| Engineering                                    | 2                |
| Other                                          | 10[**]           |

[*] The frequencies add up to more than 111, the number of respondents, as some people wanted more than one type of training.
[**] Other category includes journalism, nursing, heavy vehicle driving and how to become self-employed.

(around a quarter) than in other areas. People from Somalia were most interested in language training (two in ten), dressmaking (one in ten) and most of all in 'anything useful' (four in ten).

There were also gender differences in the sort of training people wanted. Three in ten women wanted training in clerical, office and business administration compared to just over one in ten men. Only men wanted training in building and design, law and engineering while only women were interested in child minder training and sewing and dressmaking.

Respondents who were looking for work at the time of the interview were asked, 'Is there any training that you could do to help you get the type of job you want'? Eight out of ten respondents said that there was training that could help them. The training that people wanted is shown in Table 7.12.

Once again, there were differences by country of origin and sex. Respondents from Sri Lanka and DRC were more likely than Somalis to want training to prepare them for retail and service sector jobs. Women were more likely than men to want training in retail and the service sector jobs, four in ten and one in ten respectively. Clerical, office and business training was more popular among Congolese (three in ten) and Tamils (three in ten) than people from Somalia (one in ten). Moreover, half of the women who wanted training wanted

Table 7.12    Training that could be done to help get job

|  | Frequencies[*] |
|---|---|
| Office/clerical/business administration | 17 |
| Retail/service | 16 |
| Information technology | 10 |
| Mechanical/electrical | 10 |
| Teaching | 5 |
| Any | 4 |
| Building/decorating | 4 |
| Art/design/graphics | 3 |
| Dressmaking/sewing | 3 |
| Language | 2 |
| Other | 10[**] |

[*] The frequencies add up to more than 67, the number of respondents, as some people wanted more than one type of training.
[**] Other category includes: security work, advice work and law.

training in clerical and office skills or business administration compared to just one in ten of the men. Tamils were more likely to want training in information technology (four in ten) than were others (less than one in ten), although there was little difference between men and women. Finally, training in mechanical and electrical skills was wanted by men from Somalia and DRC (both two in ten) but by no one from Sri Lanka.

Some of the training that respondents said they could do to help them get a job reflected areas where there were skills gaps in the local economy. However, as shown earlier, there is little correlation between training and employment outcomes especially among those who do not speak English as a first language. For training to be successful, refugees need to be in a position to use their skills and to convert their qualifications. Moreover, employers need to take their skills and qualifications seriously so that this often very highly experienced group can contribute to a local economy that is dependent on inward commuters because it is failing to make use of the skills that exist within the community.

## Summary

This chapter has demonstrated the high levels of unemployment experienced by refugee people, compared to others. This is in contrast to their pre-migration activity. Many refugees arrive in Britain with high levels of education and qualifications but are unable to use their skills in paid employment and levels of unemployment among refugees exceeded that of any other group.

Those who were working tend to be employed in low-paid work with poor terms and conditions of employment. In contrast to national trends, refugee women are more likely to be unemployed than their male counterparts though the impact of language skills on refugee employment and low levels of English language attainment among Somali women will have an effect on the overall trend. Those who have gained employment were overly reliant on informal contacts to help them get into employment. Little use is being made of the statutory job search provision and those who have used it did not, on the whole, find it helpful. Nevertheless, there was a big demand for basic information and advice relating to job seeking and employment in the UK although quite clearly the statutory sector was not meeting the needs of refugee communities.

There was a positive attitude towards training, as the majority said that they would like to take a training course. However, by and large, those respondents who wanted training were seeking training for relatively low skilled jobs, given the skills and qualifications that they had on arrival in Britain. Employment aspirations were low among refugees and many seemed resigned to the fact that they would not be able to use their skills and experience and instead looked for low paid and often temporary employment.

The skills and experiences that refugees bring with them remain largely unused in a locality where there is a skills gap between the needs of the local economy and the skills that many of the population are able to offer. Refugees bring skills that could easily be utilized within the local economy but remain unused for a variety of personal and structural reasons. Refugees themselves identified discrimination as a key barrier to the labour market.

# 8
# The Social Settlement of Refugees

This chapter is concerned with the social settlement of refugees. More specifically it explores attitudes to Britain as home, the reasons why refugees and asylum seekers were living in Newham and their social settlement within the locality. The areas to be examined are significant because they provide an indication of the extent to which different communities and sub-groups within communities are settling in Britain. One key aspect that emerges in the social settlement of refugees in Newham is the importance of immigration status.

## Perceptions of Britain as home

Views about a country as home are known to affect attitudes to settlement and settlement outcomes. It was shown in Chapter 4 that, for the majority, coming to Britain was by chance rather than by choice and the effect of this will be examined. However, one surprising aspect of the data was that the reason for coming to Britain in the first place was not influential. Those who came to Britain because they had no choice were just as likely to see Britain as home as those who came as a result of family ties (four in ten among both groups).

In total less than half (43 per cent) of all respondents saw Britain as home. Country of origin was more strongly correlated with perceptions of Britain as home than other variables (Cramers V = 0.406). A higher proportion of Tamils saw Britain as home (seven in ten) than Somalis (four in ten) or Congolese (two in ten).

The basis of the asylum claim also affected perceptions of Britain as home. The data reflects the typology constructed by Kunz (1981) that the reasons for flight would in turn affect settlement due to the level of orientation felt by refugees towards the homeland and its people.

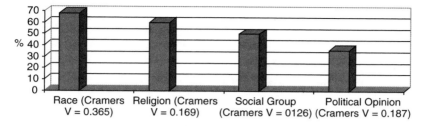

Base number = 176

*Figure 8.1*  Whether respondents saw Britain as home by basis of asylum claim.

Figure 8.1 shows the proportions perceiving Britain as home by the basis of the asylum claim. The association was strongest among those seeking asylum on the basis of race.

Immigration status was also a factor that determined whether or not respondents saw Britain as home. The more secure the immigration status, the more at home people were in Britain. Nearly two-thirds of those with refugee status (63 per cent) and just over half of those with ELR (51 per cent) said that they saw Britain as home. The proportions among those on temporary admission and those appealing against a Home Office decision on their case was much less, 27 per cent and 33 per cent respectively.

There were a number of different factors that influenced people's perceptions of Britain as home. The responses are shown in Table 8.1.

There were differences in responses by communities. Congolese found Britain the most culturally alienating and this is not surprising given that the DRC has no colonial links with Britain. In contrast, three Tamil respondents actually mentioned the British contribution to the current situation in Sri Lanka. In the words of one Tamil man 'The British government has got a responsibility to look after Sri Lankan refugees because they created this problem when they were ruling Sri Lanka.'

Those who identified limited rights or immigration status as affecting their capacity to settle were most likely to be on temporary admission and were therefore in a precarious situation. In the words of one respondent 'We have limited access and we don't have full rights as citizens to do what we want.'

Somalis were the group most likely to identify attachment to their homeland as the reason for not seeing Britain as home. Eight in ten who said that their reasons for not seeing Britain as home were:

Table 8.1   All the reasons why Britain is either seen as home or not seen as home

|  | *Frequencies* |
|---|---|
| *Do not see Britain as home* | |
| Different culture | 28 |
| Have my own country/Home is where I was born | 19 |
| Racism | 12 |
| Cannot as a refugee | 12 |
| No decision on asylum case/no refugee status | 11 |
| Climate | 10 |
| Only here temporarily/will go home | 9 |
| Britain second home | 6 |
| Different language | 6 |
| Limited rights | 5 |
| Lonely/miss family | 4 |
| Different food | 3 |
| Other | 2 |
| *See Britain as home* | |
| Living here now | 18 |
| Feel settled | 14 |
| Free/safe country | 12 |
| Second home/ future home | 10 |
| No choice | 5 |
| No plans to move | 3 |
| Taken care of here | 3 |
| British government has a responsibility | 3 |
| Know nothing else | 1 |
| Other | 2 |

Base number = 178

because they had their own country; they were only here temporarily; that they will go home; Britain is a second home or home is where they were born; were from Somalia. Attitudes towards home, especially the desire to return home, are known to affect settlement. The myth of return concept is one that is prevalent, using Kunz's (1981) typology, among 'majority identified' communities (Zetter, 1999).

The majority of those who saw Britain as home because they felt settled were Tamils (eight in ten). One of the reasons for feeling settled was the large number of South Asians living in the locality. One Tamil noted how he felt at home in the area where he lived because: 'I find a lot of Asian people, shops, temples and so I get a feeling that I am in Sri Lanka.' Tamils were also showing other tentative signs of acculturation in terms of economic participation, and as we shall see later in this chapter, housing tenure.

## Aspirations for return migration

The majority of respondents (71 per cent) said that given the right circumstances they would like to return home, 19 per cent said that they might want to return home while 10 per cent said that they definitely did not want to return to their country of origin. The determining factors for virtually all respondents who would like to go home were peace and/or democracy. Of the 10 per cent of respondents who did not want to return to their country of origin, the reasons for not wanting to return home included the length of time already spent in Britain and having children who do not know the homeland and might therefore experience difficulties on return.

Table 8.2    Whether or not respondent would like to return home, by country of origin, length of residence, employment status, immigration status and perceptions of Britain as home

|  | Whether or not respondent would like to return home | | | |
|  | *Yes (%)* | *Maybe (%)* | *No (%)* | *Total number* |
|---|---|---|---|---|
| *Country of origin* Cramers V = 0.204 | | | | |
| Somalia | 74 | 21 | 5 | 58 |
| Sri Lanka | 55 | 29 | 16 | 58 |
| DRC | 83 | 7 | 10 | 60 |
| *Length of residence* Cramers V = 0.117 | | | | |
| Less than 5 years | 76 | 17 | 7 | 94 |
| 5 years or more | 66 | 21 | 13 | 82 |
| *Current employment status* Cramers V = 0.273 | | | | |
| Paid employment/self employed | 64 | 24 | 12 | 25 |
| Unemployed | 83 | 6 | 11 | 81 |
| Student | 73 | 20 | 7 | 30 |
| Looking after home/family | 48 | 40 | 12 | 25 |
| Other | 50 | 43 | 7 | 14 |
| *Immigration status* Cramers V = 210 | | | | |
| Refugee/Exceptional leave to remain | 63 | 26 | 11 | 97 |
| Temporary admission/ Appealing | 81 | 10 | 9 | 78 |
| *Whether sees Britain as home* Cramers V = 0.484 | | | | |
| Yes | 47 | 31 | 22 | 77 |
| No | 90 | 9 | 1 | 98 |

A number of factors affected whether or not refugees wanted to return home. Table 8.2 shows that people who had been in Britain for five years or more were less likely to say that they definitely wanted to return home than those who had been in Britain for less than five years. The strength of the association, as indicated by Cramers V, was very weak. Those who were unemployed were more likely to want to return home than those who were working or studying. A larger proportion of Congolese wanted to return home than did Somalis and Tamils. A smaller proportion of those with refugee status and exceptional leave to remain said that they wanted to want to return home than did others.

Finally, nearly half who said that they saw Britain as their home said that they would like to return to their homeland compared to 90 per cent of those who did not see Britain as their home. The association between desire for return migration and perceptions of Britain as home was stronger than the association found with any of the other variables.

Table 8.3   Whether or not respondent would like to return home, by grounds for asylum

| Basis of asylum claim | Whether or not respondent would like to return home | | | Total number |
| | Yes (%) | Maybe (%) | No (%) | |
| --- | --- | --- | --- | --- |
| Race Phi = 0.206 | 58 | 27 | 15 | 59 |
| Religion Phi = 0.160 | 60 | 31 | 9 | 35 |
| Political opinion Phi = 0.259 | 80 | 13 | 7 | 112 |
| Social group Phi = 0.259 | 64 | 30 | 7 | 77 |

Theoretically a relationship between attitudes towards return migration and the grounds for an asylum claim might be expected. The data in Table 8.3 show that the association was stronger for those whose grounds for asylum was on the basis of political opinion or social group. However, an examination of Phi shows a weak level of association in all instances.

## Living in Britain: areas of residence, housing and households

Refugees and asylum seekers involved in this study will have arrived spontaneously and as such will not have received any statutory assistance in finding suitable accommodation. Moreover, housing policy including entitlements for housing benefits, has changed in recent years so asylum seekers are no longer eligible for local authority housing (Zetter and Pearl, 1999). Some single asylum seekers are provided with housing under the 1948 National Assistance Act and some families receive support under the 1989 Children Act but much of the housing used has been unsuitable (Audit Commission, 2000b). Although the 1999 legislation has changed housing provision for destitute asylum seekers, supported under the NASS, for those with ELR, refugee status and asylum seekers not receiving housing support the situation remains the same.

### Areas of residence

Refugees and asylum seekers compete with others for housing. For ethnic minority people housing is complex and harassment, discrimination and abuse can effect choices (Radcliffe, 1999). People from refugee communities, like other ethnic groups, tend to live in greater numbers in certain wards in Newham. Although the available information is necessarily restricted by limitations in the Census data, it was possible to extrapolate data about people born in Sri Lanka. Table 8.4 shows that while people born in Sri Lanka were dispersed around the borough more than half of those born in Sri Lanka lived in just three wards in Newham: Wall End, Central and Kensington.

Research has shown that voluntary migrants, such as Pakistanis in Britain and Koreans in the United States, tend to follow a pattern of chain migration. As a result, new arrivals are often helped by relatives both in terms of their migration and their initial settlement (Kim and Hurh, 1993; Shaw, 1988). Thus new arrivals tend to live in areas where there are other people from their own ethnic community. The situation for refugees and asylum seekers is often very different. Most refugees arrive in Britain spontaneously and have little control over their destination and this means that many arrive in Britain without family and kinship networks. Where refugees, such as the Vietnamese, have arrived as part of a programme a propensity for secondary migration to areas with larger proportions of people from the same ethnic

Table 8.4   Proportion of those born in Sri Lanka living in each ward in Newham, 1991 Census

|  | % | Number |
|---|---|---|
| Beckton | 0 | 0 |
| Bemersyde | 0.8 | 14 |
| Canning Town and Grange | 1.0 | 19 |
| Castle | 5.1 | 94 |
| Central | 17.4 | 320 |
| Custom House and Silvertown | 1.0 | 19 |
| Forest Gate | 1.2 | 22 |
| Greatfield | 1.3 | 23 |
| Hudsons | 1.4 | 25 |
| Kensington | 14.0 | 256 |
| Little Ilford | 6.6 | 122 |
| Manor Park | 2.2 | 41 |
| Monega | 5.4 | 99 |
| New Town | 1.1 | 20 |
| Ordnance | 0.2 | 3 |
| Park | 0.6 | 11 |
| Plaistow | 1.3 | 23 |
| Plashet | 0.6 | 11 |
| St. Stephens | 7.0 | 128 |
| South | 2.0 | 36 |
| Stratford | 0.4 | 7 |
| Upton | 3.3 | 61 |
| Wall End | 25.3 | 464 |
| West Ham | 0.9 | 17 |
| Total | 100.1* | 1835 |

* Figures rounded up
*Source*: Bloch (1994)

group has been observed (Bell and Clinton, 1993; Robinson and Hale, 1989; Stalker, 1994).

The pattern of secondary migration was also found among refugees in this study. Four in ten of all respondents moved to Newham after they had already lived elsewhere in Britain. Those who did move within Britain tended to do so if they had arrived in Britain initially because they had no choice over their asylum destination and then moved to Newham because they had friends or family in the area.

Respondents were asked to state all the factors and the main factor that influenced their decision to live in Newham. The responses demonstrate the importance of social networks, but also the importance of living in a locality where there were other members of the same

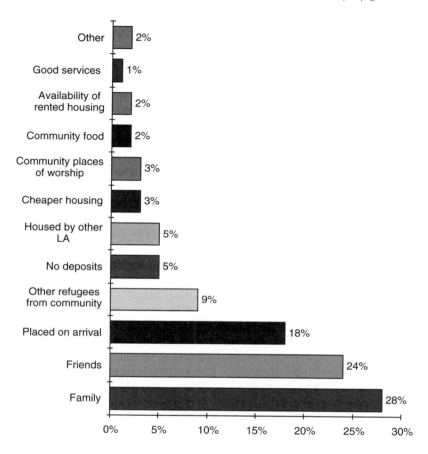

Base number = 176

*Figure 8.2* Main reason for living in Newham.

community. The factor mentioned most often, as one of the reasons for living in Newham was having friends in the borough (51 per cent). The second largest proportion mentioned family (31 per cent) The presence of other refugees from community influenced 28 per cent of respondents. Other reasons for living in Newham were, being placed on arrival (21 per cent), no deposits required by landlords for private rented housing (11 per cent), cheaper

Table 8.5    Number giving main reason for living in Newham, by refugee community

|  | Somalia | Sri Lanka | DRC | Total (%) |
|---|---|---|---|---|
| Family | 20 | 20 | 9 | 28 |
| Friends | 13 | 13 | 16 | 24 |
| Got placed in Newham on arrival | 5 | 2 | 25 | 18 |
| Other refugees from community in Newham | 5 | 8 | 2 | 9 |
| No deposits on rented housing | 5 | – | 3 | 5 |
| Got housed in Newham by another local authority | 8 | 1 | – | 5 |
| Cheaper housing | – | 6 | – | 3 |
| Community places of worship | – | 6 | – | 3 |
| Availability of rented housing | 1 | – | 2 | 2 |
| Community food | – | 3 | – | 2 |
| Good services for refugees in Newham | – | – | 1 | 1 |
| Other | – | – | 2 | 1 |
| Total number | 57 | 59 | 60 |  |

*Source*: Bloch (1999c, p. 119).

housing available than in other parts of London (11 per cent), being placed in the area by another local authority (5 per cent) and getting a job in Newham (3 per cent). The main factor that resulted in an individual living in Newham are shown in Figure 8.2.

Having family or friends in Newham was stated by more than half, as their main reason for living in the locality. Nearly one in ten said that they lived in the borough because there were other refugees from their community living there already.

The differences between the three communities were very marked and there was a strong association between the main reason for living in Newham, and country of origin (Cramers V = 0.466). Table 8.5 shows that people from the DRC were most likely to live in Newham because that was where they got placed on arrival, while Somalis and Tamils came to Newham due to family ties. Among the Somali community, placement in Newham by another local authority was also an important reason for coming to live in the borough.

Community ties were strongest among Tamils from Sri Lanka. Virtually all Tamil respondents gave their main reason for living in Newham as either kinship or friendship ties or other factors that related to the community such as other refugees already living in the borough, the availability of places to worship and community food. This helps to explain why there is a concentration of Tamils in particular wards in the borough.

Social networks, especially family, were also important for Somalis, particularly Somali women. Of those who stated family as the main factor influencing their decision to live in Newham, three-quarters were women. This is explained, in part, by the greater propensity for Somali women to be on family reunion. The reasons for living in Newham, among Tamils and Somalis, is in contrast to those expressed by Congolese and is a reflection of their more developed networks due to colonial connections and a longer migration history. Refugees from the DRC were more likely to be living in Newham because they got placed in the borough on arrival and so it was a matter of chance rather than choice.

Living in close proximity to other members of the same community can affect settlement. An ethnic enclave is seen as a haven and as a first and necessary stage in the process of adaptation (Thomas, 1992). Marcuse (1996, p. 38) states that: '"Enclaves" is a term often given to areas of spatial concentration, which are walled in socially if not physically, but which have positive consequences for their residents'.

Self-segregation into enclaves is not seen necessarily as a barrier to settlement, so long as those living in the enclave have equal access to the structures of the host society. This includes access to education and employment outside the enclave (Weiner, 1996). Enclaves can be a barrier to settlement depending on migration flows, attitudes towards settlement, acquisition of host society language skills and whether or not the migrants see their time in the new society as permanent or temporary. If the sojourn is seen as temporary then there is little incentive to move away from the ethnic community but if it is permanent then there is more reason (Al-Rasheed, 1994; Robinson, 1986). According to Weiner (1996, p. 54): 'The central question to be asked is what are the incentives for migrants to learn the language of the host society and, more broadly, to adopt behavioural patterns that make them more acceptable to the host population?'

Ethnic enclaves have a function and can be positive if migrants are able to move away from them rather than becoming ghettoized in them (Weiner, 1996). Certainly networks were very important in explaining the clustering of refugees in particular areas. In the following chapter, the role of community organizations in the everyday lives of refugee people will be explored and it will show the strength of the links between community involvement, economic activity and settlement in Britain.

## Housing tenure

One of the ways in which people from minority ethnic groups disperse and leave the ethnic enclave is through changes in their housing tenure, especially owner occupation (Shaw, 1988).

Housing tenure among refugees differs markedly from that of the rest of the population (Carey-Wood *et al.*, 1995; Gammel *et al.*, 1993). According to the 1991 Census, 50 per cent of the population in Newham were owner-occupiers and 31 per cent were in council housing. Among refugees in this study, the pattern of tenure was very different. More than half (54 per cent) were in private rented housing. 23 per cent were renting from the council, 13 per cent from a housing cooperative or association, 7 per cent were owner occupiers and 3 per cent were in other sorts of housing such as tied accommodation.

When comparisons are made with the Home Office survey of refugees, it is evident that the tenure pattern of refugees in Newham differs from that of refugees nationally (Carey-Wood *et al.*, 1995). The Home Office study found that 37 per cent of respondents were local authority tenants, 25 per cent were in private rented accommodation, 20 per cent rented from a housing association or cooperative and 12 per cent were owner occupiers. Thus, the Home Office survey found a higher incidence of social housing and fewer refugees in private rented housing.

One possible explanation for the discrepancy in housing tenures found in the Home Office survey and the study in Newham is that respondents in the Home Office survey had all arrived in Britain in the 1980s. Since the late 1980s the reinforcement of the policy trend of limiting the construction of new housing stock and selling existing stock under the 'Right to Buy' scheme has resulted in a reduction in the quantity and, therefore, the availability of social housing (Doling, 1993; Glennerster, 1992). Moreover, asylum seekers have also had their eligibility for social housing curtailed since the Home Office data were collected as a result of the 1993 and 1996 Acts (Zetter and Pearl, 1999).

Housing tenure varied by country of origin and length of residence. All of the owner-occupiers in the sample were Tamils from Sri Lanka and eight in ten of them had arrived in Britain before 1990. A higher proportion of owner-occupiers were in paid employment, spoke English fluently, saw Britain as their home and were less likely to want to return to their country of origin than were others. Moreover, there was a stronger association between tenure and perceptions of Britain as home among Tamils (Cramers V = 0.518) than among Somalis (Cramers V = 0.248) and Congolese where there was virtually no association.

Although the numbers of owner-occupiers are very small, the data suggest that they are moving towards enculturation, the process of cultural change that allows migrants to accomplish the goals of assimilation (Strand and Woodrow-Jones, 1985). Conversely, respondents in private rented housing displayed the least signs of acculturation but they also tended to contain the most recent arrivals to Britain. As a result, those in private rented accommodation were more likely, than were others, to be unemployed; to want to return home and not to feel settled in Britain. Respondents from DRC were most likely to be in private rented housing, followed by Somalis, then Tamils.

Housing mobility tends to be high among refugee groups. One reason is the high proportion in private rented housing where they are potentially vulnerable. More than half of those who had been in Newham for less than two years had moved accommodation as many as three times or more. More than half of those in private rented housing had been in their present accommodation for less than a year while only one in ten had been in it for three or more years. The pattern for people in social housing or owner occupied housing was almost the reverse.

## Household composition

Nearly a quarter of all respondents lived alone (22 per cent) while 41 per cent lived with either their spouse or partner. The rest lived with their children or in shared housing with friends or acquaintances. The household composition of people from Somalia differed from that of the other two communities. Less than one in five Somali respondents lived with a spouse or partner compared to half of the Congolese and half of the Tamil respondents. Moreover, nearly half the Somali men interviewed lived on their own and more than half the Somali women were lone parents. Informal discussions with members of the Somali community in Newham suggest that many marriages break-up once a couple is in the UK because of the stress caused by the inability of men to carry out their traditional role as provider. When men lose their status within the family unit enormous pressure can be placed on the marital relationship (Harrell-Bond, 1986).

In total, 22 per cent of respondents lived on their own and there was little difference between communities. Those who lived in households with more than one person tended to live almost exclusively with members of their own ethnic group. Indeed, only three per cent of the sample living in multiple occupied households lived in households with someone from a different ethnic community than their own and most of those were living with friends in shared private rented accommodation.

### Language spoken at home

Given the overwhelming propensity for people to live in households with members of their own community, it is not surprising that more than 90 per cent of respondents spoke their first language at home, most of the time. Less than 7 per cent of respondent's spoke mainly English at home. However, many households were multi-lingual as Figure 8.3 shows.

Figure 8.3 shows that 31 per cent of those who lived in multiple-occupation households spoke English at home and seven per cent mainly spoke English at home. Those who spoke English at home were more likely to be male than female, more likely to be Congolese than Somali or Tamil and they were more likely to have been living in England for four years or more than for less than four years. Most importantly, more than three-quarters of those adults who spoke English at home at least some of the time lived in households with children. Thus, having children in the household increases the likelihood of the English language being spoken at home at least some of the time.

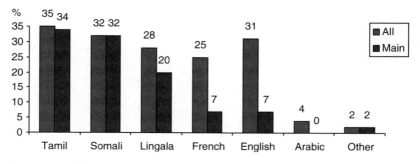

Base number = 140
*Figure 8.3*   All and main languages spoken by respondents at home.

Research carried out with Chinese migrants in Thailand found that language was an important indicator of cultural assimilation. Moreover, it found that different languages were used in different environments and was seen as a way of maintaining ethnic identity (Bun and Kiong, 1993). In Newham, some respondents were monolingual, especially Somali women, and so they were unable to use language in different settings in the same way.

The data show a strong propensity for refugees to live in areas and in households with members of their own ethnic community and to speak their mother tongue at home most of the time. Living in households with children increases the likelihood of English being spoken at home at least some of the time although there is a little evidence of monolingual households where English is the language spoken. Other research has also found this pattern among new immigrants, especially those living in ethnic enclaves where there is a tendency to speak the first language at home, despite multilingual abilities. Moreover, research has also found little inter-group marriage and the maintenance of the first language can, in some instances, conflict with the evidence that other dimensions of acculturation are taking place, especially employment outside of the ethnic enclave (Bun and Kiong, 1993; Kim and Hurh, 1993; Robinson, 1986).

## Life in Newham: social interaction

The extent to which migrants have active social contacts with others from their own community, from other migrant communities and with members of the host society is an indicator of adaptation. Robinson (1986) describes uniplex relations, that is contacts with the ethnic community, and multiplex relations, contacts outside of the immediate community, to indicate the stages in the assimilation process. Uniplex relations occur at the very early stages of migration, often immediately after arrival. Where interactions are limited to this kind of social interaction it is associated with a ghetto rather than an ethnic enclave, which also implies contacts with others from outside the community through shared associations and interests. This interaction is associated with the ethnic enclave. Whether migrants move from primary group contact to acculturation will depend on the aims and objectives of the migration and whether or not they are compatible with acculturation.

This section will explore social contacts. The data will show that respondents generally found it easy to meet people from their own

Sequential change

| Arrival |
|---|
| Secondary group contact: Uniplex relations |
| Shared membership of instrumental associations |
| Primary group contacts: Multiplex relations |
| Acculturation |
| Shared identity |
| Intermarriage / Political absorption |
| Total assimilation |

*Source*: Robinson (1986, Figure 10.1, p. 181)

*Figure 8.4*   A model of ethnic association.

community but hard to meet people and make friends from the wider society. Robinson devised a typology, adapted in Figure 8.4, which suggests that refugees in Newham are not progressing past the first stage in the settlement process.

Meeting members of the host population and having contacts with this group is an indication of the extent to which minority ethnic communities are adapting and settling in the host society. Robinson (1986) set up a model of assimilation that runs through five stages. The first step in the process is communication in the language of the host society and the second is secondary group contact, which usually takes the form of contacts with members of the host society in the workplace and the area of residence. This is different from primary group contact that includes membership of clubs and associations frequented by members of the host society.

The third stage in the settlement process is dependent on the absence of any legal restrictions, which create barriers such as rules surrounding the rights of guest workers in Germany or the old apartheid system in South Africa (Robinson, 1986). In the absence of legal impediments to settlement, access to instrumental associations such as trade unions will take place along with primary group contacts. At this stage the aims and objectives of the migration become important. According to Robinson (1986, p. 182):

If a group has sought migration purely as an economic expedience and does not foresee permanent settlement in the core society, it is unlikely to allow primary group contacts to develop to the extent that they threaten its culture and prospects for return migration. Encapsulation will ensure that the group retains its culture and its prospects for return migration.

If the aims and objectives of the migration are compatible with acculturation then this will take place and can then be followed by shared identity and assimilation. The next section will look at the interactions with other refugees.

## Meeting people and making friends

Though most, with the exception of Somali women, had developed greater proficiency in English language only a small minority of refugees were making secondary group contacts. Though nearly everyone had made new friends since coming to live in the UK (93 per cent), 90 per cent of those who had made new friends said that their new friends were mainly from their own community. Only two per cent said that their new friends were mainly British while eight per cent said that they were mainly other refugees.

Refugees, on the whole, found it easy to meet members of their own community but difficult to meet British people. While 86 per cent found it easy or very easy to meet people from their own community only 26 per cent said the same about meeting British people. In contrast, only four per cent found it difficult or very difficult to meet members of their own community while 51 per cent said they had difficult meeting British people.

There were differences by country of origin and by sex as Table 8.6. shows. Respondents from Somalia, found it much harder to meet British people than did those from the DRC and Sri Lanka. The proportional differences were most marked between Somali women and women from the Tamil and the Congolese communities. The most likely explanations are variations in English language skills, the greater propensity of Somali women than others to be lone parents and cultural and religious differences among this group.

An analysis of Cramers V shows a strong association between the ease or difficulty with which respondents met British people by country of origin (0.488). The relationship between the variables is particularly evident when controlling for sex. Among women, the

Table 8.6   The ease or difficulty with which respondents met British people, by country of origin

|  | Easy | Neither easy nor difficult | Difficult | Total number |
|---|---|---|---|---|
| *Men* | | | | |
| Somali | 3 | 9 | 18 | 30 |
| Tamil | 8 | 14 | 9 | 31 |
| Congolese | 17 | 6 | 10 | 33 |
| *Women* | | | | |
| Somali | 0 | 0 | 30 | 30 |
| Tamil | 8 | 8 | 12 | 28 |
| Congolese | 9 | 6 | 11 | 26 |
| Total (%) | 26 | 24 | 50 | |

strength of association is 0.575 while for men it is 0.438. Not surprisingly English language was found to be an important determinant of the ease with which refugees met British people. The strongest association between the variables was found with Somalis (0.522). Among Congolese it was 0.348 and among Tamils is was 0.335.

Length of residence was also influential in determining the ease with which respondents met British people, even among those who spoke English. Three-quarters of those who spoke English fluently and found it easy or very easy to meet British people had been living in Britain for five years or more. In contrast, no one who had been in Britain for less than two years and spoke English fluently found it easy or very easy to meet British people.

Finally, whether a respondent arrived alone or with others also affected whether or not they found it easy or difficult to meet British people. People who arrived alone, on the whole, found it easier to meet British people. Although the reasons for this difference are not clear, it could be hypothesized that the isolation caused by arriving alone forced people to make more social contacts whilst those who arrived with others remained in their immediate social circles.

The data show little progression from the first stage of assimilation, as shown in Robinson's typology, which is communication, into the second stage, contacts with the host population in the locality among refugees in this study. This is due in part to the interaction with immigration status and so legal impediments to settlement do exist among refugees in Newham. However, cultural alienation and racism are significant and in many cases harder to deal with.

## Summary

The data show that the migration and settlement experiences of refugee communities are diverse. Indeed, the data indicate that different communities and sub-groups within communities are moving through the settlement process at different stages although some, notably Somali women, are not moving through the process at all and remain isolated and marginalized both from the host society and from their own community.

On the whole, people did not see Britain as home though this did vary by community. Most people wanted to return home, and aspirations for return migration are known to affect settlement in the country of asylum.

Congolese were more likely to find it easy to meet British people than were others, in spite of language and fewer traditional contacts with Britain. In some ways this contradicts the theoretical literature that suggests that the ability to make contacts with members of the host society is a step towards assimilation. While Congolese found it easier to meet members of the host society, they were also less likely to see Britain as their home than were others. The propensity for Congolese to be on temporary admission and self-identified cultural differences meant that Congolese were least likely to see Britain as their home, although length of residence did mitigate against cultural differences to some extent.

Tamils were most likely to see Britain as their home while Somalis found it most difficult to settle for a number of reasons including language skills, isolation of women caused by language and being a lone parent and their marginalization from both the host society and their own community. One of the indictors of this is the difficulty they face meeting British people but also aspirations for return migration and a lack of perception of Britain as home. The immigration status of respondents, at the time of the survey, influenced perceptions of Britain as home and asylum seekers were less likely to feel settled than were those with refugee status or with ELR. However, nearly three-quarters of respondents said that they would like to return home.

The greater propensity for Congolese to be on temporary admission helps to explain the anomaly in their settlement experience. While they as a group have shown the greatest improvement in English and find it easier to meet British people, both factors which are associated with settlement, they were still less likely to see Britain as home than were others and immigration status was an important factor. Thus, the data shows that the three communities had had very different settlement experiences in Britain.

Refugees were generally operating within very tight knit social circles with people from their own community and, for many, social networks were the reason why they had elected to live in Newham. Refugees tend to cluster in specific localities and secondary migration is one way in which this occurs. This is particularly the case among refugees who have moved to Newham to be near family members, friends, members of their own community and to a locality where there is access to community places of worship and community food. Although Newham is an area with large numbers of refugees, there is still a tendency for different communities to remain separate from each other. Nearly everyone lived in households that consisted exclusively of members of their own community and the community language was spoken at home most of the time.

Most refugees do not choose to come to Britain, do not settle here and do not want to stay. Moreover, they can struggle to make contacts with members of the host society and remain isolated within very tight social and kinship networks with members of their own community. In Chapter 9 the dependence on community organizations will illustrate just how close knit many refugees are within their immediate community networks as well as the key role that these networks play in the lives of refugee people.

# 9
# Refugee Community Organizations and Volunteering

The voluntary sector is known to be a crucial component in the settlement of refugees (Balloch, 1993; Carey-Wood *et al.*, 1995) and has been of paramount importance in the lives of refugee people. It has been especially crucial in the absence of formal and ongoing statutory reception and resettlement provisions. The provision for forced migrants on arrival tends to be ad hoc and much of the responsibility in the past has been placed on community organizations (Renton, 1993; Wahlbeck, 1997a). Moreover, because many refugees arrive in the host society without kinship ties and support networks, the role of community organizations is key in the early stages of settlement. As we saw in Chapter 4, the majority of respondents had not made a positive choice about coming to the UK and more than half had arrived alone. Moreover, only a few had heard about organizations that could help them on arrival. As a result, refugees who arrive spontaneously in the UK and seek asylum, actively seek out people from their own communities and community organizations to help them with many of their needs in the early stages of settlement. This chapter will examine the role of refugee community organizations in the lives of forced migrants in Newham.

## The role of refugee community organizations

The voluntary sector has a number of roles of which one is to cater for the diversity of need within the community. Refugee community groups and organizations tend to emerge to fill the gaps in mainstream provision. For such organizations to form there have to be sufficient numbers of a particular community in any given locality. Research carried out in Germany, a country that has operated dispersal policies since 1993, found that only the longer-established communities were able to set up a structure of self-help organizations. This was because compulsory dispersal to Länder (states) around the country left insufficient numbers of any one community to build up organizations (Düvell, 1994). One of the concerns about the current UK policy of dispersal is that asylum seekers are removed from access to community-based organizations that tend to be located in the larger urban centres, particularly in London.

The functions undertaken by refugee community organizations are diverse. Activities include the provision of information, advice and advocacy, mediation between clients and other agencies, interpretation and translation, opportunities for social, cultural and political activities, the chance to meet and exchange news from home as well as education and training (Carey-Wood *et al.*, 1995; Duke *et al.*, 1999; Wahlbeck, 1997b).

Community organizations often provide specialist services where statutory and generic voluntary provision is not appropriate or does not meet the needs of a group or community. Refugee community groups are usually managed by people from the same ethnic group and tend to be specific to religion, nationality, ethnic group and in some instances political ideology. Some refugee community organizations cater for the needs of specific clients such as women, disabled people and older people. At the time of the study, funding for community organizations came from a number of sources including the Single Regeneration Budget as shown earlier. The other main sources of funding for community organizations are local authorities, the Home Office and the London Boroughs Grants Unit. In addition, other public and private programmes support work with refugees, though insufficient funding is a major obstacle to the work of this sector (Wahlbeck, 1997b).

## Refugee community organizations in Newham

Newham has a very active network of voluntary and community based organizations. However, there is less provision for the Congolese community than for the longer established Somali and Tamil communities. Community groups tend to have a local rather than a national or international remit and tend to be orientated towards host society settlement. However, some organizations were also part of an active international diasporic network concerned with political activities in the country of origin.

At the time of the survey, the London Borough of Newham funded a Refugee Centre that housed a number of voluntary organizations and there was also a refugee network that acted as an umbrella organization. Most of the community groups that were in operation, however, were small organizations with small premises working on a daily basis in isolation from other groups.

The main organizations working with Somali refugees were Newham Somali Association, Newham South Somali Association, Somali Elderly and Disabled Project, Somali Women's Development Project and the Somali Urur Organization. Among Tamils the main organizations were Newham United Tamil Association, International Tamil Refugee Network, Tamil Welfare Association Newham and Saiva Munnetta Sangam UK. For Congolese there were just two main organizations, the Community of Zairean Refugees and the Zairean Refugee Action Group. There were also a few very small community-based and cultural-based organizations as well as services attached to statutory services such as Health Advocacy projects and advice and information provided at community places of worship.

In addition to community-specific organizations, there are also generic voluntary sector groups such as the Citizen's Advice Bureaux and Law Centres that provide a service to all members of the society. Refugees tend not to use the generic advice services because they are unable to provide advice in the range of community languages and there is the view that they do not understand the uniqueness of the refugee experience (Bloch, 1994).

Thomas (1992) argues that one measure of the separation or ghettoization of minority communities is the extent to which parallel groups that have the role of meeting the needs of the community have emerged. The greater the role and dependence on the voluntary sector, the more enclosed the community within the ethnic enclave. In Newham, the voluntary sector was providing functions that ranged from information and advice to social and community activities. There were differences in activities and the levels of involvement in such activities between communities, though what the data shows is the important role that community organizations have in the lives of refugee people.

## Using refugee community organizations

Most people (87 per cent) had heard of local refugee organizations in Newham, although the assistance of some voluntary organizations in identifying respondents will have biased the response to this question. Nevertheless, as many as 80 per cent of respondents who had not been contacted through a voluntary organization had still heard of local refugee organizations, so the differences were not that great. The majority of people had heard about local refugee organizations through friends (65 per cent), followed by family members (25 per cent), leaflets (13 per cent), through a local newspaper (6 per cent) and only 2 per cent as a result of a referral from another agency.

Eighty per cent of those who had heard of refugee organizations had been in direct contact with one or more organization. Contact with the voluntary sector was directly correlated with English language skills. All of those who spoke no English had been in contact with a voluntary organization compared to 57 per cent of those who spoke English fluently. Women were slightly more likely than men to have been in contact with a refugee community organization. Controlling for country of origin showed a strong association between contact with community groups and language among Somalis (Cramers V = 0.602) and Tamils (Cramers V = 0.580) though the strength of the relationship among Congolese respondents was weak (Cramers V = 0.118).

The data show the importance and even dependency on community organizations, especially among those who do not have sufficient command of the English language to deal with bureaucratic situations. This reflects other research that emphasizes the importance of English as a means of gaining access to welfare and other services (Bloch, 1993; Law, 1996). Thomas (1992, p. 222) also stresses the importance of community groups and the link between contact and language when he writes that:

> The immigrant can draw on experiences of those who have preceded him/her and can access information about the new society in his or her own language. Established ethnic groups provide many of the services offered by mainstream settlement and social service agencies, perhaps even more effectively.

As language skills improve, so the need for community groups will decline. Clearly, the use of the voluntary sector in Newham reflects this thesis, as the more proficient respondents were in English, the less likely they were to use the voluntary sector.

### Information and advice

The provision of information and advice was one of the key tasks of community organizations in Newham. Most people who had been in

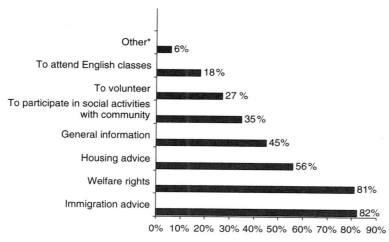

Base number = 124
*The category 'Other' included help with filling in forms, advice about children's education and to receive food donations
*Figure 9.1* Different reasons for contacting refugee organizations in Newham.

contact with community organizations had contacted them for assistance with the initial problems of immigration and welfare. Figure 9.1 shows the reasons for contacting community organizations.

Those who were fluent in English tended to contact community organizations to volunteer, receive general information, to meet people and to participate in social activities. Those who did not speak English or spoke a few words of the language were most likely to contact community organizations for advice about welfare rights, immigration or housing. Duke (1996a, p. 9) also highlights the importance of the links between language and the voluntary sector when she writes that:

> Their mediating role cannot be overstated, especially given the language problems that most new arrivals have. It is much easier for them to make contact with their community groups whose members speak their own language than it is for them to contact British agencies directly.

There were also differences in the use of community organizations that related to the reason why Britain was the country of asylum. Those who said that they had no choice over their asylum destination were more likely to contact voluntary organizations to meet people from their own community, to participate in social activities and to receive general information than were people who came to Britain because they had family. So community organizations have a social role in helping to alleviate the isolation, that can be caused by exile. In addition, they fill a gap for those without kinship networks by providing general information.

### Community organizations and the statutory sector

Community organizations often provide a service to a particular client group, instead of the statutory organizations. One example of this is the case of social security benefits. Just under three-quarters of refugee people interviewed were claiming social security benefits and three-quarters of claimants had received help with their claim. Those who had received help making a claim had obtained help from family members, friends from their own community or their community group advisor. No one had received any help from an officer of the Benefits Agency. Once again language was a key variable as Table 9.1 shows.

Table 9.1   Help making a social security claim, by level of spoken English

|  | None (%) | Few words (%) | Simple sentences (%) | Fluent (%) | Total (%) |
|---|---|---|---|---|---|
| Yes | 95 | 91 | 79 | 41 | 73.5 |
| No | 5 | 9 | 21 | 59 | 23.5 |
| Total number | 19 | 23 | 56 | 34 | 100.0 |

Clearly community organizations were fulfilling the basic role of helping refugees through the claiming process instead of this being undertaken by the Benefits Agency. This pattern of information provision has also been identified among long standing voluntary migrants who tend to rely on informal and community networks rather than the statutory provision offered by the Benefits Agency (Bloch, 1993). The Benefits Agency, in spite of their remit under the 'citizen's charter', was not seen as able to provide for the diversity within any given multiethnic locality while community organizations were seen as providing a service that was accessible in an environment that was non-threatening.

The fieldwork in Newham preceded the introduction of the NASS and so the Benefits Agency was still responsible for administering benefits for all forced migrants as they still are for those claimants with refugee status or ELR. At the time of the study, the local office of the Benefits Agency had one outreach worker whose responsibility it was to liase with community organizations. However, the outreach worker had little contact with refugee groups but instead concentrated on a few organizations working with long-standing ethnic minority groups.

Effective outreach work is known to be a successful way of providing benefits advice and help through the claiming process to people from ethnic minority communities (Bloch, 1993). The most successful model was one where an officer of the Benefits Agency undertook outreach work, on a regular basis, within a community organization using translators and interpreters from the organization. One of the prerequisites of this type of provision was a routine so customers of the Benefits Agency knew who would be arriving from the Benefits Agency and when they would be arriving.

While the services provided by community organizations are crucial in refugees gaining access to entitlements, the nature of the provision is not unproblematic. Law *et al.* (1994) have warned against over dependence on community and voluntary organizations as they can disempower ethnic minority people leaving them reliant on community advisors. Moreover, community organizations take away the need for statutory organizations to meet the diverse service delivery requirements of the communities they have a responsibility to serve. Certainly, a balance needs to be achieved between community self-help and statutory provision. In Britain, in the 1990s, the welfare ideology has been that of neo-liberalism that includes the notion of the role of civil society. This advocates the function of the local community and individual responsibility rather than the welfare state and other statutory sector organizations in the provision of services. One of the key aspects of this model is individual empowerment through labour market participation and community activity. The high levels of unemployment among refugees will certainly impede individual empowerment. Nevertheless this model has been employed in the ad hoc approach to refugee settlement.

In the future, dispersal policies will make it is even more crucial for statutory agencies to work towards meeting the diverse needs of the communities. This is because dispersal will make the organization of community self-help more difficult and new arrivals will not be in a position to draw on the experiences and knowledge of earlier cohorts of forced migrants.

## Participation in community activities

For refugees, community organizations often have a wider remit than just the provision of information and advice. Community organizations have the very important role of facilitating social, cultural and political activities for forced migrants. According to Duke (1996b, p. 475):

> One of the important roles of the community groups is to provide cultural and social activities, directly linked to the members' particular origins. These offer refugees a chance to maintain their own customs and religion, speak their own language, celebrate their heritage and traditions and exchange news from their home countries.

Kunz (1981) argues that refugees' activities in exile will be influenced by the circumstances of their migration and their resultant attitudes towards their country of origin. For example, refugees who flee due to their political activity are likely to continue their activism in the host country in an effort to influence events in their country of origin. Chileans are a good example of a community that continued with its political activities in exile. An orientation towards events in Chile manifested itself in the nature of community organization. Community activity was political in nature and concerned with overthrowing the dictatorship, certainly in the early years of exile. However, the Chilean associations did not remain static but instead developed over time. According to Joly (1996, p. 173):

> as the period of exile lengthened the Chileans abroad became involved in more diverse social, cultural and sports activities and many loosened their direct connections with political parties ... A few of the associations then began to address issues pertaining to life in the host society.

Wahlbeck (1997b), in his study of Kurdish associations, found that most organizations were associated with a political party. Moreover, on arrival to the host society, many Kurdish refugees actively seek out associations representing their political views. However, the politicization of community groups did alienate women, who felt that they were not doing enough to meet the needs of women, and those men who were non-politically orientated. Indeed, Wahlbeck (1997b) notes that the consequence of this was that community groups were not providing an equal service for all refugees. The nature of community provision will depend on the circumstances of exile and some groups have been consistently oriented towards issues within the host society. This was the case among Vietnamese community groups (Joly, 1996).

### Differences in community association

In Newham there were differences among the three communities in terms of community association. Nearly two-thirds of those interviewed (64 per cent) had participated in activities with their own community and Tamils were the most likely to be involved. Table 9.2 shows that nearly all the Tamil people interviewed attended at least one community specific activity that was usually either the Tamil Christian Church or the Temple.

Members of the Tamil community were much more involved in cultural activities than were others. Community groups working with refugees from Sri Lanka organized events like Tamil New Year celebrations and Tamil cultural events. Comparative research in Denmark and Britain found that the Tamil support community, which existed in Britain, impacted on the settlement experience (Preis, 1996). Moreover, Preis (1996) argues that the traditional narratives of Sri Lanka affect life in exile among this group and the desire to maintain tradition is all the more important due to the experience of colonialism and then exile as part of a minority group.

Refugees from the DRC were the most involved in political activities, which also correlates with the fact that they were almost exclusively seeking refugee status on the basis of their political opinions. It is too early to ascertain what the pattern of ethnic association will be among Congolese. If it follows the same course as that of the Chileans (see Joly, 1996) the emphasis will shift either to settlement in the host

Table 9.2  Attendance at social, religious, cultural or political groups, by country of origin

|  | Somalia | Sri Lanka | Congo | Total % |
|---|---|---|---|---|
| Religious | 4 | 48 | 21 | 66 |
| Cultural | 8 | 21 | 0 | 26 |
| Social | 3 | 0 | 15 | 16 |
| Political | 1 | 0 | 21 | 20 |
| Total number | 16 | 55 | 39 |  |

*Source*: Bloch (1999c, p. 127)

society or return migration, should the situation allow it, rather than political activity in the host society.

Somalis were less involved in community activities than others and there was a clear gender divide with Somali women much less involved than Somali men. A similar pattern of participation among women was found in research carried out by the Home Office. According to Carey-Wood *et al.* (1995, p. 88), women were often excluded because 'community groups are organised by men, address issues of more concern to men in the community, and exclude women from some activities on cultural, social or religious grounds.'

Al-Rasheed (1993), in her study of Iraqi women in Britain, also found a gender division in participation in community-based activities. She notes (1993, pp. 101–2) that:

> While men seek contacts with other men to minimise their isolation in exile, many unaccompanied women avoid these contacts and find themselves in greater isolation. In other words, the refugee community acts as a support network in the case of men refugees whereas it could reinforce marginality and liminality in the cases of some women.

More than half of those who were not involved in community-based activities did not attend because they were not aware of their existence. This was particularly the case among Somali women who were generally very isolated.

The longer respondents had been in Britain, the more likely it was that they participated in a group. Just over half (56 per cent) of those who had been in Britain for less than two years attended a group. Eighty one per cent of those who had been in Britain for between two years and five years and 79 per cent of those who had been in Britain for five years or more attended a community-based group.

Nearly three-quarters of those who saw Britain as their home (72 per cent) attended a group compared to 58 per cent of those who did not see Britain as their home. Finally, those who attended groups were more likely to find it easy or very easy to meet British people. This suggests that they were more settled in life in Britain. Figure 9.2 shows the effect of gender on participation, especially in the case of Somali women. In fact the association between attendance and country of origin was strong (Cramers V= 0.520). However, the relationship was even stronger, among women, when sex was controlled for (Cramers V = 0.692).

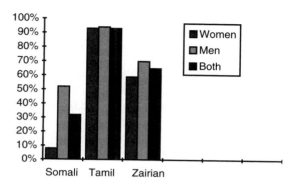

Base number = 111
*Source*: Bloch (1999c, p. 126)
*Figure 9.2* Percentage attending a social, religious, cultural or political group, by sex and country of origin.

One very striking feature of the data is that among Somali women with children only one woman attended a group and she was living with her spouse. All the other Somali women with children were lone parents and none of them attended any groups with other members of the Somali community. This mirrors the findings of Duke's research, which showed that, as a group, lone parents were least likely to participate and that cultural factors were also influential in determining whether some women attended groups, particularly those organized by men (Duke, 1996a). Thus it can be seen that this group remains more isolated and marginalized not only from the host society but also from their own community.

Those respondents who were not participating in any religious, cultural, social or political group were asked their reason or reasons for not attending. More than half of those who did not attend a group had not heard about such activities in the locality. Eight in ten who did not know about groups were from Somalia (six in ten were women from Somalia) and two in ten were Congolese. Length of residence in Britain was not a determining factor among the Somalis, but the Congolese respondents who had not heard about groups were the most recent arrivals and had all been living in Britain for less than two years. Other reasons for not participating in community-based activities included personal reasons, not having the time, preferring to remain separate and not being interested.

The survey data show that members of the Tamil community were more involved in community-based activity than are others. However, the majority are still within the ethnic enclave as the ethnic community is providing the social, cultural and most significantly, religious life for members of the Tamil community in Newham. Thus among members of this group, there has been little entry into the host society. Nevertheless, those participating in such activities tended to feel more settled in Britain than those who did not attend. In terms of Robinson's (1986) model of assimilation, it would seem that some refugees in Newham are very much encapsulated within the ethnic community and within the associations of their own community. For others, however, the model is more associated with marginalization where they are isolated from both multiplex and uniplex relations.

## Voluntary activity

In order to provide services to communities, the voluntary sector relies largely on volunteers who provide most of and, in some cases, all of the personnel resources of community organizations. In this section, the voluntary activity among respondents will be examined. Volunteering is an important mechanism through which refugees can achieve self-esteem and feel they are contributing. It also provides valuable experience. However, previous research has shown that the domain of volunteering is a male one that provides men with valuable standing within their own communities (Al-Rasheed, 1993). There are cultural differences however, and in Newham, this was explicit when considering participation in voluntary activity.

### Volunteering

A quarter of respondents had, at some point, been involved with their community in the capacity of a voluntary worker, of which half were involved at the time of the survey. This is fewer than the 37 per cent who had, at some point, been involved in the voluntary sector at the time of the Home Office survey (Carey-Wood *et al.*, 1995). The majority of volunteers were men (31 out of 46). Of the 15 women who had been involved in voluntary work, nearly all (13) were Tamils. Among male volunteers, the distribution by country of origin was more evenly distributed. Women are therefore more excluded than their male counterparts from the benefits of voluntary work that helps to re-establish the social roles and past work patterns of individuals and helps them to regain some of the self-esteem lost by being dependant on social assistance (Galvin, 2000). Many factors affected the propensity to volunteer, although length of residence was especially important. More than seven in ten of those who had been involved in voluntary work had been living in Britain for five years or more. Proficiency in spoken English was also a factor. Given that much of the role of the voluntary sector is to provide advice, information and advocacy to different communities, it is not surprising that there was a correlation between participation and the standard of spoken English. Nearly all of those who had been involved in voluntary work spoke English either fluently or at the level of simple sentences. Immigration status was also a contributory factor. Those on temporary admission were less likely than were others to have been involved in voluntary work. Finally, a higher proportion of those who saw Britain as home (35 per cent) had carried out voluntary work than those who did not see Britain as their home (19 per cent). This suggests that feeling settled also motivated people to volunteer. Clearly it was those refugees who had been resident longer and were more settled in Britain who had participated in voluntary work. Volunteering therefore corresponded with other indictors of acculturation.

### Type of voluntary work

The sort of voluntary work that was engaged in differed, though many carried out a range of duties. There were differences to be found by community. None of the Congolese respondents had been involved or were involved, at the time of the survey, with interpretation or translation work. Equal proportions of Sri Lankans and Somalis were or had been involved with interpretation and translation work. Advice and advocacy work was evenly distributed among the three communities while seven in ten of those involved with administrative and clerical work were Tamils; the rest were from DRC. All voluntary activities carried out are shown in Table 9.3.

The sort of voluntary work that people did reflected the needs of the communities and so the emphasis on advice, advocacy, interpretation and translation were not surprising. However, one area that is important to note is the absence of campaigning around issues affecting refugees in the UK. Interviews with voluntary workers suggested that the reason why there was an absence of campaigning work was due to the immediate and time consuming needs of refugees in the basic areas of welfare rights that left little time for campaigning, policy work or

Table 9.3   Type of voluntary work carried out (past and current volunteers)

|  | *Frequencies* |
| --- | --- |
| Advice/advocacy | 14 |
| Admin/clerical | 14 |
| Interpretation/translation | 13 |
| Management Committee | 7 |
| Visiting/helping people | 5 |
| Teaching | 4 |
| Social events | 3 |
| Driving | 2 |
| Women's groups | 1 |
| Fund raising | 1 |

Base number = 46

community development activities. Using Miller's (1989) typology of participation in the decision-making process, refugees could in theory present their interests through homeland organizations but in reality this was not a major part of their work. Moreover, those who had been involved in consultation exercises felt that they were merely a mechanism for statutory bodies to claim that they were exploring the needs of the communities rather than actually affecting real change.

The expressed reasons for doing voluntary work varied. Among those engaged in voluntary work at the time of the survey, the majority (nine in ten) did it simply to help their community. Five in ten carried out voluntary work to gain skills, training and experience, two in ten to meet people, two in ten to learn about the problems faced by refugees and less than one in ten were involved to remain active. A substantial amount of time was given to voluntary work. Half volunteered for ten or more hours a week and just over half had been engaged in voluntary work for three years or more.

Of those who had been involved in voluntary work, but were no longer involved, the reasons for stopping were most often to become a student, to take up paid employment or for family reasons (two in ten respectively). Other reasons given for the cessation of voluntary activity were personal reasons, family commitments and simply having had enough. Women were more likely than were men to have stopped doing voluntary work for family reasons, while men were more likely than were women to have stopped because they had either found a job or to become a student.

The data show that the voluntary sector provides a range of functions, both for the recipients of the service and also for the volunteers themselves. The fact that so many saw it as an opportunity to gain new skills or enhance existing ones demonstrates that it was seen as a mode of training. Moreover, the fact that four in ten of those who had stopped doing voluntary work had either found a job or become a student indicates that it did lead to other activities and helped to provide opportunities for people from refugee communities.

## Summary

This chapter shows that community groups and community-based activities play an important role in the lives of refugee people in Newham. Most people had received help from community groups – especially those who lacked English language or literacy skills or the confidence to use English. Those without English language skills tended to contact their community group for advice and information while those who spoke English tended to use the group as a way of meeting new people and engaging in social activities. The data shows how important the voluntary sector is for refugees and that there is little direct contact made with the statutory sector.

There were differences between communities in terms of their participation in cultural, social, religious and political activities. Members of the Tamil community were the most involved with community social and cultural activities, while Somalis were the least involved. Congolese were more involved in political activities than were others and this is an indicator of their level of identification with their homeland. This reflects the political nature of their exile in Britain and their relatively recent migration.

Tamils were most involved in community-based activities, although their activities were almost exclusively contained within the ethnic enclave. Somalis found it very difficult to settle for a number of reasons that included language skills, the isolation of women caused by language and being a lone parent and their marginalization from both the host society and their own community. The marginalization of Somali women was apparent by the difficulties they experienced meeting British people and their lack of involvement in community activities.

For some refugees participation in voluntary work was important for re-establishing themselves in exile and for providing assistance to members of their own communities. In addition voluntary work was a mechanism through which refugees gained experience and transferable skills that could be used in the UK labour market. This is demonstrated by the propensity for some former volunteers to go on and find work or to study. However, volunteers were already showing signs of acculturation and so such activities represent a continuation of that process.

Community-based activities do, however, marginalize some women and this is most notable among Somali women, though it was also apparent to a lesser extent among women from DRC. Tamil women, in contrast, tended to be more involved in community activities and in voluntary work. The explanation for this is in part cultural, in part religious, in part due to the migration experience, length of time in exile and aspirations for the migration.

# 10
## Conclusion

This chapter will first present the main findings of the case study in the areas of social and economic settlement. The findings demonstrate the experiences of refugees living in Britain and in many key areas reflect the theoretical paradigms of migration and settlement presented in Chapter 5. The data also provides new insight into the factors that affect social and economic settlement in the UK. Second, this chapter will present the views of refugees themselves about the factors that affect the settlement of members of their own community and the things that could be done to improve life for refugees in the country of asylum. Drawing on the research findings and the expressed concerns of refugee people, strategies that could be implemented in order to improve the situation of refugees in the UK will be suggested. These strategies will be related to the current situation of forced migrants under the 1999 Act and under the temporary protection schemes that have been utilized in Europe since the 1990s. Finally, the likely direction of policy in light of the European harmonization project and the implications of current developments in the UK case will be explored.

This research has shown that the phenomenon of refugee migration and the resultant settlement outcomes and experiences are dependent on a number of inter-related factors. Earlier research reviewed in Chapter 5 showed that there were a number of personal and structural factors which were either known or thought to affect the settlement experience of refugees and the settlement process itself. Some of the findings in this study verify previous research while other findings add new insights into the refugee experience particularly the importance of structural factors in the life of refugee people.

## Key findings: economic settlement

### Language, training, education and employment

One of the key aims of urban regeneration programmes is to help disadvantaged groups into the labour market through language learning and appropriate skills training and these are important factors in the acculturation process. In terms of language, most refugees were able to gain access to language training and as noted earlier, there was a notable improvement in language skills among respondents. Those who had attended language classes tended to be positive about their classes, although some students felt dissatisfied by the lack of understanding of the refugee experience and the lack of student support. The changes in the rules reducing the hours of attendance to 16 hours a week from 21 in order to be eligible for social security will impact on the intensity of language classes. This is of particular concern, given that a third of those who had attended English language classes in Britain thought that more hours would improve language learning. Other things that would improve courses mentioned most often were teachers from their own community, different level classes and longer courses.

The 1996 Act introduced changes to eligibility for benefits that affected access to language learning. Under the Act, those who were no longer eligible for benefits, because they applied for asylum from within the country rather than at the port of entry, were no longer eligible for free language tuition. Gaining English language provision under the 1999 Act will be even more problematic for asylum seekers. As a result, those who arrive in Britain without language skills will find them more difficult to obtain and will not progress as easily to the first stage of acculturation.

In terms of training, it was noted in Chapter 6, that the rationale was to provide members of the local community with the necessary skills to access jobs. People from minority ethnic communities were known to be disadvantaged in terms of getting onto training in the first place, but they were also disadvantaged in terms of their training outcomes. This research shows that refugees were even more disadvantaged than were members of other minority ethnic communities. Given the high levels of long-term unemployment experienced by refugees, it is surprising that such a small proportion have participated in training. Moreover, no one in employment had got a job as a result of a training placement and there was virtually no relationship between employment and the

type of training taken among those who were working and had participated in training. One positive finding about training was that a higher
proportion of those who had done training had participated in the
labour market than those who had done no training at all.

The position of refugees in the labour market cannot be divorced
from the local economy. As we have seen, Newham is one of the most
economically deprived areas in Britain. The traditional industries have
declined and the loss in local employment in industry and manufacturing has not been replaced by expansions in other areas of the
economy. Ethnic minority employment is known to be hypercyclical.
This means that in times of economic decline, levels of unemployment
rise faster among minority communities than among members of the
white population. Therefore it is not surprising that in an area like
Newham unemployment rates among refugees were very high and
were in fact higher than the average among minority communities in
general. In a comparative study of Vietnamese refugees in Finland and
Canada, Valtonen (1999) noted that the state of the economy when
the migration took place was a key component of the economic integration of refugees. Those who arrived when the economy was strong
integrated into the economy with relative ease compared to those who
arrived when there was an economic slump.

Refugees who were working, were mostly employed in the secondary
labour market and for the most part their jobs were also located in
Newham. In contrast to some other refugee communities, notably East
African Asians (Robinson, 1986) and Soviet Jews (Gold, 1992), there
was little evidence of self-employment or employment in the ethnic
enclave. However among Tamils, community contacts were an important route through which people found employment so the enclave
was beneficial. Moreover, there was little evidence of employment of
refugees in the primary labour market that Portes and Manning (1986)
maintained was more of a possibility for refugees than for people from
other minority ethnic communities.

Among those who were employed, participation in the labour
market was related to the key variables that affected settlement; that is
community and length of residence. Immigration status was also an
important determinant of labour market participation, but as shown
earlier, immigration status was linked to length of residence and community. However people from Somalia, regardless of their immigration
status, were still unlikely to be working. As we have seen, this group
remains marginalized from their own community as well as the social
and economic institutions in Britain.

Participation in education is also known to be an indicator of settlement and not surprisingly, a larger proportion of Tamils had studied since living in Britain than had others. Once again length of residence was a key variable, but community was a stronger determinant than was length of residence. Linked to this were attitudes towards settlement in Britain. Those who felt more settled were more likely to have been involved in education in Britain which again suggests that the ethnic enclave helps to give people the confidence to get on with their lives in exile.

The data showed that people did experience problems completing educational and training courses. Some of the expressed reasons related to the difficulties that refugee people face in exile making it hard to concentrate on their studies. The personal and practical problems faced by refugees were recognized by service providers but limited resources made it impossible for them to alleviate the difficulties.

## Skills base

Many refugees come to Newham as highly qualified and experienced members of the workforce in their country of origin. Since being in Britain most have been unable to use their skills even though they were living in a locality where there is a skills mismatch between the needs of the local economy and the skills base of the general population, which is far lower than that possessed by refugees. Refugees have a range of skills and qualifications that could be used in Newham but remain unused. Occupational down adjustment is known to be a feature among refugees, but for refugees in Newham, there is virtually no movement out of the least desirable secondary sector jobs.

Refugees experience many problems in gaining access to the labour market. One of the problems for refugees was that their skills and qualifications were not recognized by employers. Other problems that refugees faced were: a lack of experience in the UK labour market, low employment aspirations based on the experiences of other refugees, discrimination, language skills, lack of information and the state of the local economy. What was worrying was that refugees seemed unable to gain access to the same or even similar level jobs to the ones that they had before coming to Britain. In addition, for the most part, they were not looking for comparable jobs or seeking training that would allow them to gain access to comparable jobs. Instead, based on the experience of refugees who had come to Britain earlier, many seemed resigned to the fact that their economic prospects were not good and so the sorts of training that was wanted was preparation for low-skilled, low-paid jobs. Moreover, those who were seeking employment, particularly the newest arrivals, tended to look for employment through informal networks rather than through formal methods. This has the affect of continuing the pattern of occupational down adjustment among refugees.

Given the types of jobs that refugees in Newham obtained, there is little hope that there will be much short-term upward occupational mobility among refugees. Thus the skills that refugees have on arrival to Britain, which could be beneficial to the local economy, remain largely wasted.

## Key findings: social settlement

### Refugee migration

The migration experience of refugees to Newham varied. While most came to Britain because they had no choice, that is, they had no control over their destination, some refugees did come to Britain because they had family already living here. Those who came to Britain because of family ties were from the Tamil and the Somali communities and this reflects their longer history of migration to Britain due to colonial ties. This is in contrast to the Congolese community which, with the exception of a few respondents, came to Britain because they had no choice.

Work carried out by Kunz (1973) noted the differences between acute and anticipatory refugees. It was hypothesized that anticipatory refugees, who were better able to plan their flight than were acute refugees, would have a different attitude towards migration and settlement in the host society precisely because the conditions of their flight differed. In this research some respondents came to Britain due to family ties and, in some cases on family reunion visas, and so it was hypothesized that their attitudes towards settlement and their experience of settlement would differ from those who came to Britain because they had no choice. The initial reason for coming to Britain definitely influenced the attitudes of refugees towards Britain as a migration destination. Those who came to the UK as a consequence of family networks were more satisfied with Britain as the country of asylum than were those who had no initial choice. However, the reason for coming to Britain did not affect whether or not respondents saw Britain as home. The same proportion of those who came to Britain due to family ties or because they had no choice saw Britain as home. Instead, immigration status and length of residence were most influential in affecting attitudes towards Britain as home. In terms of immigration status, those with refugee status or exceptional leave to remain felt more secure about their right to stay in Britain, which in turn meant that they were more likely to feel settled. Length of residence was also important, because the longer respondents had been living in Britain, the more accustomed they became to the life. This meant that they felt more settled and resulted in a greater probability of them seeing Britain as home. In addition, those who had been in the UK longer had in some cases started families or had children that had spent most of their lives in Britain and this too influenced their views about Britain as home.

The reason for coming to Britain did affect whether or not respondents would have preferred a different asylum destination. Those who came to Britain due to family ties were much less likely to say that they would have preferred a different country of asylum. The destinations preferred by those who would have wanted to go elsewhere verified some of the theoretical literature because it pointed to the importance of family ties, the language of the host society and historic ties.

However, what was much more important than any of the theoretical factors highlighted by previous research, was the immigration policy of potential receiving countries and the prevailing attitude towards refugees. Ultimately, structural factors and perceived attitudes of host societies towards refugees were of greater importance than were social networks. Refugees wanted to be in a country where their situation was recognized and where they were accepted as refugees.

Once within Britain, kinship and social networks were influential in determining where people settled. This was especially the case among the Tamil community whose decision to live in Newham was, for the most part, determined by pre-existing social networks, as well as the presence of an already existing Tamil community. However, factors relating to community activity including places of worship and the availability of community food were instrumental in the decision to live in the locality. Congolese were least likely to specify networks and community related factors as influencing their decision to live in Newham; in fact four in ten of Congolese respondents lived in Newham because they got placed in the borough on arrival and have not moved subsequently.

The secondary migration patterns among refugees in this study mirrored that found among Vietnamese refugees (Bell and Clinton, 1993; Robinson and Hale, 1989; Stalker, 1994). Refugees from Vietnam were initially dispersed around the country and then migrated to a few urban centres to form larger communities. The same pattern was evident among refugees in this study who came to Britain because they had no choice, lived in another area in the first instance and then relocated to Newham because they had friends or family in the area. Thus, although networks were not a major factor determining the asylum destination of refugees, they were important when it came to deciding where to live once in Britain.

### Structural barriers in the country of asylum

Once within a particular host society there are many factors which are known, through previous research, to affect refugee settlement. Some factors are structural such as the policies of the host society while others are personal and relate to the characteristics and experiences of the individual.

The ability of people from migrant communities to settle is dependent on the policies of the host society, which needs to ensure that there are no legal constraints, limiting the rights of minority groups within the country of migration, that would impede settlement (Robinson, 1986). Indeed, some argue that laws need to exist to ensure that all members of the society are in a position to participate in the social and economic institutions of that society (Weiner, 1996).

This research has shown that immigration status and the resulting lack of citizenship rights experienced by some, especially those on temporary admission, served to impede settlement. There is a hierarchy of rights associated with different statuses though only forced migrants who are naturalized have full citizenship rights. Refugees have most favoured alien status which confers economic and social rights, those on exceptional leave to remain have less rights and are excluded initially from family reunion while asylum seekers on temporary admission have very limited rights.

The rights of asylum seekers have been further eroded since the time of the fieldwork for this case study under the 1999 Immigration and Asylum Act. Clearly, the national government is not committed to ensuring that asylum seekers have the same access to the social and economic institutions as other members of the society. Instead, policy changes under both the 1996 and 1999 Acts have continued to limit rights especially in the area of benefit entitlements but also in terms of freedom to decide where to live due to dispersal.

Under the Asylum and Immigration Act, 1996, changes were also made in the area of employment. Under the legislation, penalty fines were introduced for employers who take on anyone without the correct documentation. This will make it more difficult for people from visible minorities, including those with refugee status, to gain employment (Morris, 1997). This is because employers may be reluctant to pursue documentation or take the risk of employing someone who is not eligible for work. Thus for refugees, who have economic citizenship rights in theory, legislation exists which may result in their exclusion from labour market participation, one of the key determinants of settlement. Labour market participation is important in terms of enabling economic independence and because it helps to facilitate contacts with members of the host society.

The use of Temporary Protection with refugees from Bosnia and Kosovo, in the 1990s, also highlights some of the structural problems associated with this status. First, both programmes included dispersal around the country which resulted in secondary migration away from the dispersal areas to areas with pre-existing communities. Second, those with temporary protection status remained insecure about their status and had to enter the asylum determination process in order to be recognized as a refugee. With the Kosovars, temporary protection was granted for a year, in the first instance, so there was little opportunity to do much more than live in limbo during this time. There is little or no incentive to integrate under this scheme though clearly this is not the objective of government policy.

The research showed the importance of structural factors, most notably state policies, in terms of attitudes towards Britain as home and the desire for return migration. Those with temporary admission were finding it more difficult than were others to feel settled in Britain although the data did show that immigration status was not the only factor at work. Many of the personal characteristics of refugees and asylum seekers, as well as factors relating to community, affected the settlement experience.

### Factors affecting settlement

Earlier research pointed to a number of key determinants in the settlement of refugees in the host society and their ability to gain access to the social and economic institutions in the country of asylum. These included: language skills, length of residence, gender, household composition, employment, education, the presence of an ethnic community and participation in community activities. Tamils and Somalis arrived in Britain with better English language skills than Congolese and this was related to their historic colonial ties with Britain, which meant that members of these communities were more likely to have learned English at school than were Congolese. Language on arrival has been identified as a factor affecting settlement outcomes (Desbarats, 1986; Stein, 1979).

In this research, language skills were found to be crucial but what was more important than English language skills on arrival, were English language skills acquired over time. Congolese, on arrival to Britain were multilingual and the most educated group and this enabled them to attain English language skills relatively quickly. In fact Congolese showed the greatest improvement in their English language skills out of the three communities in this study. The group that fared worst, in terms of language, were Somali women. Most Somali women arrived in Britain without any formal education and, due in part to their status as lone parents, were unable to gain access to English language training. Moreover, there are cultural and religious constraints on Somali women that can make it more difficult for them to participate in activities outside the home. The result has been that Somali women are the group least likely to have acquired English language skills. Moreover, they were also the group that tended to be most isolated from members of the host society and were often marginalized from their own communities as well.

The longer history of migration of Tamils and Somalis to Britain has meant that there are larger and more established networks of refugees and voluntary sector activities for members of these communities than exists for Congolese. In terms of the settlement experience, community and community involvement were crucial. Robinson (1986; 1993) argued that the presence of an ethnic community or enclave was a vital component in enabling settlement as it provided help to new arrivals.

An ethnic enclave, according to Gold (1992) is a spatial concentration of an ethnic community within a particular locality. Gold (1992) emphasized the social rather than the economic function of ethnic enclaves. Indeed, as we have seen, some enclave theorists have been criticized for their tendency to over emphazise the economic function of enclaves (Schmitter Heisler, 1992). Work carried out by Gold (1992) and Portes and Manning (1986) with Jewish refugees to the United States found that many new arrivals found employment within the enclave. This was not the case among refugees in this study, where the minority of those who were employed worked in secondary sector jobs outside the enclave. Secondary sector jobs are characterized by low pay and poor terms and conditions of employment. However, the existence of the enclave was important as demonstrated by the Tamil community.

Many of those from the Tamil community who were employed had found their jobs through Tamil friends. Moreover, nearly all the Tamil respondents interviewed were involved in religious and/or cultural activities pertaining to their community and were the group most likely to see Britain as home and least likely to say that they would return home should the situation permit return migration.

There were large differences to be found among the three communities in terms of community activity and participation. While an ethnic enclave existed for Tamils in Newham there was no such community available for members of the Congolese and Somali communities. The case of the Congolese in Newham is anomalous. This is because Congolese showed some signs of acculturation, through language learning, but experienced barriers to settlement because the aims and objectives of their migration were not compatible with acculturation. Congolese were more involved in activities pertaining to their community than were Somalis, but there was a strong tendency for Congolese to be involved in political activity relating to their homeland rather than the social and cultural activities which are associated with ethnic enclaves.

Congolese are what Kunz (1981) describes as self-alienated refugees who often continue their political activity in exile. Involvement in such activity is thought to conflict with the aims and objectives of acculturation and certainly Congolese were less likely to see Britain as home and more likely to want to return home than were others.

The situation of the Somali community in Newham was different from that of the Tamil and Congolese communities. Somalis were, on the whole, isolated and marginalized from both their own community and from the host society. Only a minority of Somalis participated in community activities and the main reason for this lack of participation was because members of this community were not aware that such activities existed. Lack of English language skills, especially among the women, as well as the propensity for many women to be lone parents, made it virtually impossible for them to settle socially or economically in the host society. Thus, for the Somali community, the long history of migration, colonial links and the presence of family were not helping in the settlement process.

The different settlement experiences of Tamils, Congolese and Somalis, make it difficult to make generalizations about the settlement of refugees as a group. As stated earlier, there are many factors that affect settlement. Some factors are structural, some personal, some relating to the community and some relating to the initial reasons for migration and Britain as the migration destination.

In terms of the acculturation process, members of the three communities had very different experiences. With the exception of Somali women, nearly everyone in the sample has moved to the first stage in the acculturation process: the attainment of the host society language. For the Tamil community, the enclave was providing the social basis of life in exile and a stepping stone for some into economic independence through employment outside the enclave. Employment outside the enclave results in contacts with members of the host society that Robinson (1986) argues is the second stage in the acculturation process. Congolese are the group who found it easiest to meet British people which is an indicator of acculturation, but contradicting this, was the fact that, on the whole, Congolese were not settled in Britain and retained strong ties with their homeland. The Somali community remains the most marginalized from the host society. Somalis were less likely to participate in the labour market, less likely to speak good English and were less likely than others to participate in community activities.

Refugees are not, on the whole, progressing into the second stage in the acculturation process. While some are able to make contacts with members of the host society and some are employed or studying, for the most part, refugees remain unemployed and therefore economically dependent on the state, which is a serious threat to refugee integration (Valtonen, 1994). Moreover, the fact that the minority of respondents had refugee status means that for most, even if there was a desire to integrate, there is a structural barrier to successful integration caused by state policy. As we have seen, immigration status was an important determinant of settlement and attitudes towards settlement, but it should not be forgotten that community and length of residence were also related to immigration status. What the research showed was that the settlement experience of refugees in the host society was very complex as a range of pre-migration and post-migration experiences influenced refugee settlement.

## Factors that affect settlement: the views of refugees

### Factors that affect settlement

The interaction of refugees with the members of the host society (primary group contacts) has been explored in relation to settlement.

Table 10.1   Factors that affect settlement for different communities

|  | Somali | Tamil | Congolese | Total (%) |
|---|---|---|---|---|
| Immigration status | 11 | 8 | 54 | 41 |
| Language | 27 | 27 | 16 | 39 |
| Racism/ discrimination | 1 | 14 | 8 | 13 |
| Different culture | 5 | 11 | 3 | 11 |
| Lack of relevant skills/ qualifications/training | 7 | 13 | – | 11 |
| Unemployment | 4 | 9 | 4 | 9 |
| Lack of services | 5 | 1 | 5 | 6 |
| Lack of confidence | 4 | 4 | 1 | 5 |
| Weather | 2 | 4 | 2 | 4 |
| Lack of resources | 2 | 4 | 2 | 4 |
| Homesick/not ready to settle/not here by choice | 2 | 3 | 1 | 4 |
| Isolated | 5 | 1 | 1 | 4 |
| Housing | 3 | 1 | 1 | 3 |
| Lack of knowledge about legal system | – | 3 | – | 2 |
| Lack of experience | 1 | 1 | – | 1 |
| Child care | 2 | – | – | 1 |
| Access to education | – | – | 2 | 1 |
| Feel like an outsider | 2 | – | – | 1 |
| Other | 2 | 4 | – | 4 |
| Nothing | 2 | 7 | – | 5 |
| Don't know | 3 | 1 | – | 2 |

However, respondents were asked whether there were any factors that affected the ability of refugees from their community to settle in Britain in order to ascertain what the key factors were for refugees themselves. The responses were spontaneous and qualitative and respondents could state as many areas that they thought relevant, so the total number of responses adds up to more than the sample size.

Table 10.1 shows that there was a range of different concerns expressed by respondents from the three communities, although lack of refugee status among Congolese respondents and language among others were stated most often as the factors affecting settlement.

The majority of those who said that the main factor affecting settlement was immigration status had either temporary admission or were appealing against a Home Office decision on their case (seven in ten). One Somali male alluded to his own experience when he stated: 'I have been granted exceptional leave to remain, which is for a one-year term. Therefore it is difficult for me to settle in Britain.' In the words of a Congolese female: 'If you are not accepted as a refugee or resident, you are not able to do whatever you would like so long as your application is under consideration.'

Lack of security over residency definitely affected people's capacity to get on with their lives in Britain in exile. The following statements illustrate the effect of this insecurity on people's lives:

- Residency status, because they may have something to invest but cannot do so because they are not sure of residency.
- Cannot settle down properly because of lack of residency status.
- The immigration system limits and discourages the ability of refugees to settle.
- The majority are not refugees and worry about their future.

Language as an impediment to settlement was the second most frequently mentioned factor and it was a more immediate concern of Somalis and Tamils than it was among those from the DRC. Three in ten of those who mentioned language spoke no English or a few words of English and they were nearly all Somali women. Those who mentioned language also talked, in some cases, about the impact on other aspects of their lives. For example, one Tamil stated that: 'I think language is a great barrier to most of the refugees from Sri Lanka. In my case, I had a good local government job but I was unable to get a similar job due to lack of language.'

Racism in general, and discrimination against refugees in particular, was mentioned by 13 per cent of respondents and the majority of those who mentioned it were Tamils. One Tamil respondent described the affect on him as an individual when he stated that: 'Some of the well-qualified Sri Lankans are unable to get suitable jobs because they are treated as second class citizens in Britain. In my case I couldn't get a teaching job because my qualifications were not recognized here.'

As well as mentioning racism and discrimination as a factor affecting settlement, Tamils were also the most likely to mention cultural differences. This would imply that Tamils felt more alienated than did others from British culture, which contradicts the data presented in Table 8.1 which showed that Congolese felt that cultural differences was the factor which prevented them from seeing Britain as home, but this was not the case among Tamils.

Nevertheless, the responses by Tamils indicate a community that is starting to acculturate in terms of active participation and networks. However, members of the Tamil community are unable to gain access to the wider community because of the barriers, both in terms of racism and in terms of culture, that seem to be preventing such interactions.

Tamils and Somalis mentioned a lack of relevant skills and qualifications, as a factor affecting settlement, but this was not an issue raised by Congolese. This is not surprising because, on the whole as we have seen, Congolese were much better qualified on arrival to Britain than were refugees from the Somali and Tamil communities. Tamils were most likely to find that they did not have transferable qualifications and, in some cases, as the following quote illustrates, this led to jobs that were not commensurate with skills.

I finished my degree in Sri Lanka and I was about to get a teaching job. Because I came here I couldn't get a professional job like teaching. I wanted to train myself for teaching in Britain but I was told I had to do further education which involved a long period [of study] so I decided to do other jobs like cashiering jobs.

Being unable to obtain employment commensurate with skills has been identified by others as a problem for refugees in Britain and elsewhere as we have seen. Motivation to retrain will depend on aspirations for the migration. Al-Rasheed (1992) carried out research with the Iraqi community in Britain and concluded that there had been a notable decline in their occupational position. One of the reasons for the decline was that people saw their stay as temporary and, as a result, long-term economic success and development were not considered a possibility.

Thus refugees, depending on how they perceive their migration, may be reluctant to get their qualifications converted to their UK equivalent as this requires an investment in the form of a financial commitment and further study. One respondent noted that: 'Most professional people like doctors, lawyers and teachers are not in a position to get into their profession straight away as they have to waste time getting British qualifications.'

Length of residence was also important. A larger proportion of those who stated that unemployment affected settlement of their community had been in Britain since 1992 or earlier. Among those who identified unemployment as a factor, seven in ten had been in Britain since 1992 or earlier and only three in ten had been in Britain since 1993. Thus, it would suggest that issues around unemployment and skills become increasingly pertinent to people over time, perhaps as refugees realize that they are not adjusting occupationally to the British economy.

Four per cent of respondents mentioned personal reasons such as being homesick, not feeling ready to settle or the fact that they were not here by choice as factors which mitigated against the successful settlement of members of their own community. This ties in very strongly with the theoretical literature that highlights the differences between voluntary and involuntary migrants and acute and anticipatory migratory situations that result in different attitudes and settlement experiences (Berry, 1988; Kunz, 1973; Weiner, 1996). While refugees still hope, and in some cases, intend to return home should the situation enable return migration, the consequence of this hope will be an impediment to settlement in the host society (Al-Rasheed 1994; Robinson, 1986).

One Somali summed up the problem when he said that: 'It is difficult to adjust to the environment. Somali refugees do not come here as a matter of choice and therefore it is not easy to cope with the culture and the behaviour of the British people.'

Some people mentioned a whole host of inter-related factors that affected settlement. In the words of one Tamil woman: 'I think language and culture plays an important role as well as the weather. Because of the language, most of the Sri Lankans are unable to get good jobs here. The vast difference in culture restricts the social life of Sri Lankans. Also, the cold weather gives you so many health problems.'

### Ways of improving life in Britain for refugees

Respondents were asked their views about ways of improving life in Britain for members of their own community. The responses to the question were spontaneous and qualitative and some people mentioned more than one thing. Respondents identified a range of things that could improve their lives as Table 10.2 shows.

The ways that life for refugees could be improved highlights the different concerns of the three communities. Refugees from DRC were most likely to say that providing refugee status and processing claims more quickly would improve life and this was not surprising given that most of this group were on temporary admission and therefore had fewer rights than most. In the words of one Congolese, the government

Table 10.2   Most frequently mentioned ways of improving life for refugees in Britain, by country of origin

|  | Somali | Tamil | Congolese | Total % |
|---|---|---|---|---|
| More employment opportunities and support for self-employment | 9 | 20 | 21 | 28 |
| Provide refugee status | 5 | 6 | 34 | 25 |
| Training | 17 | 16 | 8 | 24 |
| Setting up social/leisure facilities | 7 | 2 | 31 | 22 |
| Education | 4 | 8 | 22 | 19 |
| Child care | 0 | 10 | 20 | 17 |
| Greater awareness of refugees and their treatment including discrimination | 2 | 7 | 19 | 16 |
| Language | 12 | 11 | 3 | 14 |
| Process claims more quickly/ resolve uncertainty | 3 | 3 | 15 | 12 |
| Housing | 8 | 6 | 3 | 9 |
| More rights for refugees and respect for rights | 0 | 6 | 10 | 9 |
| More opportunities and support for job seeking | 1 | 3 | 10 | 8 |
| Help for children | 9 | 1 | 2 | 7 |
| Better use of existing skills/ recognition of qualifications | 5 | 6 | 0 | 6 |
| More information and advice | 4 | 2 | 5 | 6 |
| More resources to help settlement process and help integration | 3 | 0 | 6 | 5 |

should: 'Consider or answer applications as soon as they come into the country because without status you can not think of integration. We are stuck.'

Congolese expressed the most concern about the way in which refugees were treated in Britain. One in ten of the Congolese respondents also said that more rights would improve the lives of refugees and nearly one in three felt that the treatment of refugees was problematic, particularly the suspicion that exists that asylum seekers were not in fact political refugees but were instead economic migrants. Finally, more than half of the Congolese respondents felt that the setting up of social and leisure activities would improve life in Britain. The lack of activities for Congolese was due, in part, to the fact that they were a new migrant community and so social networks were not in place for members of this group. The need for vocational training and language training was mentioned most often by Tamils and Somalis and this reflected the fact that these groups arrived in Britain with fewer qualifications than did Congolese. One respondent made the links between employment and language and noted that: 'English language support could be given to professionals for example advanced English course may be conducted to boost the chances of finding similar jobs here.'

Issues around employment were mentioned most often and the need for help with employment and for making sure equal opportunities worked in practice. One Tamil respondent noted that: 'Sri Lankans who have a good educational background should be given an opportunity to prove themselves. Because they don't get a fair chance they end up unemployed. This makes them frustrated and some claim social security benefits until they find a suitable job. Equal opportunity policy must be in reality not in papers.'

Others noted that if the government helped refugees to get into employment then they would not be a burden on the state and so it would be beneficial all round. According to one respondent: 'The British government must organize effective methods of employment training schemes which can guarantee a job after finishing off such a scheme so that the government can cut down on social security benefits hence refugees may not be a burden to the British government.'

Congolese were more concerned than with others with the need to provide more educational opportunities and this reflected the fact that they were a new group and many have had their education interrupted as a result of their flight. One respondent alluded to the structural problems affecting access to grants at the time of the survey noting that the rule that dictates that only those who had been resident for three years were entitled to grants was problematic and should be abolished.

The responses of refugees about ways of improving their lives in Britain also included many diverse suggestions including issues around family reunion. One of the problems faced by those without refugee status is that they are not entitled to immediate family reunion. As one respondent noted: 'Immediate family members i.e. husband, wife, children under 21 should be allowed to reunite with their families in the UK without any conditions because the long delays and uncertainty put refugees, who have already suffered a lot, in a depressed situation.'

The concerns of refugees and asylum seekers were personal, structural and in some cases very practical in nature. Strategies that could be adopted to help refugees settle are discussed below.

## Policy recommendations and the 1999 Act

### Structural barriers to settlement

The research has shown that there is a need to reconsider national as well as local policy decisions that affect the lives of refugees in Newham. On a structural level, the importance of immigration status and the resultant citizenship rights and security of residence have a huge impact on settlement and attitudes towards settlement. Throughout the research there was a relationship between immigration status and settlement. Those with refugee status were generally the most settled while those on temporary admission were the least well settled. If there is to be a commitment on the part of the national government to assist asylum seekers in the settlement process then there must also be a commitment to processing claims much more quickly. The situation, as it stands at present, leaves many in a state of limbo though one of the current objectives of the government is to speed up the determination process. So long as this does not affect the consideration given to each case, the effect on asylum seekers can only be a positive one.

Rules surrounding access to welfare leaves some asylum seekers without any means by which to support themselves, as new arrivals are not allowed to work legally in Britain. With the introduction of the 1999 Act all asylum seekers are excluded from the benefits system and are instead dependent on vouchers if they are assessed to be destitute. Relying on vouchers limits the choices that are available to asylum seekers and makes it more difficult for them to participate in any social activities. It also makes asylum seekers visible and therefore increasingly vulnerable to racist attacks. There has been a rise in racist attacks on refugees in the UK.

In the UK context, parallels can be drawn between the inst. racism experienced by Asian and African-Caribbean people as a quence of the Immigration Acts in the 1960s and the current trea of asylum seekers. The legislation in the 1960s and the 1990s iden ..es groups for differential treatment under the law and gives credibility to negative stereotypes (Institute of Race Relations, 1999). One of the arguments for asylum legislation has been the maintenance of good race relations. However there is no evidence to suggest that this is the case. In fact restrictive immigration controls have the opposite effect because they create suspicion and fear (Brochmann, 1992).

The media influence the way in which refugees and asylum seekers are perceived and can contribute to hostility towards foreigners (Schönwälder, 1999). The UK media contribute towards the negative perceptions of asylum seekers and refugees by reporting that many are in fact 'bogus' and that they come to Britain for what they argue are its generous welfare provisions (Kaye, 1999). The fight at the funfair, between refugees and local neo-fascists, in Dover in August 1999 was extensively reported in the national press. What remained unreported was the increase in racist attacks on refugees and asylum seekers in Britain.

The passing of the Immigration and Asylum Act, 1999 is likely to ensure the continued vulnerability of refugees and asylum seekers in Britain. Indeed, asylum seekers form the most vulnerable of Britain's minorities with few rights and no security of status. Combined with their pre-migration experiences, this means that while refugees and asylum seekers are increasingly vulnerable to racist attacks they may also be reluctant to seek the protection of the police. Increased violence against refugees and asylum seekers and lack of contact between refugees and asylum seekers and the police has been noted by the Chief Inspector of Lewisham police. He also noted the priority of developing a strategy for facilitating access to the criminal justice system among refugee people.[1]

The marginalization of asylum seekers is likely to increase with the dispersal policies that have been put in place to 'relieve the burden of provision in London' (The Stationery Office, 1998, 8.22). It is the emphasis on the pressure that asylum seekers place on local authorities in London and the South East and the ease with which asylum seekers

---

1. Refugee and asylum Seekers Forum, London Borough of Lewisham. Tuesday 28 September 1999.

are identified through dispersal and vouchers that makes them especially vulnerable to racism. Dispersal policies are already used in some other European countries and evidence shows that when asylum seekers are excluded from mainstream society they become targets for racism. Arson attacks on refugee hostels in Germany have been well documented (Schönwälder, 1999).

Certainly this policy initiative should be reconsidered in the UK context if there is to be a commitment to the safety of all members of society.

### Social settlement: community and dispersal

There is no formal reception and resettlement assistance available to spontaneous asylum seekers. Many arrive in Britain without social networks and prior to the 1999 Act asylum seekers tended to settle in areas where there were existing refugee communities. For those with pre-existing social networks the choice of where to live was influenced by these networks. With the introduction of dispersal, asylum seekers are excluded from the utilization of networks and therefore from the experiences of those who proceeded them. Moreover, they are not in a position to access community organizations for information, advice, social and cultural activities and to act as a volunteer. Dispersal when used in the past, with Vietnamese refugees, was found to be problematic as refugees in the dispersal areas experienced a number of problems including problems accessing services, lack of employment possibilities and social isolation. There is no reason to believe that the situation of current asylum seekers will be any different and so dispersal itself should be reassessed.

We have seen how crucial community organizations were to the refugees in Newham and how important their role was in the early stages of settlement. For those not involved in the dispersal scheme, community organizations are still extremely important but rely on tenuous local funding and the motivation among refugees to volunteer their services to these community groups. As a result, the services provided by community organizations can be limited and this needs to be addressed. Secure and adequate funding would certainly improve the situation of community organizations and enable them to carry out much more reception and resettlement work in areas where there is a concentration of any community. Community groups are especially important given the evidence that refugees in Newham, on the whole, did not make use of the statutory services that were available to members of the community. Informal networks and the community sector provided refugees with information about claiming social security benefits and employment and only a tiny proportion of respondents had made use of the statutory information provision available in the locality. One of the basic conditions of citizenship is access to and the use of statutory services. This is not the case among refugees and so there is a need to ensure that these services are accessible to all members of the population.

Moreover refugees, like others, do not have homogeneous information needs. Information needs are dependent on a number of factors including language and literacy skills, confidence, culture and religion. Some refugees will require face-to-face oral information and advice in their first language. Indeed, the research showed that literacy in the first language among some groups, most notably Somali women, was very limited and so they were entirely dependent on verbal information. Thus, more trained interpreters within statutory agencies and better funding of community sector groups is necessary, so as to reduce the dependency on family members (including children), friends and volunteers. For others, written information is suitable and appropriate. The key point for service providers is to ensure that they have an understanding of the communities they are trying to reach and the diversity within communities which often vary by gender and age.

In the dispersal areas, access to information and advice is necessarily limited by the lack of community development and the problems encountered by the statutory and non-governmental organizations with a responsibility for providing services to diverse communities in the cluster areas.

### Economic settlement: language, education, training and employment

At the moment many asylum seekers are unable to gain access to language training. English language training needs to be available to all asylum seekers on arrival in Britain. For those who are eligible for English language training, recent policy changes have resulted in a reduction in the amount of language training that refugees can participate in and still claim benefit and this needs to be rectified. Indeed, the more hours of English language training that is available, the better. English language training would be improved by the provision of child-care facilities because at present some groups, especially Somali women, are excluded from much language learning provision. Moreover, there need to be child minders from refugee communities, so that parents can feel more confident about leaving their children.

Training child minders from refugee communities would help to provide refugees with employment.

A favoured initiative to help with language provision was teachers from refugee communities. English teaching should be carried out by bi-lingual members of refugee communities and given the number of qualified and experienced teachers from refugee communities living in Newham, such an initiative could be easily implemented with appropriate training. Such a strategy would ensure that teachers had an understanding of refugee experiences but also it would create employment for refugees in Newham and would help those with teaching skills from their country of origin to use those skills.

Refugees need help and advice about how to get their qualifications recognized in Britain. Moreover, conversion courses that would upgrade qualifications to their UK equivalents are essential if refugees are to use their skills and experiences in the local economy. Indeed, this is one of the key objectives of urban regeneration programmes and to date they have not enabled refugees to participate in the labour market at the level to which they were trained. In November 2000, the Immigration Minister Barbara Roche announced a scheme to re-train doctors from refugee communities to enable them to practice their profession in the UK. Such schemes are welcomed and should become more widespread as they will help to facilitate employment and therefore the successful settlement of refugees.

Problems were found with the training schemes that refugees participated in. One of the major problems with training, for those with under-utilized skills, is that it is not equipping local people with the skills necessary to obtain the well-paid jobs in the locality. Much of the training that refugees have participated in prepared them for low-skill jobs with poor employment prospects. Links between trainers and local employers would help to ensure that refugees obtain the sorts of training that would help them get into the more desirable jobs for which some were already qualified.

More work trials and work placements are necessary, as a lack of work experience in Britain was one of the main barriers that refugees felt that they faced in trying to gain access to the labour market. Moreover, more jobs in the statutory sector for members of refugee communities would help to re-establish confidence. The high levels of unemployment and the downward occupational mobility that refugee people experience in the Britain provides little hope or incentive for refugees who, for the most part, have been unable to use their skills and qualifications in Britain.

The way in which funding is allocated to training providers needs to be reassessed. At the moment, the emphasis on quantifiable outcomes may be disadvantaging groups who experience more difficulties getting employment on completion of training. Money to support refugees who are on training courses should be provided, as this could help to alleviate the low rates of completion among refugees which is due, in part, to other pressures that refugees have to contend with in their daily lives.

Employers need to be educated in anti-racist employment strategies. In addition, the disincentives to employers to employ people from minority communities, as they have to engage in a process of checking documentation or risk being fined by the government if employees do not have the correct documentation, need to be removed.

More assistance and advice in setting up small-businesses should be provided. Some refugees had come to Britain with experience of being self-employed but have been unable to use their skills in Britain. Research has shown that self-employment among refugees is an important mechanism for providing family members and friends with employment, so the benefits of assistance would have an immediate impact.

Refugees who were in employment tended to be employed in low pay, low skill jobs with poor terms and conditions of employment. Indeed, low pay was identified as a barrier to employment. The sorts of jobs that are currently open to people from refugee groups means that taking employment would leave them financially worse off than they currently are claiming social security and other benefits. In order to escape the economic and social isolation associated with claiming benefits, refugees must have access to well paid primary sector jobs and the scheme for doctors is certainly one positive first step in this direction.

Some of the policy recommendations would need financial resources while others, most notably the provision of refugee status, would depend on the way in which asylum cases are processed and evaluated by the Home Office. Given the skills and experience that many refugees have on arrival to Britain, placing resources in their direction would benefit the local economy in the long run. Such a strategy fits into urban regeneration schemes that aim to help disadvantaged groups.

## The implication of European harmonization

The importance of the European harmonization project in terms of policing Europe's borders and dealing with the county responsible for determining any individual asylum case was noted in Chapter 3. There are other salient issues emerging from the European policies on a national level.

The asylum problem as defined by European states revolves around the numbers who gain access to territories (Schuster, 2000). With this in mind, the priority areas for signatories of Schengen and the UK and Ireland have been the elaboration of restrictive policies and the incorporation of neighbouring countries into the regime (Geddes, 2000). Thus, the effect and the future aim of European harmonization are more restrictive border controls at both the European level and at the nation state level. One of the consequences of restricting border controls has been the criminalization of refugees who are often forced to travel with false documentation and/or the assistance of smugglers.

Other restrictive measures that have been adopted have been the creation of safety zones, tackling root causes of migration, engaging in preventative action and the use of temporary protection (Geddes, 2000; Schuster, 2000). Temporary protection, which is used increasingly in Europe, has the effect of leaving forced migrants in limbo and giving them little or no security of status. While it can make members of the host society more positive about receiving forced migrants (see Bloch, 1999a) it also ensures that governments maintain strict control over the rights afforded to these groups, which are less than those conferred on refugees, and the duration of their exile.

Ideas recently mooted by the government that set out to prevent asylum seekers arriving in Europe spontaneously, have been the rewriting of the Geneva Convention and the processing of asylum claims in the nearest neighbouring state to which refugees flee. In order to advance these ideas the Home Secretary has been talking to the relevant French and Italian ministers.

The welfare state in European countries is a key area for the operation of inclusion and exclusion (Geddes, 2000) and Schuster (2000, p. 123) notes that 'welfare has become the second line of defence in the fight to reduce the number of asylum seekers'. At present there are variable systems in operation across Europe most of them increasingly restrictive. The link between immigration and welfare have been used as a justification for immigration control (Bloch, 2000a) though there is no evidence to suggest that a reduction in welfare entitlements affects asylum migration (Schuster, 2000).

At the European level there have been discussions around the harmonization of standards for the reception of asylum seekers though to date there are no fixed plans. One concern is that such a strategy might lead to the adoption of the lowest common denominator.

The concerns, therefore, of European policy revolve around restricting access to borders and curtailing the rights and entitlements of asylum seekers who manage to gain access to European countries of asylum.

## Summary

This research has shown that much of the theoretical work that identified key variables in the settlement of refugees in the host society was borne out among refugees in Newham. This included macro- and micro-factors like colonial links and kinship networks as well as levels of education and language skills on arrival to Britain.

However, the research also showed that there were other factors affecting refugee settlement, most notably immigration status, which had a huge impact on attitudes towards settling in Britain as well as the capacity of refugees to get on with their lives in exile.

Refugees in Newham were finding it difficult to progress from the first stage in the acculturation process, the acquisition of the language of the host society, through to the second stage, employment and contacts with the host population. Indeed, Somali women had not been able to reach the first stage in the acculturation process and remained marginalized from the host society and from their own community.

This research showed that refugee settlement is very complex and that it is very difficult to make generalizations about the settlement experiences of refugees. Patterns were identified within and among the three communities that show the impossibility of adopting a blanket approach to the needs of refugees. Instead, the needs of different communities must be assessed if there is to be any real hope of assisting refugees in the settlement process and in their efforts to gain access to the social and economic institutions in Britain.

Finally, if there is to be a commitment on the part of government to the settlement of refugees in Britain then the barriers that impede settlement by limiting rights within the host society must be removed. Unless there is a reversal in the policy trend of successive governments to curtail the migration of asylum seekers and any public expenditure on forced migrants then it is difficult to see how refugees will be able to settle and contribute their skills and experience in Britain.

# Appendix: Methodology

The survey sample was obtaining using snowballing techniques. Snowballing occurs when a study obtains respondents through referrals among people who share the same characteristics (Biernacki and Waldorf, 1981). One of the problems associated with snowball sampling is it can be over dependent on one network so to ensure a wider representation of refugee people a number of starting points for the chain were identified for each community (Welch, 1975).

Initially the aim was to use six contact points for each community with ten interviews taking place at each location. However this did not work out in reality as Table A.1 shows. With the Somali and Tamil communities, some organizations were unable to facilitate ten interviews so more contact points were used. With the Congolese community there was a less well established and smaller network of organizations due to their more recent migration and so less contact points were used.

## Fieldwork

The fieldwork took place in 1996 and interviews were carried out using interviewers from the three communities who were trained in survey methods and the administration of the questionnaire. The interviewers were encouraged to comment on drafts of the questionnaire and were also involved in the translation of the questionnaires into community languages (Somali, Tamil and Lingala). Moreover, the interviewers acted as gatekeepers to some of the organizations that facilitated interviews and so they had an important role in the research process.

Quotas for gender, age and length of residence were specified for each of the communities. In the end, the interviewers were unable to meet the quotas exactly but they came close enough to ensure that different experiences by the quota variables or characteristics were recorded by the fieldwork. The final sample is shown in Table A.2.

There were different problems faced by the interviewers from the three communities in terms of fulfilling their quotas. Interviewers from the Somali and Tamil communities could not find enough respondents who arrived in the UK after 1992 as refugees living in Newham from these two communities tended to have arrived in the UK before 1993. Among the Congolese community the problem was meeting the quota for age. This is because Congolese migration is recent and so the age of the community tends to be young. As a result, the Congolese interviewer could only locate 12 interviewees aged 35 and older.

Table A.1   Organizations acting as gatekeepers and the number of successful interviews carried out via each organization

|  | Frequency | Percentage |
|---|---|---|
| *Somali community* | | |
| Health advocacy project | 10 | 6 |
| Newham Somali Association | 9 | 5 |
| Somali Women's Development Project | 6 | 4 |
| Newham College of Further Education | 10 | 6 |
| Somali Cultural Association | 1 | 1 |
| Contacts among those who meet to chew | | |
|     Qat socially | 9 | 5 |
| Newham Refugee Union | 2 | 1 |
| Newham Somaliland Association | 4 | 2 |
| Other | 2 | 1 |
| *Sub total* | 53 | 31 |
| Missing: 7 | | |
| | | |
| *Tamil community* | | |
| Manor Park Christian Centre | 12 | 7 |
| Tamil Welfare Association (Newham) | 4 | 2 |
| Newham College of Further Education | 8 | 5 |
| Dance school at a local community centre | 1 | 1 |
| Temple | 17 | 10 |
| Mother and toddler group | 5 | 3 |
| Newham Refugee Centre | 3 | 2 |
| Health Advocacy Project | 1 | 1 |
| Other | 5 | 3 |
| *Sub total* | 56 | 34 |
| Missing: 4 | | |
| | | |
| *Congolese community* | | |
| COREZAG | 33 | 20 |
| Chez Tonton Jacque (a cafe in Plaistow where | | |
|     Zairians meet) | 9 | 5 |
| University of East London Zairian Students group | 6 | 4 |
| Newham College of Further Education | 12 | 7 |
| *Sub total* | 60 | 36 |
| Total | 169 | 101* |
| Total number of missing cases: 11 | | |

Eleven respondents did not want the survey interviewer to record the organization to which they were affiliated because they were concerned that they might be traced back and identified.

* Total percentage does not add up to 100 per cent as numbers were rounded up or truncated.

Table A.2    Survey sample by year of arrival, age and sex

|  | *Frequencies* | *Percentages* |
|---|---|---|
| *Arrived in the UK* | | |
| 1992 or earlier | 104 | 60 |
| 1993 or later | 70 | 40 |
| * Missing: 6 | | |
| *Age* | | |
| 34 or younger | 109 | 62 |
| 35 or older | 67 | 38 |
| * Missing: 4 | | |
| *Sex* | | |
| Male | 94 | 52 |
| Female | 85 | 47 |
| *Missing: 1 | | |

# Bibliography

Al-Ali, N., Black, R. and Koser, K. (2001) 'The limits to "transnationalism": Bosnian and Eritrean refugees in Europe as emerging transnational communities', *Ethnic and Racial Studies*, vol. 24, no. 4, pp. 578–600.

Al-Rasheed, M. (1992) 'The Iraqi community in London', *New Community*, vol. 18, no. 4, pp. 537–50.

Al-Rasheed, M. (1993) 'The meaning of marriage and status in exile: The experience of Iraqi women', *Journal of Refugee Studies*, vol. 6, no. 2, pp. 89–104.

Al-Rasheed, M. (1994) 'The myth of return: Iraqi Arab and Assyrian refugees in London', *Journal of Refugee Studies*, vol. 7, no. 2/3, pp. 199–219.

Alba, R. and Nee, V. (1997) 'Rethinking assimilation theory for a new era of immigration', *International Migration Review*, vol. 31, no. 3, pp. 826–74.

Amnesty International (1993) *Zaire: Violence against democracy*, London, Amnesty International.

Andrews, G. (1991) (ed.) *Citizenship*, London, Lawrence and Wishart.

Anwar, M. (1985) *Pakistanis in Britain: A sociological study*, London, New Century Publishers.

Audit Commission (2000a) *A New City: Supporting asylum seekers and refugees in London*, London, Audit Commission.

Audit Commission (2000b) *Another Country: Implementing dispersal under the Immigration and Asylum Act 1999*, London, Audit Commission.

Bach, R.L. and Carroll-Seguin, R. (1986) 'Labour force participation, household composition and sponsorship among Southeast Asian refugees', *International Migration Review*, vol. 20, no. 2, pp. 381–404.

Baldwin-Edwards, M. and Schain, M. (eds) (1994) *The Politics of Immigration in Western Europe*, Essex, Frank Cass.

Balloch, S. (1993) *Refugees in the Inner City: A study of refugees and service provision in the London Borough of Lewisham*, London, Centre for Inner City Studies, Goldsmiths College, University of London.

Bell, J. and Clinton, L. (1993) *The Unheard Community*, Derby, Refugee Action.

Berry, J.W. (1980) 'Acculturation as varieties of adaptation in a new society', in Padilla, A. (ed.), *Acculturation: Theory, models and some new findings*, Boulder, Westview, pp. 9–25.

Berry, J.W. (1988) 'Acculturation and psychological adaptation: A conceptual overview' in Berry, J.W. and Annis, R.C. (eds), *Ethnic Psychology: Research and practice with immigrants, native peoples, ethnic groups and sojourners*, Amsterdam, Swets and Zeitlinger, pp. 41–52.

Biernacki, P. and Waldorf, D. (1981) 'Snowball sampling: Problems and techniques of chain referral sampling', *Sociological Methods and Research*, vol. 10, no. 2, pp. 141–64.

Bloch, A. (1993) *Access to Benefits: The information needs of minority ethnic groups*, London, Policy Studies Institute.

Bloch, A. (1994) *Refugees and Migrants in Newham: Access to services*, London, London Borough of Newham.

Bloch, A. (1996) *Beating the Barriers: The employment and training needs of refugees in Newham*, London, London Borough of Newham.

Bloch, A. (1999a) 'Kosovan Refugees in Britain: The rolls royce or rickshaw reception', *Forced Migration Review*, issue 5, pp. 24–26.

Bloch, A. (1999b) 'Carrying out a survey of refugees: Some methodological guidelines and considerations', *Journal of Refugee Studies*, vol. 12, no. 4, pp. 367–83.

Bloch, A. (1999c) 'As if being a refugee isn't hard enough: The policy of exclusion', in P. Cohen (ed.), *New Ethnicities, Old Racisms*, London, Zed Books, pp. 111–31.

Bloch, A. (2000a) 'Refugee settlement in Britain: The impact of policy on participation', *Journal of Ethnic and Migration Studies*, vol. 26, no. 1, pp 75–88.

Bloch, A. (2000b) 'It's not working: Refugee employment and urban regeneration', in Kershen, A. (ed.), *Language, Labour and Migration*, Aldershot, Ashgate, pp. 197–221.

Bloch, A. (2000c) 'A new era or more of the same? Asylum policy in the UK' *Journal of Refugee Studies*, vol. 13, no. 1, pp. 29–42.

Bloch, A. and Schuster, L. (2002 forthcoming) 'Asylum and welfare: Contemporary debates', *Critical Social Policy* , vol. 22, no. 3.

Bloch, A., Galvin, T. and Harrell-Bond, B. (2000a) 'Refugee women in Europe: Some aspects of the legal and policy dimensions', *International Migration*, vol. 38, no. 2, pp. 169–90.

Bloch, A., Galvin, T. and Schuster, L. (2000b) 'Editorial introduction', *Journal of Refugee Studies*, vol. 13, no. 1, pp. 1–10.

Böcker, A. and Havinga, T. (1997) *Asylum Migration to the European Union: Patterns of origin*, The Netherlands, Institute for the Sociology of Law, Nijmegen.

Booth, H. (1992) *The Migration Process in Britain and West Germany*, Aldershot, Avebury.

Boswell, C. (2001) *Spreading the Costs of Asylum Seekers: A critical assessment of dispersal policies in Germany and the UK*, London, Anglo-Germany Foundation.

Boyd, M. (1989) 'Family and personal networks in international migration: Recent developments and new agendas', *International Migration Review*, vol. 23, no. 3, pp. 635–70.

Bravo, M. (1993) *The Special Training Needs of Refugees*, London, The Refugee Council.

Brochmann, G. (1992) 'Control at what cost?', paper prepared for the workshop on migration into Western Europe, *What Way Forward?*, London, Royal Institute of International Affairs.

Brophy, M., Maxey, K., Abraham, T., Aybek, T., Bird, P. and Stanikzai, F. (1998) *Refugee Education, Training and Employment in Inner London*, London, FOCUS TEC.

Brubaker, R. (1992) *Citizenship and Nationhood in France and Germany*, Cambridge, MA, Harvard University Press.

Buijs, G. (ed.) (1993) *Migrant Women: Crossing boundaries and changing identities*, Oxford, Bergh.

Bulmer, M. and Rees, A. (1996) (eds) *Citizenship Today: The contemporary relevance of T.H. Marshall*, London, UCL Press.

Bun, C.K. and Kiong, T.C. (1993) 'Rethinking assimilation and ethnicity: The Chinese in Thailand', *International Migration Review*, vol. 27, no. 1, pp. 140–68.

Carey-Wood, J. (1997) *Meeting Refugees' Needs in Britain: The role of refugee-specific initiatives*, London, Home Office.

Carey-Wood, J., Duke, K., Karn, V. and Marshall, T. (1995) *The Settlement of Refugees in Britain*, London, Home Office Research Study 141, HMSO.

Cashmore, E. and Troyna, B. (1990) *Introduction to Race Relations*, 2nd edn, London and New York, The Falmer Press.

Castles, S. (1995) 'How nation states respond to immigration and ethnic diversity', *New Community*, vol. 21, no. 3, pp. 293–308.

Castles, S. and Davidson, A. (2000) *Citizenship and Migration: Globalisation and the politics of belonging*, Basingstoke, Macmillan – now Palgrave Macmillan.

Castles, S. and Kosack, G. (1985) *Immigrant Workers and Class Structure in Western Europe*, Oxford, Oxford University Press.

Castles, S. and Miller, M. (1998) *The Age of Migration: International population movements in the modern world*, 2nd edn, Basingstoke, Macmillan – now Palgrave Macmillan.

Chelliah, R. (1995) *Race and Regeneration: A consultation document*, London, Local Government Information Unit.

Close, P. (1995) *Citizenship, Europe and Social Change*, Basingstoke, Macmillan – now Palgrave Macmillan.

Cohen, R. (1994) *Frontiers of Identity: The British and the others*, London, Longman.

Collinson, S. (1993) *Europe and International Migration*, London, Pinter Publishers for the Royal Institute of International Affairs.

Collinson, S. (1999) *Globalisation and the dynamics of international migration: Implications for the refugee regime*, New Issues in Refugee Research, Working Paper No, 1. , Geneva, United Nations High Commissioner for Refugees.

Community Relations Commission, (1974) *One Year On: A report on the resettlement of refugees from Uganda in Britain*, London, Community Relations Commission.

Convey, A. and Kupiszewski, M. (1995) 'Keeping up with Schengen: Migration and policy in the European Union', *International Migration Review*, vol. 29, no. 4, pp. 939–63.

Coughlan, J. (1998) 'Occupational mobility of Australia's Vietnamese community: It's direction and human capital determinants', *International Migration Review*, vol. 32. no. 1, pp. 175–201.

Crook, J. (1995) *Invisible Partners: The impact of the SRB on black communities*, London, Black Training and Enterprise Group.

Cross, M. (1992) 'Race and ethnicity', in Thornley, A. (ed.), *The Crisis of London*, London, Routledge, pp. 103–18.

Daniel, W.W. (1968) *Racial Discrimination in Britain'*, London, Penguin.

Davis, K. (1989) 'Social science approaches to international migration', in Teitelbaum, M. and Winter J. (eds), *Population and Resources in Western Intellectual Provision*, Population Development Review Supplement, pp. 245–61.

Desbarats, J. (1986) 'Ethnic differences in adaptation: Sino-Vietnamese refugees in the United States', *International Migration Review*, vol. 20, no. 2, pp. 405–27.

Doling, J. (1993) 'Encouraging home ownership: Trends and prospects', in Jones, C. (ed.), *New Perspectives on the Welfare State in Europe*, London, Routledge, pp. 64–83.

Duke, K. (1996a) 'Refugee community groups in the UK: The role of the community group in the resettlement process', paper presented to the British Sociological Association Annual Conference, *Worlds of the Future: Ethnicity, nationalism and globalisation*, University of Reading.

Duke, K. (1996b) 'The resettlement experiences of refugees in the UK: Main findings from an interview study', *New Community*, vol. 22, no. 3, pp. 461–78.

Duke, K., Sales, R. and Gregory, J. (1999) 'Refugee resettlement in Europe', in Bloch, A. and Levy, C. (eds), *Refugees, Citizenship and Social Policy in Europe*, Basingstoke, Macmillan – now Palgrave Macmillan, pp. 105–31.

Dummett, A. and Nicol, A. (1990) *Subjects, Citizens, Aliens and Others: Nationality and immigration law*, London, Weidenfeld and Nicolson.

Düvell, F. (1994) 'Fluchlingslager Heute', *1999 – Zeitschrift für Sozialgeschichte des 20 and 21 Jahrhunderts*, (1).

El-Solh, C. (1991) 'Somalis in London's East End; A community striving for recognition', *New Community*, vol. 17, no. 4, pp. 539–52.

Faist, T. (2000) *The Volume and Dynamics of International Migration and Transnational Social Spaces*, Oxford, Oxford University Press.

Finnan, C.R. (1981) 'Occupational assimilation of refugees', *International Migration Review*, vol. 15, no. 1, pp. 292–309.

Fishman, W. (1979) *The Streets of East London*, London, Gerald Duckworth and Co Ltd.

Fitzgerald, M. (1999) *Final Report into Stop and Search*, London, HMSO.

Gallagher, D. (1989) 'The evolution of the international refugee system', *International Migration Review*, vol. 23, no. 3, pp. 579–98.

Galvin, T. (2000) 'Refugee status in exile: The case of African asylum-seekers in Ireland' in MacLachlan, M. and O'Connell, M. (eds), *Cultivating Pluralism*, Dublin, Oaktree Press, pp. 199–218.

Gammel, H., Ndahiro, A., Nicholas, N. and Windsor, J. (1993) *Refugees (Political Asylum Seekers): Service provision and access to the NHS*, London, College of Health.

Gans, H. (1997) 'Toward a reconciliation of "assimilation" and "pluralism": The interplay of acculturation and ethnic retention', *International Migration Review*, vol. 31, no. 4, pp. 875–92.

Geddes, A. (2000) *Immigration and European Integration: Towards a fortress Europe?*, Manchester, Manchester University Press.

Ginsburg, H. (1992) *Divisions of Welfare: A critical introduction to comparative social policy*, London, Sage.

Girbash, C. (1991) *Manchester Vietnamese Employment and Training Survey*, Manchester, The Centre for Employment Research, Manchester Polytechnic.

Glazer, N. and Moynihan, D. (1970) *Beyond the Melting Pot: The Negroes, Puerto Ricans, Jews, Italians, and Irish of New York City*, Cambridge, MIT Press,

Glennerster, H. (1992) *Paying for Welfare: The 1990s*, Hemel Hempstead, Harvester Wheatsheaf.

Gold, A.J. (1992) *Refugee Communities: A comparative field study*, California, Sage.

Gordon, M. (1964) *Assimilation in American Life*, New York, Oxford University Press.

Goulbourne, H. (1998) *Race Relations in Britain since 1945*, Basingstoke, Macmillan – now Palgrave Macmillan.

Green, A. (1994) *The Geography of Poverty and Wealth: Evidence on the changing spatial distribution and segregation of poverty and wealth from the Census of Population, 1991 and 1981*. Warwick, Institute for Employment Research.

Griffiths, D. (1997) 'Somali Refugees in Tower Hamlets: Clanship and new identities', *New Community*, vol. 25, no. 1, pp. 5–24.

Griffiths, S. (1994) *Poverty on your Doorstep: London Borough of Newham poverty profile*, London, London Borough of Newham.

Guild, E. (1996) *The Developing Immigration and Asylum Policies of the European Union*, Amsterdam, Kluwer Law International.

Guild, E. (2000) 'Kosovar Albanian Refugees in the UK', in van Selm, J. (ed.), *Kosovo's Refugees in the EU*, London, Continuun 2000, pp. 67–90.

Hansard, London: House of Commons.

Harrell-Bond, B. (1986) *Imposing Aid: Emergency assistance to refugees*, Oxford. Oxford University Press.

Hausner, V. and Associates (1992) *Economic Revitalisation of Inner Cities: The urban programme and ethnic minorities*, Inner Cities Research Programme for the Department of Environment, HMSO, London.

Havinga, T. and Böcker, A., (1999) 'Country of asylum by choice or chance: Asylum-seekers in Belgium, the Netherlands and the UK', *Journal of Ethnic and Migration Studies*, vol. 25, no. 1, pp. 43–61.

Ho, S.Y. and Henderson, J. (1999) 'Locality and the variability of ethnic employment in Britain', *Journal of Ethnic and Migration Studies*, vol. 25, no. 2 pp. 323–33.

Holmes, C. (1978) (ed.) *Immigrants and Minorities in British Society*, London, George Allen and Unwin.

Holmes, C. (1988) *John Bull's Island: Immigration and British society, 1871–1971*, Basingstoke, Macmillan – now Palgrave Macmillan.

Holmes, C. (1991) *A Tolerant Country: Immigrants, refugees and minorities in Britain*, London, Faber and Faber.

Home Office (1998) *Asylum Statistics, United Kingdom, 1998*, London, Home Office.

Home Office (1999a) *Asylum Statistics, United Kingdom, 1997*, London, Home Office.

Home Office (1999b) *Statistics on Race and the Criminal Justice System*, London, Home Office.

Home Office (2000) *Asylum Statistics: United Kingdom, 1999*, London, Home Office.

Iganski, O. and Payne, G. (1996) 'Declining racial disadvantage in the British labour market', *Race and Ethnic Studies*, vol. 19, no. 1, pp. 113–33.

Institute of Race Relations (1999) 'Lessons from Europe: How the UK government's asylum proposals will create racism and social exclusion', *European Race Bulletin*, no. 30, pp. 1–3.

Jiwani, A., Pratt, J. and Richards, N. (1994) *Stratford City Challenge Baseline Study*, Centre for Institutional Studies, Commentary Series Number 45, London, University of East London.

Joly, D. (1996) *Haven or Hell? Asylum policies and refugees in Europe*, Basingstoke, Macmillan – now Palgrave Macmillan.

Joly, D. with Kelly, L. and Nettleton, C. (1997) *Refugees in Europe: The new hostile agenda*, London, Minority Rights Group.

Jones, P. (1982) *Vietnamese Refugees: A study of their reception and resettlement in the United Kingdom*, London, Home Office.

Jones, P. (1983) 'Vietnamese refugees in the UK: The reception programme', *New Community*, vol. 10, no. 3, pp. 444–53.

Jones, T. (1993) *Britain's Ethnic Minorities*, London, Policy Studies Institute.

Juss, S. (1993) *Immigration, Nationality and Citizenship*, London, Mansell.

Kay, D. and Miles, R. (1988) 'Refugees or migrant workers? The case of the European Volunteer Workers in Britain', *Journal of Refugee Studies*, vol. 1, no. 3/4, pp. 214–36.

Kaye, R. (1999) 'The politics of exclusion: The withdrawal of social welfare benefits from asylum seekers in the UK', *Contemporary Politics*, vol. 5, no. 1, pp. 25–45.

Kershen, A. (1993) 'The Jewish community in London' in Merriman, N. (1993) (ed.), *The Peopling of London: Fifteen thousand years of settlement from overseas*, London, Museum of London, pp. 138–48.

Kim, K.C. and Hurh, W.M. (1993) 'Beyond assimilation and pluralism: Syncretic sociocultural adaptation of Korean immigrants in the United States', *Ethnic and Racial Studies*, vol. 16, no. 4, pp. 696–713.

King, M. (1993) 'The impact on Western European border policies on the control of "refugees" in Eastern and Central Europe', *New Community*, vol. 19, no. 2, pp. 183–99.

Knox, K. (1997) *A Credit to the Nation: A study of refugees in the United Kingdom*, London, Refugee Council.

Koser, K. (1996) 'Recent asylum migration in Europe: Patterns and processes of change', *New Community*, vol. 22, no. 3, pp. 151–8.

Koser, K. (1997) 'Social networks and the asylum cycle: The case of Iranians in the Netherlands', *International Migration Review*, vol. 31, no. 3, pp. 591–611.

Koser, K. and Black, R. (1999) 'Limits to Harmonization: The "temporary protection" of refugees in the European Union', *International Migration*, vol. 37, no. 3, pp. 521–43.

Kunz, E.F. (1973) 'The refugee in flight: Kinetic models and forms of displacement', *International Migration Review*, vol. 7, no. 2, pp. 125–46.

Kunz, E.F. (1981) 'Exile and resettlement: Refugee theory', *International Migration Review*, vol. 15, no. 1, pp. 42–51.

Kushner, T. (1993) 'Jew and non-Jew in the East End of London: Towards an anthropology of "everyday" relations', in Alderman, G. and Holmes, C. (eds), *Outsiders and Outcasts*, London, Gerald Duckworth and Co Ltd, pp. 32–52.

Kushner, T. and Knox, C. (1999) *Refugees in an Age of Genocide*, London, Frank Cass.

Kymlicka, W. (1995) *Multicultural Citizenship: A liberal theory of minority rights*, Oxford, Clarendon Press.

Law, I. (1996) *Racism, Ethnicity and Social Policy*, London, Prentice Hall/Harvester Wheatsheaf.

Law, I., Karmani, A., Deacon, A. and Hylton, C. (1994) 'The effect of ethnicity on claiming benefits: Evidence from Chinese and Bangladeshi communities', *Benefits*, no. 9, pp. 7–11.

Layton-Henry, Z. (1984) *The Politics of Race in Contemporary Britain*, London, Allen and Unwin.

Layton-Henry, Z. (1992) *The Politics of Immigration*, Oxford, Blackwell.

Leslie, D., Drinkwater, S. and O'Leary, N. (1998) 'Unemployment and earnings among Britain's ethnic minorities: Some signs for optimism', *Journal of Ethnic and Migration Studies*, vol. 24, no. 3, pp. 489–506.

Levy, C. (1999) 'European asylum and refugee policy after the Treaty of Amsterdam: The birth of a new regime' in Bloch, A. and Levy, C. (eds), *Refugees, Citizenship and Social Policy in Europe*, Basingstoke, Macmillan – now Palgrave Macmillan, pp. 12–50.

Liebaut, F. with Blichfeldt, T. (2000) *Legal and Social Conditions for Asylum Seekers and Refugees in Western European Countries*, 4th edn, Copenhagen, Danish Refugee Council.

Liebaut, F. and Hughes, J. (1997) *Legal and Social Conditions for Asylum Seekers and Refugees in Western European Countries*, 3rd edn, Copenhagen, Danish Refugee Council.

Local Economic Policy Unit (1996) *Improving Work Placements and Positive Outcomes for Trainees from Minority Ethnic Groups and Trainees with Disabilities*, London, LEPU, South Bank University.

Loescher, G. (1993) *Beyond Charity: International co-operation and the global refugee crisis*, New York, Oxford University Press.

London East Training and Enterprise Council (1996a) *London East Economic Assessment*, London, LETEC.

London East Training and Enterprise Council (1996b), *Economic Bulletin, Number 3*, September 1996, London, LETEC.

Macdonald, I. (1993) 'Current law and practice in the UK', in Robinson, V. (ed.), *The International Refugee Crisis: British and Canadian responses*, Basingstoke, Macmillan – now Palgrave Macmillan, pp. 158–74.

Macpherson, W. (1999) *The Stephen Lawrence Inquiry*, London, Home Office.

Malik, F (1990) *A Survey of the Armenian Community in London*, London, Social and Community Services Group, London Research Centre.

Marcuse, P. (1996) 'Of walls and immigrant enclaves', in Carmon, N. (ed.), *Immigration and Integration in Post-Industrial Societies: Theoretical analysis and policy-related research*, Basingstoke, Macmillan – now Palgrave Macmillan, pp. 30–45.

Marshall, T. (1989) 'Cultural aspects of job hunting', *Refugee Issues*, London, The Refugee Council.

Marshall, T. (1992) *Careers Guidance with Refugees*, London, Refugee Training and Employment Centre.

Marshall, T.H. (1950) *Citizenship and Social Class and Other Essays*, Cambridge, Cambridge University Press.

Meehan, E. (1993) *Citizenship and the European Community*, London, Sage.

Merriman, N. (1993) (ed.) *The peopling of London: Fifteen thousand years of settlement from overseas*, London, Museum of London.

Metcalf, H., Modood, T. and Virdee, S. (1997) *Asian Self-Employment: The interaction of culture and economics*, London, Policy Studies Institute.

Miles, R. and Clearly, P. (1993) 'Migration to Britain: Racism, state regulation and employment', in Robinson, V. (ed.), *The International Refugee Crisis: British and Canadian responses*, Basingstoke, Macmillan – now Palgrave Macmillan, pp. 57–75.

Miller, M.J. (1989) 'Political participation and representation of non-citizens', in Brubaker, R.W. (ed.), *Immigration and the Politics of Citizenship in Europe and North America*, New York, University Press of America, pp. 129–43.

Modood, T. (1998) 'Ethnic diversity and racial disadvantage in employment', in Blackstone, T., Parekh, B. and Sanders, P. (eds) *Race Relations in Britain; A developing agenda*, London, Routledge, pp. 53–73.

Modood, T. and Bertoud, R. (eds.) (1997) *Ethnic Minorities in Britain: Diversity and disadvantage*, London, Policy Studies Institute.

Modood, T., Beishon, S. and Virdee, S. (1994) *Changing Ethnic Identities*, London, Policy Studies Institute.

Montgomery, J.R. (1996) 'Components of refugee adaptation', *International Migration Review*, vol. 30, no. 3, pp. 679-702.

Moody, A. (2000) 'New deal and ethnic minority participants', *Labour Market Trends*, Feburary.

Morris, L. (1997) 'A cluster of contradictions: The politics of migration in the European Union', *Sociology*, vol 31, no. 2, pp. 241–59.

Morrison, J. (1998) *The Cost of Survival: The trafficking of refugees to the UK*, London, Refugee Council.

Morrison, J. (2000) *The Trafficking and Smuggling of Refugees: The end game in European asylum*, Geneva, UNHCR.

National Coalition of Anti-Deportation Campaigns (2000) www.ncadc. demon.co.uk

Newham History Workshop (1986) *A Marsh and a Gasworks: One hundred years of life in West Ham*, London, Newham Parent's Centre.

Owen, D. (1994) 'Spatial variations in ethnic minority group populations in Great Britain', *Population Trends*, vol. 78, pp. 23–33.

Panayi, P. (1993a) 'Germans in London', in Merriman, N. (ed.), *The Peopling of London: Fifteen thousand years of settlement from overseas*, London, Museum of London, pp. 111–17

Panayi, P. (1993b) 'Refugees in twentieth century Britain: A brief history', in Robinson, V. (ed.), *The International Refugee Crisis: British and Canadian responses*, Basingstoke, Macmillan – now Palgrave Macmillan, pp. 95–112.

Panayi, P. (1994) *Immigration, Ethnicity and Racism in Britain: 1815–1945*, Manchester, Manchester University Press.

Panayi, P. (1999) *The Impact of Immigration*, Manchester, Manchester University Press.

Park, R.E. (1950) *Race and Culture*, Glencoe, The Free Press.

Parkinson, R. (1998) *Survey of Refugee Needs in Hackney for the Hackney Refugee Training Consortium*, Cardiff, Research Consultancy Training.

Paul, K. (1997) *Whitewashing Britain: Race and citizenship in the postwar era*, Ithaca and London, Cornell University Press.

Peabody Trust and London Research Centre (LRC) (1999) *Refugee Skills-Net: The employment and training of skilled and qualified refugees*, London, Peabody Trust and LRC.

Peach, C. (1986) 'Patterns of Afro-Caribbean migration and settlement in Britain', in Brock, C. (ed.), *The Caribbean in Europe: Aspects of West Indian experience in Britain, France and the Netherlands*, London, Frank Cass, pp. 62–84.

Peach, C. (1998) 'Trends in levels of Caribbean segregation, Great Britain, 1961–91', in Chamberlain, M. (ed.), *Caribbean Migration: Globalised identities*, London, Routledge, pp. 203–15.

Portes, A. (1995) 'Children of immigrants: Segmented assimilation', in Portes, A. (ed.), *The Economic Sociology of Immigration*, New York, Russell Sage Foundation, pp. 248–80.

Portes, A. (1999) 'Conclusion: Towards a new world – the origins and effects of transnational activities', *Ethnic and Racial Studies*, vol. 22, no. 2, pp. 463–77.

Portes, A. and Manning, R.D. (1986) 'The immigrant enclave: Theory and empirical examples', in Olzak, S. and Nagel, J. (eds), *Competitive Ethnic Relations*, Orlando, Academic Press, pp. 47–68.

Pratt, J. and Fearnley, R. (1996) 'Stratford City Challenge', in Butler, T. and Rustin, M. (eds), *Rising in the East: The regeneration of East London*, London, Lawrence and Wishart, pp. 327–52.

Preis, A.B.S. (1996) 'The vagaries of refugee resettlement: Power, knowledge and narrativity', *Anthropology in Action*, vol. 3, no. 1, pp. 4–8.

Radcliffe, P. (1999) 'Housing inequality and "race": Some critical reflections on the concept of "social exclusion"', *Ethnic and Racial Studies*, vol. 22, no. 1, pp. 1–22.

Rasmussen, H.K. (1996) *No Entry: Immigration policy in Europe*, Denmark, Copenhagen Business School Press.

Ravenstein, E.G. (1885) 'The laws of migration', *Journal of the Statistical Society*, Vol. 48.

Refugee Council (1996) 'What sort of jobs are refugees seeking?: The impact of the Job Seekers Allowance and the 16 hour rule', *Factfile Number 8*, November 1996, London, Refugee Council.

Refugee Council (1998) *Asylum Statistics 1987–1997*, London, Refugee Council.

Refugee Council (1999) 'Catch 22', *iNexile*, vol. 5, pp. 4–5.

Refugee Council (2001) 'Statistics', *iNexile*, vol. 14, p. 3.

Renton, T. (1993) 'Refugees: The responsibilities of the UK government', in Robinson, V. (ed.) *The International Refugee Crisis: British and Canadian Responses*, London, Macmillan Press – now Palgrave Macmillan, pp. 26–33.

Rex, J. (1996) 'National identity in the democratic multi-cultural state', *Sociological Research Online*, vol. 1, no. 2, pp. 1–12.

Richmond, A. (1993) 'Reactive migration: Sociological perspectives on refugee movements', *Journal of Refugee Studies*, vol. 6, no. 1, pp. 7–24.

Richmond, A. (1994) *Global Apartheid*, Toronto, Oxford University Press.

Rix, V. (1996) 'Social and demographic change in East London', in Butler, T. and Rustin, M. (eds), *Rising in the East: The regeneration of East London*, London, Lawrence and Wishart, pp. 1–19.

Robinson, V. (1980) 'Correlates of Asian immigration: 1959–1974', *New Community*, vol. 9, no. 1/2, pp. 115–22.

Robinson, V. (1986) *Transients Settlers and Refugees: Asians in Britain*, Oxford, Clarendon Press.

Robinson. V. (1993a) 'Marching into the middle classes? The long-term resettlement of East African Asians in the UK', *Journal of Refugee Studies*, vol. 6, no. 3, pp. 230–47.

Robinson, V. (1993b) 'British policy towards the settlement patterns of ethnic groups: An empirical evaluation of the Vietnamese programme1979–88', in

Robinson, V. (ed.), *The International Refugee Crisis: British and Canadian responses*, Basingstoke, Macmillan – now Palgrave Macmillan, pp. 319–54.

Robinson, V. (1998) 'The importance of information in the resettlement of refugees in the UK', *Journal of Refugee Studies*, vol. 11, no. 2, pp. 140–60.

Robinson, V. and Hale, S. (1989) *The Geography of Vietnamese Secondary Migration in the UK*, Warwick, ESRC Centre for Research in Ethnic Relations.

Robson, B., Bradford, M., Deas, I., Hall, E., Harrison, E., Parkinson, M., Evans, R., Garside, P., Harding, A. and Robinson, F. (1994) *Assessing the Impact of Urban Policy*, London, Inner Cities Research Programme for the Department of Environment, HMSO.

Rogers, R. (1992) 'The future of refugee flows', *International Migration Review*, vol. 26, no. 2, pp.1112–43.

Rolfe, H., Bryson, A. and Metcalf, H. (1996) *The Effectiveness of TECs in Achieving Job Outcomes for Disadvantaged Groups*, London, Policy Studies Institute.

Ryan, L. (1997) *Refugee Women: Issues facing Bosnian women in Ireland*, discussion paper drafted for the Bosnian Community Development Project, Dublin.

Saggar, S. (1992) *Race and Politics in Britain*, Hemel Hempstead , Harvester Wheatsheaf.

Saggar, S. (1998) (ed.) *Race and British Electoral Politics*, London, UCL Press.

Salt, J. (1987) 'Contemporary trends in international migration study', *International Migration Review*, vol. 25, no. 3, pp. 241–7.

Schellekens, P.(2001) *English Language as a Barrier to Employment, Education and Training*, RBX3/01, Sheffield: Department for Education and Employment.

Schmitter Heisler, B. (1992) 'The future of immigrant incorporation: Which models? Which concepts?, *International Migration Review*, vol. 26, no. 2, pp. 623–45.

Schönwälder, K (1999) 'Persons persecuted on political grounds shall enjoy the right to asylum – but not in our country': Asylum policy and debates about refugees in the Federal Republic of Germany', in Bloch, A. and Levy, C. (eds), *Refugees, Citizenship and Social Policy in Europe*, Basingstoke, Macmillan – now Palgrave Macmillan, pp. 76–90.

Schuster, L. (2000) 'A comparative analysis of the asylum policy of seven European government', *Journal of Refugee Studies*, vol. 13, no. 1, pp. 118–32.

Schuster, L. and Solomos, J. (1999) 'The politics of refugee and asylum policies in Britain: Historical patterns and contemporary realities', in Bloch, A. and Levy, C. (eds), *Refugees, Citizenship and Social Policy in Europe*, Basingstoke, Macmillan – now Palgrave Macmillan , pp. 51–75.

Shaw, A. (1988) *A Pakistani Community in Britain*, London, Basil Blackwell Limited.

Siddhisena, K. and White, P. (1999) 'The Sri Lankan Population of Great Britain: Migration and settlement', *Asian and Pacific Migration Journal*, vol. 8, no. 4, pp. 511–36.

Sitaropoulos, N. (2000) 'Modern Greek asylum policy and practice in the context of relevant European developments', *Journal of Refugee Studies*, vol. 13, no. 1, pp. 105–17.

Sivard, R. (1995) *Women ... a world survey*, 2nd edn, Washington, World Priorities Inc.

Sly, F. (1995) 'Ethnic groups and the labour market: Analysis from the Spring 1994 Labour Force Survey', *Employment Gazette*, June, pp. 251–62.

Sly, F. (1996) 'Ethnic minority participation in the labour market: Trends from the Labour Force Survey 1984–1995', *Labour Market Trends*, vol. 104, no. 6, pp. 259–70.

Sly, F., Thair, T. and Risdon, A. (1999) Trends in the labour market participation of ethnic groups', *Labour Market Trends*, pp. 631–9.

Solomos, J. (1993) *Race and Racism in Britain*, 2nd Edn, Basingstoke, Macmillan – now Palgrave Macmillan.

Soysal, Y.N. (1994) *Limits of Citizenship: Migrants and postnational membership in Europe*, Chicago, University of Chicago.

Spencer, I. (1997) *British Immigration Policy Since 1939*, London, Routledge.

Spencer, S. (1998) 'The impact of immigration policy on race relations', in Blackstone, T., Parekh, B. and Saunders, P. (eds), *Race Relations in Britain: A developing agenda*, London, Routledge pp.74–95.

Srinivasan, S. (1992) 'The class position of the Asian petty bourgeoisie', *New Community*, vol. 19, no. 1, pp. 61–74.

Stalker, P. (1994) *The Work of Strangers: A survey of international labour*, Geneva, International Labour Office.

Statham, P. (1999) 'Political mobilisation by minorities in Britain: Negative feedback of "race relations"?', *Journal of Ethnic and Migration Studies*, vol. 25, no. 4, pp. 597–626.

Stein, B.N. (1979) 'Occupational adjustment of refugees: The Vietnamese in the United States', *International Migration Review*, vol. 13, no. 1, pp. 25–45.

Stein, B.N (1981) 'The refugee experience: Defining the parameters of a field study', *International Migration Review*, vol. 15, no. 1, pp. 320–30.

Strand, P.J. and Woodrow-Jones, Jr (1985) *Indochinese refugees in America: Problems of adaptation and assimilation*, North Carolina, Duke University Press.

Suhrke, A. (1997) 'Uncertain globalization: Refugee movements in the second half of the twentieth century', in Gungwu, W. (ed.), *Global History and Migrations*, Boulder, Westview, pp. 217–60.

Swedish Institute (1999) *Fact Sheets on Sweden – Immigrants in Sweden*, Stockholm, Swedish Institute (www.si.se).

Teague, A. (1993) 'Ethnic group: First results from the 1991 Census', *Population Trends*, no. 72, pp. 12–17.

Thränhardt, D. (1999) 'Germany's immigration policies and politics', in Brochmann, G. and Hammar, T. (eds), *Mechanisms of Immigration Control: A comparative analysis of European regulation policy*, Oxford, New York, Berg, pp. 29–57.

The Stationery Office (1998) *Fairer, Faster and Firmer – A modern approach to immigration and asylum*, London, The Stationery Office.

Thomas, D. (1992) 'The social integration of immigrants in Canada', in Globerman, S. (ed.), *The Immigrant Dilemma*, pp. 211–60, Vancouver, Canada, The Frasier Institute.

Twine, F. (1994) *Citizenship and Social Rights*, London, Sage.

Twomey, B. (2001) 'Labour market participation of ethnic groups', *Labour Market Trends*, January, pp. 29–42.

Uçarer, E. 1997 'Europe's search for policy: the harmonisation of asylum policy and European integration', in Uçarer, E. and Puchala, D. (eds), *Immigration into Western Societies*, London, Pinter, pp. 281–309.

UNHCR (2000a) http://www.unhcr.ch/issues/asylum/eustandards0007/gbr.pdf

UNHCR (2000b) *The State of the World's Refugees: 50 years of humanitarian action*, Oxford, Oxford University Press.

Valtonen, K. (1994) 'The adaptation of Vietnamese refugees in Finland', *Journal of Refugee Studies*, vol. 7, no. 1, pp. 63–78.

Valtonen, K. (1998) 'Resettlement of Middle Eastern refugees in Finland: The elusiveness of integration', *Journal of Refugee Studies*, vol. 11, no. 1, pp. 38–60.

Valtonen, K. (1999) 'The societal participation of Vietnamese refugees: Case studies in Finland and Canada, *Journal of Ethnic and Migration Studies*, vol. 25, no. 3, pp. 469–91.

Van Steenbergen, B. (1994) *The Condition of Citizenship*, London, Sage.

van Selm-Thorburn, J. (1998) *Refugee Protection in Europe: Lessons of the Yugoslav crisis*, The Hague, Martinus Hijhoff Publishers.

Vertovec, S. (1996) 'Multiculturalism, culturalism and public incorporation', *Ethnic and Racial Studies*, vol. 19, no. 1, pp. 49–69.

Vertovec, S. (1999) 'Minority associations, networks and public policies: Reassessing relationships', *Journal of Ethnic and Migration Studies*, vol. 25, no. 1, pp. 21–42.

Vincenzi, S. (2000) 'Italy: A newcomer with a positive attitude', *Journal of Refugee Studies*, vol. 13, no. 1, pp. 91–104.

Visram, R. (1993) 'South Asians in London', in Merriman, N. (ed.), *The Peopling of London: Fifteen thousand years of settlement from overseas*, London, Museum of London, pp. 169–78.

Wahlbeck, O. (1997a) 'The Kurdish diaspora and refugee associations in Finland and England', in Muus, P. (ed.), *Inclusion and Exclusion of Refugees in Contemporary Europe*, The Netherlands, ERCOMER, Utrecht University, pp. 171–86.

Wahlbeck, O. (1997b) 'Community work and exile politics: Kurdish refugee associations in London, *Journal of Refugee Studies*, vol. 11, no. 3, pp. 215–30.

Walker, A. and Walker, C. (1997) 'Introduction: The strategy of inequality', in Walker, A. and Walker, C. (eds), *Britain Divided: The growth of social exclusion in the 1980s and 1990s*, London, Child Poverty Action Group, pp. 1–16.

Walzer, M. (1983) *Spheres of Justice: A Defence of Pluralism and Equality*, Oxford, Martin Robertson & Co Ltd.

Weiner, M. (1996) 'Determinants of immigrant integration: An international comparative analysis, in Carmon, N. (ed.), *Immigration and Integration in Post-Industrial Societies: Theoretical analysis and policy-related research*, Basingstoke, Macmillan – now Palgrave Macmillan, pp. 46–62.

Welch, S. (1975) 'Sampling by referral in a dispersed population', *Public Opinion Quarterly*, vol. 39, no. 2, pp. 237–46.

Whyatt, A. (1996) 'London East: Gateway to regeneration', in Butler, T. and Rustin, M. (eds), *Rising in the East: The regeneration of East London*, London, Lawrence and Wishart, pp. 265–87.

Wieviorka, M. (1998) 'Is multiculturalism the solution?', *Ethnic and Racial Studies*, vol. 21, no. 5, pp. 881–910.

Wooden, M. (1991) 'The experience of refugees in the Australian labour market', *International Migration Review*, vol. 25, no. 3, pp. 514–534.

Zetter, R. (1999) 'Reconceptualising the myth of return: Continuity and transition amongst the Greek-Cypriot refugees of 1974', *Journal of Refugee Studies*, vol. 12, no. 1, pp. 1–22.

Zetter, R. and Pearl, M. (1999) 'Sheltering on the margins: Social housing provision and the impact of restrictionism on asylum seekers and refugees in the UK', *Policy Studies*, vol. 20, no. 4, pp. 235–54.

Zetter, R. and Pearl, M. (2000) 'The minority within the minority: Refugee community-based organisations in the UK and the impact of restrictionism on asylum-seekers', *Journal of Ethnic and Migration Studies*, vol. 26, no. 4, pp. 675–97.

Zhou, M. (1997) 'Segmented assimilation: Issues, controversies, and recent research on the new second generation', *International Migration Review*, vol. 31, no. 4, pp. 975–1003.

Zolberg, A. (1989) 'The next waves: Migration theory for a changing world', *International Migration Review*, vol. 23, no. 3, pp. 403–30.

Zolberg, A., Suhrke, A. and Aguayo, S. (1989) *Escape from Violence: Conflict and refugee crisis in the developing world*, Oxford, Oxford University Press.

# Index

Note: Page numbers in italics refer to figures; page numbers in bold refer to tables.

218